Getting
What We
Ask For

Recent Titles in
Contributions to the Study of Education

Black Students in Higher Education: Conditions and Experiences in the 1970s
Edited by Gail E. Thomas

The Scope of Faculty Collective Bargaining: An Analysis of Faculty Union
Agreements at Four-Year Institutions of Higher Education
Ronald L. Johnstone

Brainpower for the Cold War: The Sputnik Crisis and National Defense
Education Act of 1958
Barbara Barksdale Clowse

In Opposition to Core Curriculum: Alternative Models for Undergraduate
Education
Edited by James W. Hall with Barbara L. Kevles

Peer Teaching: Historical Perspectives
Lilya Wagner

School Law for the Practitioner
Robert C. O'Reilly and Edward T. Green

The Search for Quality Integrated Education: Policy and Research on Minority
Students in School and College
Meyer Weinberg

From Little Rock to Boston: The History of School Desegregation
George R. Metcalf

American Higher Education: Servant of the People or Protector of Special
Interests?
E. C. Wallenfeldt

School Desegregation Plans That Work
Charles Vert Willie

Education and Poverty: Effective Schooling in the United States and Cuba
Maurice R. Berube

Learning from Our Mistakes: A Reinterpretation of Twentieth-Century
Educational Theory
Henry J. Perkinson

Getting What We Ask For

THE AMBIGUITY OF SUCCESS AND FAILURE IN URBAN EDUCATION

Charles M. Payne

CONTRIBUTIONS TO THE STUDY OF EDUCATION, NUMBER 12

GREENWOOD PRESS
Westport, Connecticut • London, England

Library of Congress Cataloging in Publication Data

Payne, Charles M.
  Getting what we ask for.

  (Contributions to the study of education, ISSN
0196-707X ; no. 12)
  Bibliography: p.
  Includes index.
  1. Education, Urban—United States. 2. Education,
Urban—Illinois—West Chicago. 3. Educational
equalization—United States. 4. Socially handicapped
children—Education—United States. I. Title.
II. Series.
LC5131.P39   1984   370.19′348′0973   83-18623
ISBN 0-313-23520-1 (lib. bdg.)

Library of Congress Catalog Card Number: 83-18623
ISBN: 0-313-23520-1
ISSN: 0196-707X

First published in 1984

Greenwood Press
A division of Congressional Information Service, Inc.
88 Post Road West
Westport, Connecticut 06881

Printed in the United States of America

10 9 8 7 6 5 4 3 2 1

Copyright acknowledgment

Grateful acknowledgment is given for permission to use material reprinted from *Integrateducation*, a publication of the University of Massachusetts.

Contents

Tables   vii

Acknowledgments   ix

Introduction   3

1 **Black Bastards and White Millionaires**   7

    The Varieties of Denial   8

    The Methodology of Denial   14

    The Conservative Potential of Progressive Theory   20

    The Rationalization of Inequality   37

2 **Westside and the Production of Disorder**   43

    The Production of Disorder   50

    Reforms and the Ambiguity of Success   59

3 **A World That Asks Too Little**   75

    Student Interpretation of Teacher Characteristics   76

    The Conditionality of Student Response   82

    Student Explanations for Their Own Behavior   89

    Misbehavior among Transfer Students   94

    The Significance of Factors Other Than Demands   96

4 Alienation and the Failure to Teach   103

Students as Accomplices   117

The Institutional Roots of Teacher Exploitation   128

Elite Interests and Miseducation   144

Learning from Real Kids   149

5 Schools That Work and Research That Doesn't   155

Looking Where the Light Is Bright   180

References   189

Index   199

Tables

1. Students Absent from English Classes, by Class Period — 56

2. Responses to "What Are the Characteristics of a Really Good Teacher?" — 77

3. Responses to "How Can You Tell if a Teacher Is Really Concerned About Students Learning Something in the Course?" — 78

4. Explanations for Why Some Teachers Have More Trouble and Others Have Less Trouble Controlling the Classroom — 84

5. Explanations for Why Students Work Harder in Some Classes Than in Others — 90

6. Explanations for Variations in Student Behavior: Skipping Classes and Effort Questions Combined — 93

7. Students' Evaluation of Teachers as to Their "Concern," by Degree of Student Misbehavior — 97

8. Students' Evaluation of Teachers as to How "Snotty" They Are, by Degree of Student Misbehavior — 98

Acknowledgments

My introduction to the schools of Chicago's West Side was made possible largely by Gordon Austin, who has lived in that neighborhood and taught in its schools all of his life. He has had a great deal to do with shaping my sense of what a teacher in ghetto schools can be.

Early drafts of this work were helped by the comments and encouragement of James Pitts, Charles Moskos, Freddye Hill, and Remi Clignet. Later drafts profited from the criticism of John Stanfield, Eileen Julien, and from the particularly thorough and perceptive remarks of Mark Gould.

My debt to Arnold Feldman is of a more permanent sort and difficult to put into a few words. It will have to do to say that much of what I think most useful here is directly or indirectly attributable to his influence and to his endless and endlessly useful criticism.

I once had the good fortune to take a course under C.L.R. James. Although I was unable to appreciate the lesson at the time, I am indebted to him for constantly insisting on drawing a distinction between social apologetics and useful social analysis.

The debt to those studied is also unusually great here. The climate within inner-city schools is such that staff and students are frequently defensive, suspicious of outsiders and outside inquiry. I am thus all the more grateful for the cooperation I received from people at "Westside High." That name, of course, is a pseudonym, as are the names of staff members mentioned in the text.

Getting
What We
Ask For

Introduction

Having grown up in a small town, I was a college sophomore before I had my first experience in an inner-city school. I was a volunteer crisis teacher in an elementary school. I was given a long, narrow room with a single exit. Each morning teachers brought the least manageable of their male students to that room. My job was to guard that one exit. Not long after, I found myself teaching Afro-American history to sixth graders two or three times a week. This was at a time when many, myself included, believed that teaching relevant material like Afro-American history would have an instant and magical effect on ghetto children. I know I began with perfect confidence that I could handle the students better than the regular teachers could. Beyond that, my memories of that first class are hazy now, a blurred vision of objects whizzing through the air and a relay race going on in the back of the room. I do not recall whether I ever got to distribute the handouts I had prepared. I do remember very distinctly, though, that it was a Friday, that I went home and went to bed around three in the afternoon with a pitcher of Kool-aid and a bowl of cheese popcorn, and that I stayed there until late the next day.

That was some years ago. I have since observed or participated in schooling for the disadvantaged and their children at several different levels of the educational system and in several different capacities. This book is an attempt at making sense of my experience. It is, more particularly, an attempt at suggesting a more hopeful vision of the prospects for urban education than the visions to which most of us have grown accustomed.

There are essentially three sections to this work. The discussion of educational inequality has been but one aspect of a larger debate over questions of race and class and social equity. The first chapter examines portions of that debate. Where has it been? Where is it going? What does it portend for our understanding of inner-city education? How questions are framed and discussed by scholastics both reflects and helps shape how issues are approached in the real world, no matter how otherworldly academic debate may sometimes seem. Despite the ill feeling between urban schoolteachers and researchers, much of the real damage done by teachers results from the fact that their thinking is so fundamentally similar to that of many researchers, with whom, after all, they share a common intellectual tradition. As teachers come to see the limitations of that broad tradition more clearly, perhaps they will become increasingly able to divest themselves of ideas that have only got in the way. If social scientists come to see teachers as, in many ways, intellectually kindred spirits, they may begin to lose some of the disrespect for teachers in the public schools that has contributed to the pointlessness of much educational research.

The next two chapters draw on fieldwork done at a high school on Chicago's West Side to analyze the problem of disorder, a problem that in the inner city typically impinges on and aggravates every other problem. It is a premise of these chapters that we have as much to learn from the small successes of bad schools as from their more obvious failures. Part of what we learn is that failure is not always so unattractive to the people suffering from it, nor success so unambiguously appealing as one might suppose.

The two remaining chapters discuss the problematics of learning and teaching in the inner city. Chapter 4 draws on what I regard as the most instructive recent research to outline an explanation of why so little learning normally goes on in schools. There is still much that we do not know about that, but at least we now know that the failure to learn cannot be attributed to the inadequacies of inner-city students, or, for that matter, to the inadequacies of inner-city teachers. The final chapter approaches the same question from a more useful direction. What do we know about urban schools that *do* work?

That question reflects a hopeful change in the way we think about educational inequality. There is a story about a philosopher who rose up from his deathbed to announce to his assembled friends, "I have it! I have found the answer!" only to sink back into a coma before sharing it with anyone. Hours later he arose again, this time to ask, "What was the question?" Students of the problems of inner-city schools have often lost touch with the questions, expending enormous resources to generate the right answers, or at least partially right answers, to precisely the wrong questions. I mean particularly that the organizing question for most of the past two decades has been, "Why cannot children who are poor and dark learn as other children do?" It was a question worth asking, but in retrospect it was clearly not the most efficient way to promote positive change. A great deal of trouble could have been saved and innumerable children might have been helped had we spent somewhat less time investigating failure and more time trying to understand success, however statistically rare success might be.

There have always been schools that do well with children no different from the children other schools are failing, just as there have always been individual teachers who are able to get their children to achieve, no matter what is going on around them. Until very recently, however, such teachers and schools have been relegated to the margins of the ongoing discussion about urban education, treated as interesting but not meaningful exceptions to the all-important general pattern. Like urban teachers, researchers have made a cult of failure, a cult whose doctrines held that variations in school resources don't have any effect on learning; that schools themselves really don't have much to do with who learns how much; that the child's background is what matters; that reform is ultimately possible, but only after heaven and earth move in tandem.

In the last few years that has begun to change. Perhaps there are no more successful urban schools than there were years ago, but they are certainly getting much more concentrated attention. Virtually every major teachers' journal has published since 1979 at least one discussion of effective urban schools. Of course, some success stories are built more on skillful public relations than on performance, and it is true that we have more description than convincing analysis. Still, we have learned a good deal just by changing the question. For one thing, while the better schools employ a wide variety of instructional and organizational approaches, they are not on the whole doing things that cannot be done with the human and material resources available to any big-city system. Beyond a threshold, it is the sane organization of resources that matters. It is also clear that sanity has to begin at the level of school governance. The quality of school leadership, and the ethos established by it, seem much more important than particular instructional methods.

By the same token, the particular details of what we learn about successful schools are far less important than what they do to our collective expectations for urban schools. The doctrine of the ineducability of the children of the urban poor has been made into a staple of our culture by a generation of I-taught-in-the-ghetto combat novels and a steady stream of journalistic exposés of the mindlessness, the violence, the Keystone Kops disorganization of inner-city schools—all of this assented to and legitimated by the academic establishment. Much of this was done with the earnest intent to contribute to reform, but taken together it has helped to create a climate of despair about the prospects for urban education, a climate which has become in its own right more pernicious than the particular problems being described. The most important thing about schools that do work is that they call into question the grounds for that despair; does it arise from a collective willingness to believe in the intellectual incapacity of those who are poor and dark? If poor children can be taught somewhere, then why not everywhere?

Whether this new attention given to the successes, rather than the failures, of urban education will lead to real change, I cannot say, but it opens possibilities that have not existed before. Ronald Edmonds, who has played a particularly important role in raising the level of discussion, points out that who learns what is a matter of political choice. Perhaps in the future, as in the past, we will choose not to educate the children of the urban poor. But it is worth something to know that we are in fact making a choice, that we are not merely tolerating miseducation because we just don't know how to do better.

1

Black Bastards and White Millionaires

Three-quarters of a century ago, W.E.B. DuBois, in *Souls of Black Folk,* complained about sociologists gleefully counting Black bastards and prostitutes (1961:20). For most of the twentieth century, the remark remained an accurate characterization of the way in which the social sciences typically approached matters of race and class inequalities. It was an approach that too frequently assumed that understanding inequality is essentially a matter of describing those who suffered from it.

The approach is different now. With some pushing and squeezing, for example, we can place most explanations for the various problems of inner-city schools into two broad categories. One school of thought, long the more orthodox and squarely in the tradition of counting Black bastards, contends that the problem results from cultural or genetic or psychological inadequacies in the preschool life of the children. There are endless arguments over just which preschool factors are critical, but there is an underlying agreement that the problem in the inner-city school is the inner-city child. The other school of thought contends that the institution itself causes the problem. Probably the most common version traces the problem back to low teacher expectations, while the most radical versions trace those expectations back to the school's role in reproducing and legitimating the social order.

How we choose to see educational inequality is related to how we see inequality itself. In other areas of the social sciences and on virtually all the enduring questions touching on social inequality, there are similar arguments between traditional and less traditional ways of seeing. Indeed, the less traditional styles are now well enough entrenched as to have generated a reaction in the form of such neoconservative approaches as supply-side economics, genetic interpretations of racial inequality, and sociobiology. The officially conservative mood of the country probably means that such theories will be on the offensive for some time to come.

What do we learn from the general debate that should be taken into account as we try to understand the failings of urban schools? Better, what does the general debate teach us about how we can study inequality, educational or otherwise, in ways that help to redress it? A comprehensive analytical review of all that has been written or said on that subject is beyond the scope of this book, but we should be able to learn something of value by looking selectively at works which either have been influential, or embody influential themes. Part of what we learn is that the styles of thought we ordinarily term radical and conservative are not always as far apart in their implications for change as they might be. We are all familiar with the principle in social affairs, having almost the force of law, that holds that new orthodoxies will come to have some of the odor of the old, a principle from which not even the changing orthodoxies of social scientists are exempt.

The Varieties of Denial

We can start with an illustration of the challenges to conservative orthodoxy. Mark Chesler's review (1976) of theories of racism reflects some of the most common concerns. He looks at theories according to where they fall on two issues, victim-system control and the degree of embeddedness of racism. The first is concerned with whether the root cause of racial inequality is seen as being within the control of victims or of the control of the larger social system. That is, has it to do with the personal and cultural characteristics of the deprived or with authority relations and patterns of resource allocation within the broader society? In more popular, if somewhat misleading terms, Chesler is asking how victim-blaming is the theory.

Chesler's second dimension overlaps with the first. Degree of embeddedness refers to whether racism is central or peripheral to American society. Discussions of race relations often center, for example, on tensions in interpersonal relations. Prejudice is often presented as the core of the problem and is often understood as a function of ignorance or as a function of certain personality types—authoritarian personalities, perhaps—or as the irrational scapegoating response of people who feel their social position slipping away. If one says that the problem reduces basically to irrationality or ignorance or warped personalities, the implication is that racism is personal, not part of the system; it is relatively peripheral to our national life. On the other hand, racism might be seen as one reflection of core American values about competition or as built into the capitalist system, implying in either case that it is woven into the fabric of our institutional life. Chesler's survey of the literature finds that research on racism has ordinarily taken approaches that were high on victim-blame and low on embeddedness.

Chesler's thinking reflects two of the questions most at issue in critiques of traditional thinking about inequality. How is a particular problem of inequality connected to features of our core institutions? What role is played by the overprivileged in determining the life-chances of the underprivileged? In order to stress the moral and political overtones of the problem, I prefer to approach essentially the same issues with a slightly different language. Our concern is with those theories that purport to explain either the existence of inequality or the "deviant" behavior of those on the bottom of inequality structures. Many of our misgivings with traditional theory stem from a single characteristic—the persistent tendency to either deny or minimize the possibility that there is some causal significance to the relationship between Haves and Have-nots. These theories, which I call denial theories, treat the top and the bottom of the social order as separate spheres, each floating along quite independently of the other.

It helps to think of denial theories as coming in at least four varieties. First are the attribute theories, where the explanations take as their independent variables (that is, their causes) some internalized characteristic of Have-nots. These are more commonly called victim-blaming theories, but that terminology will not be used here, for reasons to be discussed later. Then there are the opportunity theories, treating the differential distribution of opportunity structures as the independent variable but breaking off the analysis before inquiring as to how those structures are created and maintained. Third are the mystical theories, which give unreasonable weight to the subjective characteristics of Haves, thus diverting attention from their objective behavior. Finally, there is what might be called the thesis of the Redneck-as-Patsy (hereafter RAP), which looks strictly at lower-status Haves. They strike a variety of notes, but all forms of denial theory contribute to what James Baldwin called the Chorus of the Innocents.

Since attribute theories have probably been the most influential, we will discuss them first. Consider the sheer range and variety of questions on which social scientists have traditionally ended up explaining stigma with stigma. Why are some people poor? Because they have not developed the relentless future-time orientation of "normal" people, or because their essentially matriarchal backgrounds failed to give them the achievement orientation so necessary in our competitive society. Why are some people sexually promiscuous? Because they have internalized subcultural norms that sanction such behavior. Why can't some children learn to read? Because their home backgrounds do not offer the intellectual nourishment conducive to learning. Why were North American slave revolts not as successful as those elsewhere? Because, according to one persistent school of thought, these slaves had internalized the attitudes of their masters to a degree that made revolt unthinkable. Why are Chicanos poor? A number of studies make it clear that their culturally induced tendency to passively accept whatever fate befalls them is at the core of their troubles. (See Romano 1968 for a well-done critique of these studies.) The notion of self-concept deserves special mention. It ranks second only to the Black family as an all-purpose, economy-size, universal independent variable for explaining anything and everything.

Viewed historically, the sociology of inequality has changed less than one might expect, especially on racial questions. Both the Social Darwinism of the late nineteenth century and the crudely racist theories of the early twentieth were denial theories. (See Jones 1973 for a summary of the latter.) Arguing that racial inequality is attributable to God and Nature is the most unequivocal method of denying that such inequality has anything to do with what whites do to Blacks. Modern attribute theorists simply substitute Culture and Personality for God and nature, yielding a denial more subtle in form, more acceptable to contemporary sensibilities, but hardly more original in substance. The characteristic policy implication logically flowing from attribute theory, of course, is that the poor should be changed, not the relationship between the poor and nonpoor.

A subcategory of attribute theory consists of the historical-cultural theories, which take the position that it is the relationship between Haves and Have-nots that accounts for the disabilities of the Have-nots but which place that relationship in the past. Once upon some distant time, Haves so mistreated the Have-nots that the Have-nots had to change their culture in order to adapt. Today, however, it is that unfortunately warped culture that accounts for their disabilities. Daniel P. Moynihan's work on the Black family (1965) is among the more familiar examples.

It will be useful to have a category to pose against denial theories. Let us refer to that opposing category as progressive, meaning only those theories that see as their causal variable either something ongoing that is done to those on the bottom of inequality structures by those on the top or see as their causal factor some aspect of the standard arrangement of core social institutions. Here it is the relationship between those of different social status that accounts for who winds up where, or who exhibits the higher rates of "undesirable" behavior. In Mark Chesler's terms, theories are progressive to the extent that they stress high system control and high embeddedness. Progressive theories should be divided into two categories. Some are concerned only with face-to-face interactions between Haves and Have-nots. Others are more complex, treating cases where the relationship between Haves and Have-nots is such that those on top may never come into direct contact with those on the bottom.

Midway between attribute and progressive theories is an approach that illustrates the second category of denial theories. These are those borderline theories that do not refer to the internalized attributes of Have-nots as their causal variables, but yet do not refer explicitly to what Haves do to Have-nots. Robert Merton's theory of anomie (1957), or the theory of delinquency that Cloward and Ohlin (1960) derive from it, or Liebow's treatment (1967) of the impact of the economic situation on family life in the urban Black lower class would all fall into this category. All of them use the differential distribution of opportunity as their independent variables, but in all these cases the distribution is treated as a given. No consideration is given to whether and how privileged classes create and maintain that distribution. If attribute theories blame the victim, opportunity theories blame no one at all.

The two remaining categories of denial theory, mysticism and the RAP thesis, both play important roles in educational theorizing. By way of explaining them, we could hardly do better than begin with Gunnar Myrdal, or rather with Oliver Cox's response to Myrdal. Myrdal's *An American Dilemma* (1944) signaled the triumph of a new theoretical orthodoxy. Shortly after Myrdal's book was published, Cox (1948) responded that the new orthodoxy was a dubious improvement over the old. Myrdal adopted the position that racial inequality has to be understood as a moral conflict, as a contradiction of basic American ideals. In principle, he says, American racial problems were solved long ago. In principle, retorts Cox, all the moral problems of the Western world were solved by the Sermon on the Mount. He goes on to point out how conveniently the moral focus minimizes the question of power differentials, the question that Cox regards as key: "If the race problem in the United States is preeminently a moral question, it must naturally be resolved by moral means, and this is precisely the social illusion which the ruling political class has constantly sought to produce" (1948:538).

This type of thinking is what Cox refers to as mysticism. He appears to use that term to refer to work which is simply vague or which shows an over-reliance on subjective, especially moralistic, explanations, thus obscuring the objective nature of the relationships between whites and Blacks, a relationship which, according to Cox, has to be understood more in terms of power differentials and economic interests than of moral conflict.

The mystical element in Myrdal with the most contemporary relevance is his tendency to treat racial beliefs as primary causal agents. Despite the warnings of Cox and others (Merton 1949, Deutscher 1966), a large proportion of the discussion on race relations continues to reveal a subjectivist bias. Chesler's review of sociological interpretations of racism concludes that "much more research and theory has been developed on minority adaptations and attributes and on white attitudes than on the other approaches." Taken as the tendency to reduce racial relationships to attitudes and their expression in interpersonal relationships, mysticism has enjoyed a remarkable hold on American thinking about race.

One familiar nonacademic example is the politics of image among minority groups, the politics of building bridges of interracial cooperation, to use a term from the 1940s. The civil rights movement of the 1960s can be seen as a progression from the politics of changing hearts and minds to a politics addressing structures of dominance and exclusion. To take a more contemporary example, interracial friction has lately become a matter of more active concern on college campuses. As I have known them, the discussions still ordinarily frame those issues in mystical terms. Tension in interpersonal relationships ("Why must the Black students always eat together?") gets traced back to group attitudes and having the "wrong" attitude is assumed to be immoral. The solution, of course, is to get to know one another better. Change our attitudes. Get more diversity in the student body.

Now, it is almost necessarily true that the tenacity of such tensions stems in good measure from the fact that we already know quite a bit about one another, but little attention is paid to that knowledge nor to approaches to racism stressing differentials in power. The argument, for example, that Black students having an all-Black meeting is an expression of racism equates defensive, situationally specific exclusion by a relatively powerless group with more inclusive historical patterns of exclusion controlled by the powerful and aimed at perpetuating systematic subjugation of one group by another. Treating narrow similarities of interpersonal behavior as equivalent while ignoring the radically different contexts in which they occur misses quite a few distinctions and, as Oliver Cox would note, just those kinds of distinctions that would be most discomfiting to the socially privileged.

The stress on good interpersonal relationships as a solution to racial problems is, or at least once was, as common among academics as among college students, a point made by James Pitts (1974) while discussing research on "racial isolation." That research proceeds from the assumption that racial problems are caused by the isolation of Blacks, by their lack of favorable personal contact with whites. Interestingly, as Pitts points out, much of what would be called "solidarity" if it occurred among any other group gets called "isolation" when it occurs among Blacks. Thus we expect racial tensions to abate as we get more equal status contacts between members of different racial groups. We expect school problems to wither as we integrate schools. In the spirit of Oliver Cox, John Stanfield (1982) has suggested that the focus on school desegregation avoids discussion of differences in power between racial groups. In educational research, one of the most useful ideas of the last decade has been the idea that teacher expectations do a lot to shape student performance. That idea, though, is too easily mistaken for the entire explanation, encouraging us to look no further than interpersonal feelings between teachers and students, ignoring the institutional constraints under which they operate.

Attribute theories are the purest form of denial theory since they deny outright that there is any relationship there to be analyzed. Mystical theories grant the existence of a relationship, but proceed to analyze it in terms I assume to be ordinarily superficial. The same is true of our final category, the RAP thesis. Myrdal repeats the once common argument that the class of whites from whom Blacks have the most to fear is the poorer class, the rednecks, while whites of higher status tend to be more enlightened. For Cox, the RAP thesis turns the world inside out, substituting the more vicious and dramatic expressions of inequality for the possibility that those of higher status create, maintain, and profit most from the racial status quo. It is easy enough to find more recent examples of the RAP thesis. Thus, when the problems of bad schools are not seen as resulting from the cultural characteristics of the children, they are likely to be seen as resulting from poor teachers rather than, say, poor superintendents. The horrors of prison life are more likely to be explained as a function of brutal guards than of the decisions of state legislatures. During the 1960s the popular media managed the neat trick of virtually blaming the Vietnam War on hard hats; that is, on the working class. (See the discussion in Sennett and Cobb, 1972.) In general, the higher one ranks in the hierarchy, the smaller one's chances of being studied as a possible cause of social problems, a problem noted by Alvin Gouldner (1968) among others.

Both the RAP thesis and attribute thinking encourage a Good Person–Bad Person conception of social issues. If only we had more dedicated teachers, more humane prison guards, a more intelligent working class. Defining matters so turns us not only from analysis of the distribution of power but also from analysis of the consequences of particular social structures. During the civil rights movement the media, with the aid of the movement in its early years, so successfully reduced racism to a problem of Bad Persons, that they were unable to adjust to the emergence of less simplistic conceptions of the factors sustaining racial privilege, conceptions stressing not bad people but bad structures maintained by perfectly wonderful people. The Bad Person conception of social problems should be considered a distancing mechanism, a way of saying that the people who are problematic are not like us, not like the civil, literate, and concerned people who produce and read social theory. Much of what one hears in liberal circles nowadays about the "moral majority" is just this kind of distancing device. If the students I have taught recently are any guide, the tendency is to write the "moral majority" off as hopelessly stupid, which is to say that the problem with this world is that there aren't enough intelligent people—that is, people like my students.

In addition to the denial of responsibility inherent in the content of the theory, there is a parallel denial in its preferred mode of presentation. Denial theory has historically been associated with the claim to scientific objectivity, a claim which, whether it comes from jurists, journalists, or social scientists, amounts to a refusal to acknowledge responsibility for the consequences of one's thinking. In turn, the claim to objectivity is associated with the traditional preference for a language that imitates the language of science—calm, dispassionate, void of emotion-laden terms and of the first person singular. It is literally a style which implies that there is no one there to accept responsibility. It is therefore highly disarming. Quite silly ideas, once wrapped in the antiseptic, sleep-inducing language of the professional journals, can sound persuasive even to a fairly critical audience. It is rhetoric that derives its power precisely from not appearing to be rhetorical.

We have now discussed four means by which social scientists either deny or minimize the causal significance of the Have–Have-not relationship: opportunity theory, attribute theory, subjective mysticism, and the RAP thesis. The first looks at differential distribution of opportunity but does not examine the sources of that distribution. Attribute theory, in its pure form, simply denies outright that what Haves do to Have-nots is the source of Have-not troubles. The mystical approach admits that that behavior is the source, but implies that what Have-nots should do about it is change the thought patterns of the Haves. The RAP thesis again admits that what is critical is what Haves do to Have-nots, but suggests that the really dangerous Haves are not the really well-off Haves, but rather those just a little better off than the Have-nots. Clearly, all of this seems to be missing some of the logical possibilities.

Clearly, too, any theoretical perspective diverts attention from some of the logical possibilities. Every way of seeing is a way of not seeing. Still, when the overwhelming insight produced by three-quarters of a century of theory is that no one has much complicity in human suffering except the sufferers and those closest to them, we are justified in being more than normally skeptical.

The Methodology of Denial

If we wanted to fully account for the traditional dominance of denial thinking we would have to take a hard look at its usefulness as ideology and at the reward structure of the social science professions. We will skip that discussion, though, in order to concentrate on the methodological underpinnings of denial. We can start with the parallel between inequality as portrayed in the professional literature and inequality as it is understood in the popular culture. That consistency is often striking. In 1968, a fifteen-city survey found that the majority of white respondents felt that Blacks miss out on jobs, promotions, and good housing as a result of discrimination. The survey also asked, "On the average, Negroes in (——— city) have worse jobs, education and housing than white people. Do you think this is *mainly* due to Negroes having been discriminated against, or *mainly* due to something about Negroes themselves?" (emphasis added, Campbell 1971:12–13). On this item 19 percent of the whites respond that it is mainly discrimination, as against 56 percent saying that it is mainly something about Blacks themselves. As seems to be the case with more formal theories, the relational aspect is acknowledged, but the attributes get most of the attention.

Sociologists, of course, do use a more elegant language. Where the layperson might say that "those people" could get off welfare if they did not spend all their money on liquor and Cadillacs, the sociologist will intone something about subcultural norms and deferred gratification. There is little difference between the theory of differential association and what thousands of mothers say every day about the bad effects of running with the wrong crowd. Small wonder that students come to regard sociology as an elaboration of the obvious. Rather than transcending our culture, we relabel it, rediscovering as theory verities of the culture learned at mother's knee.

The underlying similarity between much sociological thinking and the thinking of laypersons results more from the fact that the two are molded by a common culture than from the accuracy of folk wisdom. The problems created by this are not so much a matter of explicit values or ideological leanings in any narrow sense. One should look for the structure of cultural bias not so much in one's attitude toward this or that, but rather in the type of questions that seem interesting, the kinds of definitions that come most readily to mind, the kind of interpretations that seem plausible—in short, in the diffuse rather than the specific influence of culture. Given a stronger methodology, this would matter little. Given the methodology we have, it matters a great deal.

It is often observed that relatively few of our studies are longitudinal, which increases the probability that we will confound the time-order of the variables whenever interpreting data that is only correlational. We can see this in the argument that poverty is due partly to cultural characteristics of the poor that make them nearly unemployable (Banfield 1968:48–54, 105–6; Davis 1966). Such arguments are generally based on little more than the fact that certain "negative" work attitudes and behaviors are correlated consistently with social class. As Ryan notes (1971:119), "culture" has been defined in any number of ways, but sociologists generally use the term such that whatever else it may refer to, it refers to patterns of behavior which are transmitted from one generation to another. Thus, placing a cultural interpretation on the fact that lower-class men have higher rates of absenteeism from work than middle-class men assumes that the factors leading to the disparity were present before the men actually entered into the world of work; it was something they learned from their equally shiftless fathers, perhaps.

A longitudinal study suggests a different interpretation. Powell and Driscoll (1973), examining the effect of long-term unemployment on middle- and upper-class professionals, find that as the period of unemployment lengthened, their subjects went longer and longer periods between attempts to find a new job, came to describe themselves as listless and apathetic, and became cynical about attempts to help them. In short, they began to exhibit some of the attitudes and behavior that nonlongitudinal studies often attribute to lower-class culture. In nonlongitudinal studies, the time-order of variables has to be guessed, and where the subjects are among the Have-nots, the guess will more often than not turn out to be something about the attributes of the subject.

The Powell and Driscoll study illustrates a couple of important points. Until recently, there has been a tendency to contrast actual data on lower-class life with idealized images of the middle classes. Thomas Cottle writes, "One finds, for example, mountains of articles on inner city schools but nary a molehill on the problems in suburban high schools, apart from drugs, long hair, and dress codes. There is more than one can read on working class patterns, but surprisingly little on the upper middle class" (1969:60). That is less true today, but it is quite right that we have a long tradition of making the most flattering assumptions about life at the top of the heap and how one gets to enjoy it. Consider that the classical literature on occupational mobility proceeded as though brownnosing, backstabbing, and skill at workplace politics played no role in middle- and upper middle-class life, hardly the assumption around which most of us organize our lives.

More importantly, Powell and Driscoll illustrate the critical point that one of the consistent characteristics of the research supporting denial theory is that it downplays questions of social process, questions about how and in what order things occur, so that the unsavory attributes of Have-nots almost inevitably come out pictured as the cause of inequality rather than as the consequence of a possibly exploitative process.

Education is the area most at issue here, so let us consider how questions of process are ignored in that area. The U.S. Commission on Civil Rights (1973) conducted a study involving the observation of over four hundred classrooms, aimed at discovering whether there were any important differences in how teachers interacted with students of different ethnic background. They found that Mexican-American students as compared to Anglos were significantly less likely to be praised by the teacher, to be asked questions by the teacher, or to have their contributions to classroom discussions elaborated on by the teacher. Obviously, this suggests the possibility that differences in educational achievement between Mexican-American and Anglo students may be due to differences in classroom treatment rather than to differences in cultural background. That is, the study suggests that the process of classroom interaction may be the significant cause of disparities in achievement.

A more traditional study by Audrey Schwartz (1971) finds that the value-orientations of Mexican-American high school students differ in some respects from the orientations of Anglo students. She finds, too, that values and school achievement are correlated: the more the values of a Mexican-American student tend to be like those of an Anglo, the higher his or her achievement tends to be: "While it is recognized that pupils' values and achievement are substantially interdependent, the findings of this study suggest that affective factors in the cultural background of many Mexican-American students hinder their general academic achievement" (p. 460). The point about the interdependence of the variables, which is not elaborated further at any point in the article, is probably correct. All the rest of it is wishful, if not racist, thinking. The article offers no data on processes of cultural transmission and no data indicating that values and achievement are causally related. It would make just as much sense to interpret a correlation between values and achievement as meaning that the same school experiences that shape achievement shape values as well. Here again, in the attempt to derive actual processes of causation from static correlations there is the danger of confounding the time order of the variables. The type of classroom processes indicated by the Civil Rights Commission study could not have shown up here because the method eliminated the possibility.

Another work on the subject uses the same sleight of hand. Justin (1974) uses a questionnaire to measure fatalism and the unwillingness to defer gratification among Mexican-American high school students. As usual, he finds higher levels of both among them than among a comparable sample of Anglo students. As usual, he goes on to suggest that this is at the root of their educational problems. As usual, he ignores the question of what social processes are taking place in the classroom. He therefore lacks the data to make any causal argument, but, as usual, he makes the argument anyway.

These examples illustrate the powerful predilection among denial theorists toward methods and interpretations that minimize the significance of social process, especially processes between those of unequal status. They illustrate another point as well. Denial theory simplifies the research process considerably. By either ignoring social process or trying to infer it from static data, theorists skirt a number of difficulties. Thus the popularity of mysticism probably derives partly from the relative ease of constructing and administering an attitude scale as compared to the greater investment of time involved in the direct observation of ongoing relationships. Similarly, the RAP thesis is likely to be with us so long as there is an inverse relationship between the status of subjects and the degree of unhampered access to them on the part of researchers. One of the difficulties in educational research is that it is more difficult to get access to administrators than to teachers and students. A full-blown progressive theory would deal with, as C. Wright Mills (1959) would phrase it, the intersection of history and biography, examining both the characteristics of individuals and the larger social milieu within which they operate; this in turn would mandate methods appropriate to both levels of analysis. By contrast, denial theory is very much the lazy path to research.

Works like Justin's and Schwartz's are unimportant in themselves. They matter only as lesser imitations of the analytic style of far more influential work. For our purposes, no one work is more important than James Coleman's (1966) analysis of educational inequality, and perhaps there is no other work that better illustrates the cavalier treatment of social process and social context. Albert Murray has written: "There is little reason why Negroes should not regard contemporary social science theory and technique with anything except the most unrelenting suspicion. There is, come to think of it, no truly compelling reason at all why Negroes should not regard the use of the social science statistical survey as the most elaborate fraud of modern times" (1970:37). If that seems too strongly put, consider Coleman. Done at the behest of Congress in the mid-1960s, the Coleman report aimed at explaining the roots of racial and class disparities in educational performance. At the time, it was the second costliest research project ever undertaken in this country. The numbers were dramatic—645,000 students, 60,000 teachers, and 4,000 schools were examined. "Examined" means that Coleman distributed questionnaires and tried to infer the roots of inequality from responses to them and from performance on standardized tests. He expected to demonstrate that most differences in learning were the result of unequal school facilities—textbooks, science labs, money spent per pupil, library resources, and so forth. He found, of course, that on the whole such things mattered little. The key determinant—not correlate, determinant—turned out to be family background, the socioeconomic status of the child's family. The school characteristic that made the most difference was the social mix of the student body; students learned more when they went to school with more affluent classmates.

More than any other, Coleman's work has been used as the foundation for the notion that the primary cause of what children learn in school is what they bring with them, an idea that has been called "an educational truism" (Greer 1974:94). Coleman was even used as support for the notion that schooling does not matter, which he does not say. (As recently as 1978, *Urban Education* thought it necessary to devote a special issue to arguing that schools do make a difference.) In *Inequality* (1972), Christopher Jencks, whose philosophical position is far to the left of Coleman's, reanalyzes Coleman's data to find that Coleman actually underestimated the impact of family background. Jencks notes, though, that he himself is ignoring the internal life of the school (1972:13), apparently without realizing that leaves him no grounds for talking about causes of educational inequality.

It is entirely possible that racial and class disparities in educational achievement are due partly or totally to the fact that teacher behavior varies systematically with the race and class of students, but it is nearly impossible that Coleman would have uncovered that possibility since he pays no attention to social processes in the classroom, to the internal life of the school. Indeed, given that the actual data gathering took only two months, given Coleman's reliance on those familiar tools of the survey researcher, the standardized test and the questionnaire—neither of which is a particularly good tool for getting at questions of process— Coleman virtually had to come up with an attribute theory. Coleman, it is true, does talk about "school quality," concluding that its impact is surprisingly small, although greater for minority students than for others. Unfortunately, he uses school quality to refer to easily quantified characteristics of the school—the number of books in the library or the amount of experience the teaching staff has had—rather than to anything that anybody is doing in the school. It sounds absurd, but support for the argument that educational inequalities must be understood in terms of the cultural inadequacies of the children comes from studies of students, not studies of the educational process. It is as if one had studied war, but ignored all that extraneous killing that goes on.

More generally, the critical step in causal analysis is usually the identification of a full range of alternative explanations, and the problem here is that of the actual possibilities, some—those stressing the denial paradigm—are more likely to occur to us than others. Neither multiple regression analysis nor path analysis will of themselves allow us to avoid the problem of alternative explanation or the related problem of fixing the time-order of the variables. (On the use and abuse of statistical procedure in studies of inequality, see Howard Taylor 1973; 1976.) For all practical purposes, our ability to construct a convincing argument hinges on our ability to generate alternative explanations, and that unfortunately leaves far too much room for bias to operate. On the point of causality, the social sciences become a fundamentally imaginative enterprise, and most imaginations have traditionally run in directions pointed to by the popular culture.[1]

More than any other, Coleman's work has set the terms for public discourse about education and inequality for the past decade and a half.

One can attribute that to anything one wishes, but not to the quality of the research design. The methods of Coleman illustrate common tendencies in denial work: the over-reliance on nonlongitudinal methods looking at whatever factors can be conveniently quantified; the focus on central tendencies in aggregate data, masking important differences within aggregates; inferring causes from statistical manipulation; survey techniques that generate data on a great many cases, but very little data on any one case. None of this leads to seeing things that are not really there, but taken collectively it can lead to seeing only some of what is there and seeing it divorced from social process, out of context and out of focus. On methodological grounds alone, it is not hard to see why the old paradigms would come under attack (although that is not a full explanation). It may be more important for us to look at the ways in which the attacks themselves leave something to be desired.

The Conservative Potential of Progressive Theory

In reexamining the first premises that dominate American life, a number of activists and intellectuals moved in the 1960s toward a vision of the world that saw social problems as interconnected, saw major social institutions as barriers to human life, and saw imbalances of power and the venality of powerful as the driving forces behind human suffering. For those seeing the world so, the old moral hierarchies were reversed. Middle-class roots became suspect, upper middle-class roots positively embarassing. Wealth and power became measures of insensitivity, if not *prima facie* evidence of exploitation. Progressive theory climbed to a new respectability within the academy, a respectability reflected in a variety of ways. We have seen a number of critiques of various components of the denial ideology (such as Ladner 1973; Billingsley 1968; Reginald Jones 1980; Yetman and Steele 1971; Ryan 1971; Horton 1966; Chesler 1976; Colfax and Roach 1971; McCarthy and Yancey 1973; Taylor 1976). Among anthropologists, the same tensions seem embedded in the struggle over the adequacy of cultural deficit models as compared to cultural difference models (Baratz and Baratz 1972) and the adequacy of either of these as compared to a bicultural model (Valentine 1975). Among historians, we find examples of the change in Walter Rodney's remarkable reexamination of the colonial experience (1972) and in Herbert Gutman's equally striking reconsideration of slavery's impact on the Black family (1976). In sociology, progressive headway is reflected in the labeling perspective on deviance, in teacher expectation theory, in Alvin Gouldner's call for a reflexive sociology (1970), in the attempt to develop a colonial model of American race relations (Blauner 1969; Cruse 1968; Tabb 1970), and most enduringly, in the continuing disquietude with structural functionalism and the burgeoning interest in various conflict models, Marxist models in particular.

Generalizing as I have done about a long-established body of work is risky enough. It has to be riskier still to generalize about a less established body of work. Still, certain potential abuses of progressive theory can be tentatively identified. In its worst forms, progressive theory ends up caricaturing the nature of oppression and reinforcing the assumptions built into the denial paradigm; it proceeds from naive assumptions about the nature of social change and reduces the political function of social theory to a kind of elaborate public relations job.

We should note first that some of the work advertised as new is new only in the advertising. The RAP thesis, given the proper rhetorical polish, lends itself especially well to reincarnation as some sort of radical insight. Then there are those works that begin by framing problems in language that sounds progressive—white racism, dehumanization, exploitation—and then go on to discuss the matter at hand pretty much as it is discussed in the denial tradition. The progressive dimension gets acknowledged, but only that.

What of those theories in which the progressive component is not so superficial? One of the difficulties here arises from the fact that much progressive thinking is self-consciously reactive. This encourages the assumption that denial theories are inversions of the truth and thus only need to be stood on their heads. In the case of attribute theory, this is likely to lead to arguments over whether the attributes of the group in question do in fact exist. I am not sure about the value of such arguments. I will concede that continued oppression changes people and some of those changes are likely to be unpleasant. That is, attribute theories, allowing for the usual exaggeration, may have some degree of descriptive, if less explanatory, validity. It would seem preferable to focus the argument on whether the attributes have the causal significance imputed to them, on the extent to which Haves continue to create these attributes in Have-nots, on the assumption that the significance of the attribute extends across all social situations, and on the notion that it is beyond the capacity of our institutions to serve the needs of those who have the attributes.

What is troubling is that progressive analysis easily lends itself to picturing relative differences in power—and hence responsibility, if one chooses to look at it that way—as absolute. The rich and powerful, pure as driven snow a few theories ago, become the embodiment of absolute evil, while the world's losers are rehabilitated prematurely to sainthood, enduring suffering in which, due to their absolute impotence, they bear absolutely no complicity.

Consider the old argument that everything in Black life can be viewed as derivations from or reactions to white oppression. Whites act, Blacks react. (Is this an unconscious form of boasting?) Slavery involves such unusually great disparities of power that it seems to attract periodic arguments of this sort (Elkins 1968; Genovese 1974). Slaves, we are told, were so absolutely impotent that they wound up internalizing whatever their masters thought about them. What that perspective precludes, of course, is any consideration of the sustaining, creative quality of the relations among slaves. It is a short step from there to the more exaggerated discussions of racial self-concept and self-hatred. The doctrine, once dominant and still common, that Blacks live lives of unending self-doubt and self-deprecation again reflects the assumption that whites have taken so much from Blacks that Blacks have nothing left to give to one another.

We get another version of people-as-the-sum-of-their-oppression in the popularity of the idea that Blacks have no distinctive culture of their own (Berger 1970). Ralph Ellison (1963:302) saw and reacted to elements of this in Myrdal:

But can a people...live and develop for over three hundred years simply by *reacting*? Are American Negroes simply the creation of white men, or have they at least helped to create themselves out of what they found around them? Men have made a way of life in caves and upon cliffs, why cannot Negroes have made a life upon the horn of white man's dilemma?

A doctrinaire progressive perspective is likely to overlook the extent to which some of the elements of Black life are simply a matter of what Blacks choose to be. It is likely to overlook as well the fact that some aspects of white life are the result of what whites have been forced to do or influenced to do by Blacks. See, for example, Vincent Harding's essay (1975) on the extent to which Blacks have shaped the political behavior of whites since World War II.

It is not surprising that while race relations is among the most studied of all topics, we have very little in the way of systematic analysis of how Blacks relate to one another. There are exceptions, including some of the recent work on the Black family, but "most of the research on black racial dispositions fails to collect and analyze data on the types of relationships among blacks and the social positions they hold in relation to one another" (Pitts 1974:675). This is particularly true of those relationships involving race consciousness or a sense of obligation to the group.

The deemphasis on intraracial relations necessarily means that we lose touch with a vital key to understanding change. We have an absurdly large and largely unprofitable literature on Black intelligence, taking intelligence to mean performance on IQ tests. If what we generally mean by intelligence, though, is the capacity to respond effectively to one's environment, there must be dozens of more useful ways to study it. One historically more useful way to think of it among American Blacks, for example, would be to treat intelligence as the quality of social relationships among them. As with many other deprived groups, Black capacity for cooperative interaction has historically been a way of compensating for the absence of other resources, an idea not much stressed outside some of the discussions of the Black family. The early success of the southern civil rights movement was largely based on its ability to exploit some of the positive elements of such communal traditions as remained among rural southern Blacks. On a number of grounds—the crime rate in the ghetto, the inability of many community organizations to generate any constituency, the alienation of Black youth from their communities—one might wonder whether the past three decades have seen a lessening in Black capacity for cooperative behavior. My guess is that what is happening to that form of intelligence matters a great deal more than how Blacks perform on IQ tests, and we know a great deal less about it. A doctrinaire progressive perspective, one that proceeds from the assumption that the only relationship worth analysis is that between oppressor and oppressed, will insure that we continue to know little about that other kind of intelligence.

The tendency to adopt without qualification a language of exploiters/exploited or victimizers/victims ought to be viewed in light of this tendency to confuse relative power differentials with absolute ones. The terminology is a good deal simpler than the world it purports to describe. The world would appear to consist of those who exploit other people more successfully and those who do so less successfully. We properly think of drug addicts as victims, but not to the extent that we forget that they too will probably create some victims. Ignoring the fact that some benefits, relatively small though they may be, do accrue to those on the bottom in their occasional roles as victimizers oversimplifies the world and patronizes its losers. More, we may lose a key to understanding how exploitative systems sustain themselves. The extent to which losers in a system are able to work that system for some slight gain ought to be taken into account whenever we consider the intransigence of inequality systems.

Thus the idea that the proper response to decades of denial fetishism is to study the rich rather than the poor is especially unhappy in that it once again points us away from the centrality of the relationship. Rather than an exacting analysis of how winners and losers create one another, and to what extent, such a viewpoint is likely to lead to a kind of romanticism, an updating of the noble savage. To be equally unkind to both sides, the faithful court scribes of the past may come to be replaced by public relations shills for society's losers. The irony in such a development would be that in reducing the political function of social analysis

to burnishing the public image of the downtrodden, there is an implication of the very mysticism that we are presumably trying to grow
beyond.

Many of us see and justify our work as providing a theoretical and
empirical base for practitioners of social change. Equipping them with
romantic oversimplifications may well lead to disillusionment. Any number of young teachers begin their careers in inner-city schools determined
to do the best jobs of which they are capable. Some of them begin
convinced that the problems of such schools lie entirely within the schools
themselves, having nothing to do with the nature of the students (Levy
1970). Given teachers who cared and acted like it, the students would
respond in kind. Now, most of this book is devoted to arguing that this
line of thinking is substantially correct. Still, by itself, that is much too
simplistic to protect one from the day-to-day pressures of teaching in
the slums. The children *are* problems, or so it must appear from the
teacher's desk. Many idealistic twenty-two-year-old teachers will be self-
consciously cynical at twenty-five, and a theory that oversimplifies the
world by patronizing its losers contributes to the process by which that
happens. Thus, analysis that is progressive in substance and in intent
may be quite conservative in its effect beyond the academy, which is
where we came in, as it were.

We ought not be troubled by the proposition that people ordinarily
end up contributing in some fashion to the systems that oppress them.
The groups of young men now terrorizing inner-city communities are
victims of race and class suppression. They are also its agents. They are
probably more effective agents of it than the night riders of yesteryear
because they are more demoralizing, eroding the communal bonds that
gave their grandparents a measure of support in the face of more obvious
agents of oppression. There is no reason we ought not see both aspects
of the situation. One can be devoted to the human race, James Baldwin
(in Hansberry 1970:xiii) once wrote, without being romantic about it.

In these more doctrinaire forms, progressive theory merely changes
the character assigned the villain's role. Amos and Andy are out, the
Rockefellers are in. The underlying conception of villainy remains the
same; that is, a simplistic one. Lawrence Levine writes:

The familiar urge to see in heroes only virtue and in villains only malice has an
analogue in the desire to see in the oppressed only unrelieved suffering and
impotence. This ideal construct—the ideal victim—is no more convincing or
supported by what we know of human psychology and history than the ideals
of pure hero or villain. (1977:xi)

There is a defensive quality to much of this work. The moment we
"admit" that the oppressed retain a measure of control over their lives,

we imply that they have also a measure of responsibility for their condition, an uncomfortable position for many of us, and uncomfortable for perfectly good reason, given the uses to which that notion has traditionally been put. This produces certain inconsistencies. Take the literature extolling the virtues of Black family life. While a welcome response to some of the usual slander, much of it could be accused of trying to dance at two weddings, the accusation that William Ryan makes against some denial theory. On the one hand, there is clearly a desire to credit Blacks for whatever in their family arrangements is deemed good—informal adoption arrangements, flexibility of roles, the viability of extended family systems. This implies that they have managed, oppression notwithstanding, to exert some power over their own lives. On the other hand, there seems to be a reluctance to allow the possibility that they have any responsibility for the negative elements, implying absolute powerlessness.

Consider Ryan's very influential *Blaming the Victim* (1971). It is an instructive and admirably outraged work, but also a defensive one. Ryan takes several components of the denial paradigm—Black matriarchy, cultural deprivation, culture of poverty—and carefully points out their logical and empirical inadequacies, arguing forcefully and in most cases persuasively that we have to understand the problems addressed by these theories as being caused by "loot and power, money and clout." One chapter responds specifically to those who are still gleefully counting Black bastards, promoting the image of "sluttish, promiscuous, conniving welfare mother[s]" (p. 88) having babies for fun and profit; having out-of-wedlock children, that is, because they come from a culture that doesn't teach people to consider the consequences of their actions so long as their actions are immediately pleasurable, because illegitimacy itself is just acceptable within that subculture, and because public assistance is so readily available.

Ryan responds, pointing out that there is good reason to believe that the statistics that point to a higher illegitimacy rate in the Black community are exaggerated, that white illegitimacy is very much underreported, that girls from middle-class backgrounds have traditionally had greater access to abortion and to information on contraception and a greater likelihood of going through with a shotgun wedding. He argues that only a minority of unwed mothers depend on welfare and that few sane people would choose Aid to Families with Dependent Children (AFDC) as a way of life except as a last resort. He argues, in short, that the problem of out-of-wedlock birth among the urban poor is not so much one of immorality as one of subtle social discriminations that deny the poor effective equality of choice.

Even taking Ryan's comments to be substantially accurate, they are misleading. He tends to frame his responses in a way that assumes that the fundamental issue is the moral stature of the poor. So much energy goes into defending their morality that there is no discussion of the consequences of high rates of illegitimacy for the individuals and communities involved. Regardless of what we think about anyone's moral stature, the pattern of babies having babies, as Jesse Jackson puts it, would be more problematic for Blacks than for whites if only because the Black community has fewer of the resources necessary to respond to the social, emotional, and financial problems associated with high numbers of out-of-wedlock births; further, some of the vehicles by which it has historically done so—notably the extended family form—seem to be attenuating even as the number of such births is rising. (According to the 1980 census, about half the Black children in the country now live with a single parent.)

If we are to go by Ryan's portrait, the factors shaping differences in illegitimacy rates are essentially beyond the control of the poor. That almost has to be unrealistic (or from the viewpoint of, say, Malcolm X, perfectly ridiculous). It is a safe bet that variations of sexist social norms are alive and well in the ghetto and are used by some males there to legitimate irresponsible sexual behavior—whether they are more or less responsible than someone else is not my concern. I am quite sure that the lack of economic resources is a more important factor in shaping life chances, but to proceed as though that were the whole story is misleading to say the least. Ryan is very aware of the dubious argument that all problems in the Black community, including its poverty, can be traced to one form of family instability or another; and he is right to reject it, but rejecting it does not mean implicitly adopting the position that none of those problems is in any way either caused by or correctable by the poor.

Every other argument in *Blaming the Victim* proceeds along the same track, stressing the moral fortitude of the poor and those causes for their predicament that are completely beyond their control. Ryan's chapter on crime analyzes the various venalities and hypocrisies of the criminal justice system, leaving out any discussion of what is clearly a predatory life-style among segments of ghetto youth. His comments on urban housing, for example, are so bent on demonstrating that all housing problems stem from the manipulations of the powerful as to pay no attention worth mentioning to the role played by lower-class people in the deterioration of lower-class neighborhoods. Granted, it takes a whole lot of kids setting fires and breaking windows to do as much damage to inner-city housing as the Department of Housing and Urban Development (HUD) has managed to do, but the kids do play their part.

Some authors, I am sure, write this kind of defensively one-sided analysis knowingly. The ordinary picture is totally negative. Thus we may be tempted to correct the imbalance by offering a picture that is totally positive. It is not likely, though, that we can get at much of the truth by taking the average of two distortions. Then, too, it may be that what is most enlightening in lower-class life-style is the ongoing struggle between what we consider the positive and negative elements. If so, we have to have both elements in the same picture, Robert Hill's *Strengths of the Black Family* (1972) and Moynihan's work in the same volume.

Ryan is attempting to promote change by undermining the ideological undergirding for the status quo. That is arguably one of the crucial tasks of the moment, but at some point Ryan's style of attack becomes counterproductive partly because, as was suggested earlier, it minimizes the discussion of the most reliable instrument of reform the poor have—themselves—and partly because it accepts the underlying logic of the official line. Ceaselessly insisting on the humanity of those whose humanity has long been held in question reaffirms the validity of the original question and the assumptions built into it. Denial theory claims that the poor have such-and-such a noxious characteristic and thus, at least by implication, deserve their lot. We immediately start hollering, no, they don't really have that characteristic or if they do they can't help it and thus deserve a better deal than they are getting. Either position accepts the validity of drawing a connection between character and entitlement. Neither position necessarily examines the soft assumption that is built in, the assumption that there is ordinarily some connection between virtue, defined any way you want, measured by any instrument you choose, and being at the top of the social order.

Maybe we should do it the other way around. Maybe we should go out looking for poor people who are in fact demonstrably lazy, irresponsible drunkards, so that we can ask what degree of shiftlessness justifies malnutrition? How much financial irresponsibility must there be before an individual loses the right to basic medical care? Where do we draw the bottom line on entitlements? What claim does a person have on the rest of us merely by being human? Even in these aggressively conservative times, it might over the long run be better to start raising the moral questions directly than to pretend that there are no people to whom they apply, or to continue constructing empirical questions so that they lead to the moral conclusions we advocate and obviate those we fear.

The best illustration of the counterproductive nature of some of this work comes from the attacks on the recent born-again genetic theories of racial inequality. Actually, some of the attacks were so quick, so loud, that you had to wonder if the scholars weren't protesting a bit too much. The debate probably did very little to change anyone's beliefs about race and intelligence, but it may have done much to reinforce for the broader public the notions that there is some measurable thing out there called intelligence and that it does and should relate in stable and important ways to material success—questionable notions both and vastly more harmful now than the simplistic versions of racism being attacked. The mythology surrounding the idea of intelligence serves in this era the social function served by doctrines of genetic inferiority in previous eras and serves no other function, unless it be the support of that thriving little industry devoted to its cultivation and measurement. There were writers who spoke to the more basic issues (such as Persell 1977), but I suspect their voices were lost in the storm. Rushing to defend racial equality, scholars ended up shoring up even more basic tenets of the meritocracy ideology by which inequality, racial and otherwise, is legitimated.

The paradox here is that doing a cosmetic job on the poor, something presumably done in hope—and saying "hope" makes the process sound more conscious than I imagine it to be—of promoting change, may actually reinforce instruments of oppression more potent than those being attacked. One is forced to argue that according to some shared and esteemed set of values this or that bunch of losers isn't really so bad as reputation would have it, but the content of those values may be more pernicious than the reputations of the poor. Vincent Harding's essay "History: White, Negro and Black" (1974) makes a similar point. By "White History" Harding means the traditional mainstream versions of the American experience. By "Negro History"—and he is at pains to say that he does not use the phrase pejoratively, that he recognizes that much of value has grown from this school—he means an approach that "accepts much, indeed most, of the basic white assumptions about the nature of society" (p. 54) even while disagreeing with White History in peripheral ways; that is, disagreeing with the way that history ordinarily portrays Blacks. It accepts the assumption that the basic story is a good and admirable one and asks only that Blacks be allowed into it. It then supports the request for membership, for entitlement, with the now familiar litany about the contributions of Blacks to American civilization. At the extreme, one finds oneself bragging about Blacks having participated in the opening up of the West—that is to say, in the extermination of American Indians—because that, after all, was a contribution. It is a history, in Harding's phrase, that is essentially aimed at creating a portfolio of credentials, a history that fails to question the assumptions built into the credentialing process. The point of "Black History" for Harding is precisely to question the basic assumptions and the basic values.

What Harding says about "Negro History" characterizes much work done in other areas of the social sciences; it too is aimed at creating a portfolio of credentials, and thus has built into it traditional assumptions about society, including an implicit theory of social change. Demonstrate that these people are in fact worthy according to the expressed rules of the game and one generates additional pressure for change. That hope probably accounts for many of the arguments to the effect that we have hardly made any progress on this or that problem. Proponents of that stance may agree with Camus that some change becomes the basis for denying any further change. Almost certainly, that fear accounts for some of the emotional quality of the debate over the exact size of the Black middle class. Concede that it is growing by leaps and bounds and you reduce the pressure that may lead to further growth. Argue that the changes have been minimal, that those who continue to suffer do indeed have the right credentials, and you keep the pressure on.

What we make of the probable efficacy of such an approach has to depend largely upon the audiences we have in mind. Are we speaking to students? To the disadvantaged themselves? To other academics? To policymakers? Aimed at policymakers, much of this does seem particularly questionable. Is there a level of human degradation so intolerable that if only we can capture it in sufficient depth, the resulting moral revulsion is going to cause significant shifts in policy? Granted, under particular (and peculiar?) sets of circumstances, work of this kind may have some impact on policymakers, but taken as a whole it seems to constitute an unwarranted level of faith in the sensibilities of the powerful, which can be compared with what sometimes seems to be our lack of faith in the potential of the relatively powerless. As a model of change, it seems wonderfully optimistic, thoroughly mystical, reminiscent of the civil rights moralists of two decades ago or of the Russian peasants who thought all their troubles would be solved "if only the Czar knew." Their disreputable image may help legitimate the status of outgroups, but treating it as the prime cause of that status is dubious policy.

A better case can be made for the proposition that major advances for outgroups in our society have not often come because someone on the top of the social hierarchy looked down and saw that people were being unfairly excluded from the good things of life. They have more typically come when outgroups themselves agitated or threatened (Piven and Cloward 1977) and/or when it was in the interest of ruling groups that concessions be made, as with the economic advances made by Blacks during World War II or by women since then.

There is something else to be said for change that comes from the bottom up. While top-down change may improve the life conditions of those at the bottom, we have every reason to think (Rothschild-Whitt 1979) that when those on the bottom themselves participate in changing their lives, they may also be significantly changed as persons, becoming more creative and effective social participants. James Farmer has put it well. Writing on the southern civil rights struggle, he speaks of the need

...to involve the people themselves, individually, personally, in the struggle for their own freedom. Not simply because it was clear that no one else was going to confer liberty upon them, but because in the very act of working for the impersonal cause of racial freedom, a man experiences, almost like grace, a large measure of private freedom. Or call it a new comprehension of his own identity, an intuition of the expanding boundaries of his self, which, if not the same thing as freedom, is its radical source.[2] (1966:17)

From that perspective, a social science that wishes to make some contribution to the lasting empowerment of people must begin with the assumption that they, even those at the very bottom, have at least potentially some influence over the conditions of their lives. That assumption has dual implications. We do not want to become so afraid of its familiar use by conservative ideologues to justify the status quo as to render us insensitive to its potential as a point of departure for change.

That we are often afraid is clear. It is partly fear, for example, that is reflected in some of the reactions to William Wilson's *Declining Significance of Race* (1979), which argues that class factors have recently become more salient than race in determining the life chances of Blacks. I did not think Wilson argued the case terribly well,[3] but, that aside, some of the more hostile reactions clearly reflected the fear that his work lends itself to being misused. Even some of those substantially in agreement with Wilson's work felt constrained to reject it out of fear that the argument would be used to rationalize attacks on affirmative action gains of Blacks, gains that are valued—minimal and class-biased though they are. In one discussion, Wilson was explicitly asked to disavow the "Charles River crowd"—that is, conservative Ivy League intellectuals.

We have to contend with the possibility that scholarly work, no matter what its intention, will be turned to the disadvantage of those whose lives most need improving. That possibility is all the more disturbing because, first, we cannot segregate audiences very effectively (leaving aside that segregation which is built into the language we use and our publication structure) and, secondly, because many of us are convinced that there is a wondrous ideological consistency in the way in which popular media select intellectual products for broader distribution—witness the attention given in recent years to the works of V. S. Naipul (e.g. 1976), William Wilson, and Richard Rodriguez (1982)—all nonwhite writers whose work contains elements that accord well with elements of the conservative agenda.

Take the problematics of writing or talking about Black colleges. Many of them find their future threatened by either inadequate resources or by governmental pressure or by both. The author's good intentions notwithstanding, any discussion that can be construed as critical of those schools is nearly certain to fuel the flames already jeopardizing institutions, which, whatever their problems, serve functions quite necessary to the aspirations of large numbers of Black people. That kind of thought can have a chilling effect on free inquiry. Many of the public discussions about Black colleges which I have attended or participated in over the past few years had an air of defensive dishonesty and it is not difficult to see why.

We have to choose among perils and I know of no general guidelines that I find satisfying. Still, there are several points we can consider. First, if a choice has to be made, it should be an explicitly self-conscious choice, not a reflexive acquiescence to the audience of "loot and power, money and clout" peering over our shoulders.[4] Automatic self-censorship grants that audience too much control over our lives and our thinking.

Second, the chance that one's work will be abused may sometimes be the lesser of evils. The overriding fact in the case of Black colleges may be—for me, is—that institutional growth and maturity are possible only where informed, sympathetic, and critical evaluation is available. Without it, many of the more problem-ridden institutions may well collapse under the weight of their own internal contradictions. If they must be destroyed, I would prefer that it be from the outside, which means that I prefer to see them honestly criticized, knowing full well that over the short term doing so plays directly into the hands of those most hostile to their existence.

Third, refraining from criticizing hardly means that one's work will not be abused. Work that examines Black schools but shrinks from saying anything negative is quite likely to be used by interested parties at those schools as grounds for denying or ignoring very real problems. Finally, we want to be aware that when our work is used to rationalize bad policy, it may only be rationalization; that is, the fundamental pressures for the policy stem from sources more important than the ruminations of the learned.

In 1934 DuBois had Black colleges in mind when he wrote that "if the truth about a situation in a university is bad publicity, the way to attack it is to change that truth and reform or not repeat the facts upon which it is based" (DuBois 1934:117). The status of Black colleges is probably much chancier now than it was in 1934, but DuBois's advice, as applied to this question and others, deserves to be considered before we allow ourselves to be intimidated into skirting the truth. (For a commentary on Black colleges with a balance that DuBois would have appreciated, see Marable 1983.)

Not all defensiveness can be attributed to the fear of airing one's linen in public. Many outgroups have seen so much professional literature that was insulting, that slandered them and caricatured their lives—whether conceived in plain malice or well-meaning but bungling ignorance; they have seen so much purportedly written in their best interests turned against them, that their nerves are constantly on edge. They and those who try to think from their perspective are thus hypersensitive, quick to reject anything that even looks like the same old stuff. We would be foolish to expect things to be otherwise, but such a pattern does mean that now and again a particular work gets an angry response not so much because of what it actually says but because of merely apparent association with historical tradition.

Something like this seems to have happened with Gutman's *The Black Family in Slavery and Freedom* (1976). Proceeding from the position that what was done *to* slaves is critical, but not so important that we ought to forget what slaves did *with* what was done to them, the book argued (and I thought argued well) that slaves managed despite all to retain surprisingly strong and supportive kinship bonds. Some of the reaction from both the left and the right took the book to be yet another apology for slavery, an attempt to rehabilitate the southern reputation, as one conservative writer approvingly put it. Coming from the left, such an interpretation may be explained by the fact that so much of what mainstream historians have written about slavery has in fact been apologetic that some of us have become quick to see that element even when it is not there. The fact that some people on the right read the book the same way, though, means the left is well advised to keep its guard up.

As things currently stand in the debate between traditional and less traditional ways of seeing inequality, the traditionalists are still exerting too much influence on the choice of questions even if they have less to say about the answers offered. There are reflections of that influence in the way we allow ourselves to be bemused by the notion of typicality, in the persistence of attempts to prove statistical equality between groups and in what I take to be an exaggerated concern with the question of causality itself.

Identifying the causes of inequality, the central question in all this business, can mean several different things. "Causality" may refer to the factors that originally brought a pattern of behavior into being or to the factors that sustain the pattern now or, less commonly, to the factors that can change it. In a particular case, the three sets of factors may or may not be the same. Certainly, there is no reason to assume that the factors that create or sustain a pattern are the only factors that can change it. Nevertheless, exactly that assumption is frequently made by individuals on both sides of the ideological divide. (This is at least arguably a self-serving assumption, since it implies that change cannot proceed until the all-important social analysts have done their work.) Supposing for the sake of argument that the real root cause of American racism is American capitalism, it does not follow that the only way to eliminate racism is to destroy capitalism nor does it follow that if we do destroy capitalism, racism will necessarily wither on the vine. When our central concern is with change, we might often do better to address that question directly rather than entering into the ongoing debate about original causes.

A study like Coleman's, a study clearly oriented toward its policy implications, should have devoted more energy to careful delineation of the circumstances under which poor and nonwhite children *do* learn, a question that would have dictated very different research strategies, and a question which, as we shall see in chapter 5, might have helped deliver us from more than ten years of fruitless debate. Of course, we learned something about promoting positive change from Coleman—even if some of it was misleading—but hardly what we might have learned had he been less concerned with identifying the original causes of achievement. Elizabeth Freidheim takes that point further:

...Consciousness must locate the preventing structures of life rather than the causal ones. Instead of assuming that some great constellation of deterministic force moves players around the social stage, consciousness assumes the players move by free will until they are stopped by social powers greater than themselves. This changes the basic scientific question. Common science looks at the current scene and asks "Why did this happen?" ...Using consciousness as our model we must think of a desirable outcome and ask "Why didn't this happen; what prevented people from doing this?" (1979:7)

Changing our organizing question from "Why did it happen?" to "What works? What is right and possible and how do we make it real?" would almost certainly raise the level of a discussion which has sometimes been pitched at a regrettably low level. That point has been made earlier, but it is worth reemphasizing that scholars, too, can fail by asking too little, settling for standards lower than would be possible. To take the case of Black colleges again, a few of them have been accused of graduating students with degrees in education who are utterly unprepared to teach. Of the rejoinders that can be made by defenders of those schools, none is more depressing than the one that goes: "Yes, that happens, but it happens at white colleges, too, and that's more important because there are more of them." All of that is of course true, but it offers mighty slim comfort. Taking what white colleges are as the standard for what Black colleges might be is certainly settling for too little. Even knowing something of the history and the politics which lead to that kind of short-sightedness, it has to be called capitulation.

The same logic (If we're equal, we're OK) underlies the attempts to derive moral stature from statistical equality. I mean here those arguments—Ryan has several—to the effect that with such-and-such a set of factors held constant, the distribution of this or that "pathology" would be no greater among Have-nots than among Haves. Blacks aren't *really* more criminal than whites, women aren't *really* less capable than men, poor people *do* love their children as much as wealthy people. Pretty modest boasting, isn't it? Again, even if we understand why people feel constrained to make these points, it remains true that these arguments, made in the name of outgroups, reaffirm that those who have historically excluded them are to be taken as the proper measure of human worth. Fannie Lou Hamer, for most of her life a farm laborer, used to say that the *last* thing she wanted was to be equal to Senator James Eastland, which meant she was free to have a larger set of standards than those by which other people had tried to define her.

It helps sometimes to ask: Whose questions are these, anyway? What is their social origin? What groups urged their consideration upon us? Take the argument, which apparently is to be with us always, over how bad slavery was. Now, whose question is *that*? Can you picture some field hand musing to herself or himself, "How bad is my life *really*?"

Some of the work aimed at finding out what is or is not typical of some population group might also be added to a list of questionable questions. We behave as if there were a decree somewhere to the effect that once we capture the central tendency in a situation, we have mastered its enduring essence. There are purposes for which it is vital to know whether the typical Black family is unstable, but what most matters for other purposes is that too many of them are unstable, no matter what the number may be.

Progressive theory that continues to make a fetish of finding the central tendency in everything is going to be a dubious improvement over denial theory. Denial theory's tendency to minimize social process lends itself to the perpetuation of static and inflexible images of human behavior. Despite disclaimers to the contrary, cultural, personality and attitudinal attributes are persistently treated as though their implications were more or less constant across a wide variety of, if not all, social situations. This is especially true where there are grounds for treating some attribute as "typical" of some segment of the population. In part, the reduction of relative to absolute power differentials is vexing precisely because it suggests that progressive theorists may not be immune to the tyranny of the construct of typicality, which would help explain the inability to see the powers generated by weakness and the infirmities caused by power.

Casting every problem in terms of the general tendency versus the exceptions to it, rather than in terms of two or more tendencies in active opposition to one another, means that we remain insensitive to the possibility that what is most interesting in a particular case is the interplay between what we label the general tendency and what we label the exceptions to it. Whenever it is the opposing tendencies that are most significant, it follows that the phenomenon under consideration cannot be adequately analyzed without considering the particular situation in which the phenomenon occurs, its context, since it may be that context which determines which of the struggling tendencies will be most important at a given time. Thus, rather than asking whether inner-city parents are interested in their children's education, we ask: Under what circumstances do they best express whatever interest they have? Such an approach, which might be termed a dialectical approach, would allow us to replace static phrases like "disadvantaged child" or "incompetent teacher" with concepts that allowed for the possibility of people becoming very different with a change in circumstances. Progressive analysis may give us this more "flexible truth," to borrow a phrase from Lorraine Hansberry (1970:219), but not if it persists in confounding the average with the whole. If only as a hedge against losing touch with the normal dynamic ambiguity of social experience, we need to have a sense of the full range of possibilities and how they might be changing, as much as we need to have a sense of the typical.

One final point: the language employed by progressive theorists is often depressingly similar to the esoteric, impenetrable jargon that more traditional academics have long been justly criticized for. The language immediately restricts the potential audience to those who have learned the magic words—which is to say the socially privileged—thereby creating in the *form* of the work the very kinds of caste distinctions that the *content* of the work is aimed at changing. The retort that complexity of thought requires complexity of language is seldom justified. Such is the wonder of the English language that a remarkably large number of important things can be said within it—witness the writings of *Dollars and Sense* on economics or Manning Marable on political economy.

Taken as a whole, progressive theory at its most defensive smacks of the dilemma of the Helpful Outsider—the man sitting in on a feminist consciousness-raising session, the Swarthmore graduate gone South to help the poor, situations that can generate an acutely felt need to demonstrate sincerity and noble intent. People in such situations may become more strident in their denunciations of the evils at hand than the people suffering from those evils, may become too concerned with proving themselves to be able to see clearly. Similarly, for academics of progressive bent, there may be a degree of felt accusation in the contradiction between lofty social ideals and actual social position. Counting white millionaires may be one way to convince ourselves that we stand yet on the side of the angels. We should remind ourselves from time to time of the distinction between the expressive and the instrumental consequences of our work. Producing work that serves our social and emotional needs, work that makes us feel good about ourselves, is not always going to be the same as producing work that contributes to change.

The outcome of the Outsider dilemma in discussions of educational inequality is work that seems motivated by the desire to establish some kind of symbolic solidarity with the poor. This seems particularly the case in the last ten years or so. Prior to then, the really critical errors seemed to be those most wedded to the denial tradition, taking the form of exaggerated concern with the characteristics, real and imagined, of the urban poor and their children, a focus on original causation, and little concern with questions of process and organizational context. Progressive theories are harder to generalize about, but they seem to have given us new errors—the substitution of the RAP thesis (It's all the teachers' fault) for attribute theory, accepting many of the questions of the denial paradigm while rejecting the answers that paradigm offered. Thus, people may be unwilling to study urban parents on the assumption that they aren't the cause of school failure. That may be true, but parents may still be worth more attention than they get from the ideological left as a part of the solution. Too, there is a refusal to think about the extent to which the children themselves are problematic, presumably based on fear of how that idea will be used. There has also been too much concern with "Why failure?" as though what is typical is also most instructive.

At the last, this discussion seems to have come to a place at which Harold Cruse—and Franklin Frazier before him and DuBois before that—arrived some time ago. In *Crisis of the Negro Intellectual* (1967), Cruse took that class to task for its lack of originality in generating its own questions and pursuing its own answers. The same point can be made about the left in general. Think, too, of Frantz Fanon—Come, let us leave this Europe. Leave it, he said. Not quarrel with it or prove ourselves to it. Leave it and its questions and its language as well (1968:311–13).

We cannot leave it all at once nor should we. Given the current political mood of the United States, particularly, it is still the case that for a specific purpose, with a specific audience in mind, the very approaches that have been most criticized here will continue to be the most valuable. At a minimum, though, we want to make sure that there is some careful consideration of the connections among the purpose and the content and style of our work.

Anyone familiar with the literature on inequalities of race and class over the last decade could cite a good number of works to which nothing I have said is applicable. I have complained so much not because the abuses typify recent work, but because they are common enough to interfere with the contribution researchers can make.[5]

There is a contribution to be made by students of inequality. Simply the fact that the structures on inequality have grown more complex means there is a greater need for people who have the time and the resources to examine them. The national mood may offer opportunities as well. It seems not so much a genuinely conservative mood as a "nasty mood, a cynical, distrusting and resentful mood," as someone has said, coming at a time when conservatives were best positioned to profit from popular attitudes. For a while, conservative intellectuals will be able to press their agenda with great vigor and visibility. Over the longer run, though, such a mood may evolve into a greater willingness among many audiences to consider ideas that previously would have been rejected out of hand. If more receptive publics are coming into being, we owe it to them and to ourselves to present the best we can present.

How shall we study inequality in a way that helps to change it? Nothing here points to a formula, but some considerations do stand out. First, we may want to be very careful about adopting an either/or posture. Either Black bastards or white millionaires. Either cultural deprivation or teacher expectation. If denial theory taken as a body will seldom be useful, it may contain particular ideas and concerns that ought not be written off because they are embedded in an unacceptable ideological context. On the other hand, I think we have to be more cautious about inadvertently accepting the framework of inquiry generated by the denial paradigm—its assumptions, its pet variables, its static imagery, its normative orientation, and its exaggerated concern with typicality and causation in the grand sense. We have to be more careful about overvaluing essentially cosmetic work while discounting the potential for change among Have-nots themselves. Simplistic versions of progressive theory lend themselves to conservative outcomes.

The Rationalization of Inequality

I have a set of assumptions about how patterns of inequality have been changing, which should be made explicit before we go on.

During the Vietnam War era, a Jules Feiffer cartoon appeared that went something like this: A man working in a munitions factory explains that he is not killing; he's just trying to get out a product. The same goes for the man who crates bombs in that factory. He's just packaging a product. He's not trying to kill anyone. So it goes until we come to the pilot who flies the plane that drops the bomb. Killing anyone? Certainly not, he's just pushing a button. In the last panel there is a Vietnamese peasant, dead, but not killed, you might say. The consequence is there, but born of a process so fragmented as not to register in the consciousness of those involved in it. (Life imitates art. Robert Lifton's *Home from the War* [1974:346–49] contains a section which might have been written just to prove Feiffer right.)

Feiffer need not have restricted himself to the example he chose. Indeed, he proceeds from a premise virtually axiomatic among sociologists: activities in the modern world tend increasingly to be characterized by a strict division of labor with any individual involved in only one or two segments of that process. It is easier, therefore, for that individual to focus on his or her immediate segment and ignore or deny the fundamental nature of the process, all the more so if the process is morally repugnant.

We might well presume that fragmentation of social process will affect the nature of the processes sustaining inequality and exploitation as much as it does narrower productive and administrative enterprises. My political sympathies notwithstanding, for example, I stand in an exploitative relationship to, say, Jamaican bauxite workers. The exploitation of that labor enables American manufacturers to obtain bauxite more cheaply than would otherwise be the case. Some of that advantage is then passed on to me when I purchase refined aluminum products. In a perfectly objective sense, I stand in a relationship to those laborers; a substantial loss for them gets translated into a small gain for me. I participate in thousands of such relationships, of course, and in each case so many relationships intervene between myself and the initiation of the process that under normal circumstances I remain happily unaware that any relationship exists. At the extreme, the fragmentation of social process precludes any consciousness of the process whatsoever.

To emphasize the rootedness of this kind of model in our intellectual traditions, we can call it the rationalization of inequality. Max Weber took "rationalization" to refer in large part to the process by which the ethos and structure of bureaucracy become increasingly embedded in our lives. One element of that process is the kind of fragmentation of process that shows up in the shift from generalist to specialist, in the assembly-line organization of work, in organizations subdivided into departments and offices each concerned with but a tiny segment of the organization's life. Rationalization had other connotations for Weber, but fragmentation of process was certainly a key element. As applied to inequality, rationalization means that the processes sustaining inequality are shaped by chains of interaction extending across many individuals or organizational units or institutional boundaries.

The sharecroppers of a generation ago could understand their exploitation in explicitly personal terms, naming particular decisions made by particular men at particular points in time which robbed them of their substance. The system required powerful institutional support, but for all practical purposes sharecroppers found their lives held in the palm of one man's hand, the landlord's, and they knew that man's name and face and history. The landlords were generalists, we might say, and the process fairly simple. Many of the descendants of those sharecroppers, in contrast, find their life chances shaped by "structural unemployment." Who can name the person responsible for something as amorphous as "structural unemployment"? Inequalities that were once clearly done *to* people, imposed upon them, come increasingly to seem as if they just *happen* to people.

Were we to look more closely at some particular Black child, we might find that some first-grade teacher in a slum school decided he had little chance to learn much because children who looked like him, dressed like him, and talked like him seldom did well in school and so the teacher, having many other responsibilities, made only the most minimal attempts to teach him. Accordingly, some sixth-grade teacher found him so far beneath the skill level at which she had been trained to teach that she taught him nothing at all; and therefore some high school counselor later took one look at the child's record and suggested that he might do well in shop courses; and so some personnel officer four years later looks at the youngster's performance on an employment test (which is likely to be quite unrelated to the ability to do the job in any case) and suggests that the young man maybe look elsewhere and come back when he has some experience. So the young man looks at the military where some desk sergeant sees his score on the Armed Forces Qualifying Test ("We give the same test to everybody, rich or poor, Black or white. Grade 'em on the same machine.") and realizes that this boy was born for combat arms. After a tour of duty, the young man, thinking he has some experience, goes looking for that personnel officer only to find that the factory has moved south where labor is cheaper. In fact, it moved to a place right down the road from where his sharecropper granddaddy used to live. Had he found the personnel officer, though, he would have been quickly relieved of the idea that you learn marketable skills in combat arms. Either way, we add one more to the ranks of the structurally unemployed.

You can call the process racist, but there need be no racists in it. At nearly every step in the process, people can act in accord with established norms of fair play, perhaps even with the best interests of the young man at heart. There are no generalists here, only specialists in a process too fragmented to be easily identified as a process.

In terms of stability, such a system should have much going for it. Drawing again on the tradition of Weber, we would expect that as rationalization makes the experiences generating inequality increasingly impersonal, it makes those experiences increasingly less likely to generate the kind of emotional response that crystallizes easily into destabilizing discontent. Rationalized inequality does not make for a gripping ninety-second spot on the evening news. The de-dramatization of inequality hastens its depoliticization.

Rationalization should mean that the unfocused anger of Have-nots, other things being equal, should increasingly be turned on one another. Even for them, denial theory becomes more plausible even as it becomes increasingly anachronistic. For most ghetto residents, understanding the implications for their lives of capital mobility or redlining requires an act of imagination, but they can hardly miss the impact of the local street gangs or the junkies or the pimps. These people have faces. Mortgage bankers and insurance brokers, from the vantage point of the ghetto, do not. There will remain a sense that "they," some vague and faceless "they," are still rigging the game, but just who and how remain obscure.

As Feiffer implied, the ordinary propensity of Haves to deny any complicity in the problems of Have-nots ("Look, I never owned any slaves and it just so happens that my wife *likes* doing the dishes") is strengthened immensely by the rationalization of inequality. This is not just a matter of the process being obscure. Even when the linkages are made clear, the triviality of one's contribution in contrast to the enormity of an admittedly noxious process militates against any personal sense of responsibility. I think here of the recent reaction of college trustees to charges of their complicity in South African apartheid. They typically joined in the general condemnation of the cumulative product maintaining all the while that their own involvement was so negligible as to hardly be involvement at all. Small wonder that good will comes to have such a bad odor. In any case, alienation—the sense that one is not a significant part of the process—seems incompatible with a sense of moral responsibility, as much in the corporate board room as in the ghetto and a more rationalized world is inherently a more alienated one.

Steve Biko (Arnold 1979:336) quotes a passage from Karl Jaspers in which Jaspers, reflecting on the Nuremburg trials, claims that there is a solidarity among people through which we all bear a measure of responsibility for every injustice and wrong committed in the world and especially for those of which we cannot be unaware. If we do not do all that we can to prevent them, we are accomplices, violators of an absolute human command that says accept life for all together or not at all.

It is an ennobling sentiment, seldom so well expressed and it has exactly no relationship to the modern world. A social world of fragmented causality implies a moral world of collective responsibility, an idea which boasts the authority of the Old Testament. It is the doctrine of original sin writ anew. The new version, like the old, is apt to prove an indifferent moral imperative. Everybody-is-guilty simply does not move us very much. Since the Industrial Revolution we have had no comfortable niche in our ethical traditions for collective responsibility, all the more so since fragmentation means that there are no longer wrongs of which we have to be aware. A case can be made that American social thinking is moving toward greater sensitivity to what Jackall calls the real and symbolic interconnectedness of life but for the foreseeable future our moral antennae will remain attuned to the involvement of particular individuals in discrete evils, a way of saying they will be out of touch with reality as often as not.

The fragmentation of the processes sustaining inequities makes attribute thinking increasingly appealing. As the puzzle becomes more complex, the temptation becomes stronger to focus on whatever pieces are seen most conveniently. Even if some expressions of progressive theory are disappointing, it does not by its very nature virtually preclude the holistic consideration of the problems we study, consideration not only of the characteristics of people, but of the larger social contexts in which they operate. The search for the causes of social inequity has always had a moral dimension even though the professional pretensions of the searchers once made it difficult for them to admit that. The question has always reduced to: Who is responsible for the hurts of the world? As the answers to that become more complex, progressive theory, even if some expressions of it are disappointing, becomes more important insofar as it is willing to examine a broader spectrum of the social order.

The rest of this work is given over to the examination of institutions which, from the viewpoints of those closest to them, are failing—indeed depraved—institutions. It is a system of organized irresponsibility so structured that those who work very hard to create failure have little sense of doing so and thus no sense of responsibility for the fruits of their labor. In this respect, inner-city schools are perfectly modern institutions.

Notes

1. Thomas Cottle (1969:56) wonders if one of the reasons correlations so often emerge as causal certainties is that social scientists are responding to a public intolerant of tentativeness in its "experts."

2. Within the civil rights movement, the philosophy on which Farmer is drawing is associated particularly, but by no means exclusively, with the personal influence of Ella Baker and the organizational influence of the Student Nonviolent Coordinating Committee (SNCC). While the social sciences borrowed a great many themes from the activists of the sixties, the stress on individual empowerment seems to have made little lasting impression, although there are signs of renewed interest lately in the form of more concern with participatory and collectivistic structures.

3. I agree with Wilson's stress on the Black underclass, with the contention that a purely racial interpretation lends itself to reactionary uses, and with his public statements about the increasing irrelevance of Black "leadership." Implying that the insistence on a racial interpretation is *only* an attempt by that leadership and the strata that produce it to defend vested interests goes too far. More, the title is mischievous and not particularly related to his evidence. Certainly what he presents as impersonal class barriers are not racially neutral (see Payne 1980). Additionally, he is not much clearer than the rest of us about how to analyze the intersection of past racism with present advantage.

4. Given the levels of distrust across ideological lines, we have to consider the possibility that until there is some fundamental change in the distribution of power and privilege, we ought abandon the conception of an intellectual "community" that is capable of open dialogue or, for that matter, that is worth it. Perhaps the veil that DuBois used to speak of is now, as it was then, just too

thick to permit honest communication on the questions that most matter, even when all concerned are in earnest. If so, we might do better to try to create channels of communication that are narrower, better approximating the limits of our trust and thus better allowing us to speak such truth as we can see without fear of what hostile audiences will do with it.

5. This chapter has been criticized, accurately, for failing to provide guidelines for the systematic integration of the denial and progressive paradigms. That question cuts across so many different subject areas, that I am simply unable to speak to it. I do feel, though, that much of what is said here reduces to an argument for a more dialectical mode of analysis.

2

Westside and the Production of Disorder

Physically, Chicago's Westside High School is all that one expects a slum school to be—a tired building in a tired neighborhood. What is referred to as the "new" section of the building was built in the 1920s. The majority of the windows outside are broken or boarded over, as are many inside. Some classroom walls show the effects of past fires, others have desks that have been ripped from the floor. Hall lockers by the dozen have been so damaged as to be useless. The gym is a dingy, dimly lit little snake pit. Just looking at the place can make you feel weary.

Academically, Westside was, at the time of the study beginning in 1972, among the city's poorest schools. Judged by its attendance and dropout rates, it ranked well down among the worst fifth of Chicago schools. Reading scores for the all-Black student body were consistently at or near the bottom in the annual citywide testing. Reading scores for entering freshmen hovered around the sixth-grade level, just about the national norm for Black students entering ninth grade. There was a subpopulation of students classified as educable mentally retarded with even poorer skills.

The ghetto served by Westside was a fairly new one, certainly as compared to the older and—to let its residents tell it—more sophisticated Black settlement on the city's South Side. Still, the neighborhood had gone through a good deal in ten or fifteen years. Just fifteen years before, it had been the place for Blacks to move to. When the study began in 1972, it was a place to move from, if at all possible. Demographic shifts had caused the school's population to go from a high of around 5,000 to about 3,000 when the study began and half that before it finished.

In the mid-to-late 1960s when the school's population was largest, so were its street gangs. The Conservative Vice Lord supergang had been the best known, but it had to compete with a number of smaller groups.

Gang activity had largely abated by the time I came there, but had not been entirely eliminated. Certain parts of the building were still designated as belonging to this or that group.

Like the neighborhood, the school had had its ups and downs. We think of slum schools on the whole as being demoralized, but there are differences. Here or there, a successful athletic team, a single strong academic department, a popular principal, or a vigorous special program may allow students and staff to derive some measure of pride or satisfaction from their association with what is in fact a bad school. Such was not the case at Westside. Athletic glory was a thing of the past. The principal was neither much liked nor much respected. There were no programs that one might feel tempted to brag about. There were teachers around who could remember when the neighborhood had been different and the academic program superior, but that was a memory. Westside was thoroughly demoralized. Like the neighborhood, it was pretty much at the bottom, not on the way there.

The morale problems among students and staff were related in circular fashion to Westside's image as a tough school, a place with hard-to-handle students, dangerous students. Substitute teachers sometimes refused to work rather than accept a position at Westside. Certain of Chicago's high schools are supposed to be so bad that any principal who can keep one of them quiet for two years is guaranteed promotion to a higher administrative level. Westside is said to be among them. Whether any such policy exists in fact—and the career patterns of past principals suggest that it may—the rumor reflects how Westside was thought of within the city school system. Similarly, the three to five city police officers assigned to the school's security staff both reflect and add to the school's image as a difficult place to work in.

The image of schools like Westside for those who are not in them seems to be shaped largely by the more dramatic expressions of disorder—stabbings, shootings, fires set by students. These do happen, of course, and the effect of a single such incident will linger a long time. From the viewpoint of teachers in the school, though, what may be equally troubling are the more day-to-day kinds of misdeeds. Their sheer volume can overwhelm teachers, grating like sandpaper and contributing to the sense of individual impotence and collective futility that is the hallmark of slum education. Certainly the misbehavior of students contributes to the belief of many teachers that such students cannot be taught because they do not want to be taught. If they do want to be taught, you will hear many teachers say, some of them have mighty unusual ways of showing it. Faced with students who often fail to show up at all; who, when they do decide to put in an appearance, are often totally unprepared; who are frequently just too "cool" to bring a book or paper and pencil; students who often fail to observe the most minimal rules of classroom decorum or common courtesy—putting their feet up on the desks, listening to their radios in the classroom, sleeping in class, refusing to answer when spoken to or answering finally in the most insolent tone they can manage—given a daily diet of this, never certain when these minor problems will flare up into something more threatening, most of us would find it difficult to retain faith in the educability of our students. Teachers are right: if the students are interested in education, many of them have strange ways of showing it.

Such a portrait is accurate as far as it goes, but it leaves out a great deal. If many children in inner-city schools typically fail to give their teachers more than the most minimal kinds of cooperation, if such schools are typically academic disasters, what is typical hardly exhausts what is significant. There are, now and then, successes among the failures and they matter. Robert Coles (1971:528), after visiting slum schools in more than a dozen cities, says that even in the poorest schools "some really luminous and inspiring moments were to be had." That could be said of the teaching at Westside and it could be said of the way teachers and students interact as well. The students may be a pretty rebellious bunch in general, but they are not equally rebellious with all teachers. Some few teachers seem to have been given a grant of immunity. They can ordinarily count on reasonable levels of cooperation from the very students who are driving their colleagues into a state of resigned withdrawal. There is a striking difference between what goes on in the classrooms of these few and what occurs in the classrooms of other teachers, striking enough that if the average teacher got cooperation from students comparable to that given the most favored teachers, the character of the institution would be sharply altered.

It was essentially this problem that brought me to Westside. I wanted to find out whether some teachers were in fact consistently more successful than others at eliciting student cooperation—I was not all that sure that there were such teachers at the beginning. If there were, I wanted to try to explain why. That is, of course, a question which by its nature does not easily lend itself to explanation from the perspective of the denial paradigm. Psychological problems of students, their immersion in the culture of the street or features of their home backgrounds certainly play a role in shaping student misbehavior, but such factors cannot tell us much about why student behavior varies so much across situations. To explain that, it seemed to me that we would do better to look at the structure of relationships in different situations. (As I see it now, my approach to the question had too much of the RAP thesis built into it, as will become clearer at the end of this chapter.)

The experience that first led me to wonder about this problem had already led to some tentative answers. Before going to Westside, I spent a year observing classes at a street academy serving students in another section of the Westside ghetto. The Outpost, as it was called, admitted students who had either already dropped out of school or who were in clear danger of doing so. Academically and behaviorally, these students had had particularly negative school histories. Nevertheless, aside from some class skipping, student misbehavior was a minor problem. On the contrary, as compared to what one finds in the regular high schools in the area, student-teacher relationships were exemplary, warm and mutually supportive, extending beyond the confines of the school building and after school hours.

When students talked about how their experience with teachers at the Outpost contrasted with what they had known of teachers elsewhere, two themes struck me with particular force. One was that their former teachers often seemed almost to go out of their way to humiliate students, to make them feel small in various ways. Many of the teachers, that is, were seen as behaving in status-degrading ways, while teachers at the Outpost were seen as being egalitarian. Moreover, the students felt very strongly that teachers at the Outpost made a more determined effort to teach more carefully and thoroughly than was normal for inner-city schools. From what I could see, the students were right about this.

This led to two expectations. First, I thought that the more status-degrading a teacher's style, the less likely students would be to cooperate with that teacher, other things being equal. One of the more salient aspects of social interaction in almost any context is the degree to which the interaction operates as a threat to or a support for our sense of self. It seems reasonable to expect that in an inner-city high school, the differences of race, life-style, class, and status separating student from teacher, along with the general ill-humor that often pervades such schools, would lead teachers to behave in ways that, from the students' viewpoint, were status-degrading.

I had had earlier experiences which made me feel that status degradation might be an especially important part of the experience of being schooled in the inner city. When I was a teacher's aide in an elementary school serving low-income Black children, frequently when a lesson called for students to read aloud or work math problems on the board, some of the students would begin "cutting the fool." It was as if they had decided that it was better to be sent from the room than to have one's weaknesses put on display. Others would read in such low, mumbling tones that it was nearly impossible to tell if they were reading well or not. More poignant still, some would habitually slip the jackets from the sixth-grade books they could not read onto the second-grade books they could read. I doubt that many observers spend time in inner-city schools without seeing patterns which suggest that students are aware of and often embarrassed by their deficiencies. In such a situation, even if we ignore those teachers who are bluntly unconcerned with the feelings of students, it is not difficult to see how quite well-meaning teachers could unintentionally operate in a way that students would find threatening.

The quality of teaching merges with the exposure of students to status degradation. The consequences of poor teaching at one point in time translate into deficiencies which make the student emotionally more vulnerable at some later time. Still, the two are separable and it seems reasonable to expect that the quality of the teaching—amount of information successfully conveyed, skills sharpened, the sense of growth imparted—would have important implications for student behavior all apart from the issue of status degradation. To be a student is to give up a good deal, including the ability to control one's own time and movements. Where the teaching is good, there is a kind of quid pro quo; one gives up something and one gets something. Where the teaching is poor, the student is being asked to give up something for nothing. In sum, I expected the inner-city high school to be a place where status degradation and ineffective teaching undermined the legitimacy of many teachers, assuring them of more trouble than they could handle.

I was at Westside for about eighteen months from the middle of the 1972–73 school year until June 1974, with a hiatus of about two months at the beginning of the second school year. I observed classes, talked with teachers, students, and administrators, and examined school records.[1] I also conducted fairly formal interviews with students about their behavior and the behavior of their teachers as they saw it. The interviews, which typically lasted about an hour, could be called semistructured. Every student was asked the same group of core questions but not always in the same order or with the same phrasing. Since I wanted the tone to be as conversational as possible, I encouraged students to go off on tangents if they seemed interesting.

I was allowed to tape record all but one interview. Overall, the students were interested in what I was doing, were very cooperative, but frequently either nervous or suspicious as well. I am sure that there were some who never stopped believing me to be a cop of some previously unencountered type. The nervousness was expressed in a few cases by attempts to avoid me as long as possible, more often by staring throughout the interview at the floor, the ceiling or whatever printed matter might be about. Sometimes it was expressed simply by reticence. Even those students who impressed me as most self-assured often said, when asked about it after the interview, that they had been at least a little nervous, despite my attempts to set each respondent at ease before we began.

It is best, then, to assume that students weighed carefully the remarks they made in the interviews. Given the presence of the tape recorder, the kinds of things we were discussing, the unfamiliarity of the situation, and the fact that I was seldom able to establish much of a relationship with students before the interviews, that is not surprising. It is especially likely that students held back some on negative remarks about their teachers. Students were asked several times to grade their teachers on this or that characteristic and then to explain the grades. In the vast majority of cases when there was an obvious discrepancy between the grade and the student's explanation for it, the student had assigned a teacher a relatively high grade and then was unable to think of anything positive to say about that teacher. Respondents often hesitated a good while before saying something negative and a few went so far as to ask me to shut off the tape recorder temporarily.

I had done a pretest earlier and student reaction to that was quite different, possibly because I was able to establish something of an informal relationship with the students before interviewing them. They were much more relaxed about the whole affair, as indicated by less concern with the tape recorder, more cursing, and more irreverent comments like "I can't get along with her because she's a Virgo," or "I go to her class because she has nice legs." These students were sharply more critical of teachers.

The context of the interview also made a difference. Whenever I spoke to students in groups rather than individually (all of the formal interviews were done privately), the number of critical remarks about teachers escalated and they were delivered eagerly. Students competed with one another to see who could think of the shoddiest examples of teacher behavior, for all the world like their teachers sitting in the teachers' lunchroom competing to see who could offer the most egregious examples of student stupidity and irresponsibility. It was as if each group had a norm insisting that the other group be always pictured in the most disparaging terms and in the presence of one's peers that norm would be followed, even though privately expressed opinions might be somewhat different.

If students did hold back some on critical remarks, that is not all bad. One of the disadvantages of using the reports of students as a guide to teacher behavior is that such reports are certain to reflect student biases to some degree. Here, though, it is not necessary to worry much about whether students have exaggerated the negative side of their teachers.

I interviewed fifty-two students chosen randomly from school records. In addition, I did pretests with twenty students and junked another thirty interviews because of an administrative reorganization of the school's population. (Using the fifty unused interviews in the analysis that comes in chapter 3 would not have changed it significantly.) Doing the interviews took longer than I thought it should. The reasons for this are worth going into because they suggest a good deal about the nature of the school as an organization.

My sample was drawn from the program office files which were supposed to contain a class schedule and other pertinent data on each student in the school. The difficulty began right there. Every card contained some erroneous information. At the very least, the class schedule was wrong, probably more than once. The homeroom assignment might have changed several times since the card was prepared. It was entirely possible that the student's name was wrong.

After I drew up the sample, I consulted other records that indicated whether the student was a dropout or was classified DNA (does not attend). Those records, though, were unreliable and had to be cross-checked with information from the teachers. Sadly, the teachers were not always right about who had dropped out, so that I had to adopt a policy of not giving up on a name until at least two teachers said the student was out of school. Even so, I am sure I gave up on at least a few students who were in the building somewhere. Fortunately, information from some teachers could be relied upon absolutely. Some could tell you not only which of their students were attending but also which of other teachers' students were attending, what students were doing when they were not in school, and which of a student's buddies might be willing to track him or her down for you.

Once I knew which students really did come to school, there was the problem of locating them in the building. From an examination of teacher's attendance books for the English Department during the 1972–73 school year, I concluded that students skip English class about 48 percent of the time, although English is a requirement. (Treat this as a rough guide only since, as we shall see, attendance books were as problematic as other records.) After I knew that students were in fact going to school and had some idea of what their real schedules were, it normally took a few visits to classrooms before I actually encountered my quarry in the flesh.

Having caught up with the respondent, explained the study, and begged cooperation, it only remained for me to schedule a mutually agreeable time. Again, the likelihood was that the respondent would not really show up at that time, so the hunt began again. Most interviews had to be scheduled either during a gym class or a study hall. Study hall in particular was a bad joke. During most periods of the day few people showed up for study hall, and that sometimes included the study hall teacher.

The chase for students was instructive. Once I got over the unfairness of a world so inconveniently arranged for the purposes of researchers, the difficulty of locating students forced me to think more about Westside as an organization. I had gone there solidly fixated on teacher-student relationships, perfectly content to ignore the broader context of that interaction as much as possible. The chase for students made me aware of how poorly the basic machinery functioned and of how thoroughly its failure to function adequately impinged on everything else that went on in the school. It made me think about the nature of an institution so badly organized that it quite literally did not have much notion who its members were, let alone where they should be at any given time. Thinking about the nature of the organization then led me to realize I was asking some pretty poor questions.

The Production of Disorder

Disorder is, in a sense, the first fact of life at Westside. It is a wondrously, joyously disorganized place. On occasion the disorder reaches truly spectacular levels, but even on an ordinary day it attains levels that can only be reached through cooperative effort. They may snipe and sneer at one another, but administrators, teachers, nonprofessional staff, and students all manage to pull together for the perpetuation of disorder.

One need not actually enter the building to realize that Westside is a confused place. As you approach the building, weather permitting, you will ordinarily encounter students, many of them cutting class, milling about in clusters near the entrance or propping up the walls. The scene inside is much the same. Students who are supposed to be in class wander the halls as if that is what they came there to do. It is certainly not unusual to see, in one short section of corridor, fifty to a hundred students scattered about in small clusters during the middle of a class period. Late in the day, the number may double, and if there is some special activity going on, the halls may become nearly impassable. Students don't just stay out in the halls. They make them an extension of the street corner. They smoke cigarettes or marijuana, play whist or spades, listen to their radios, work on their dance steps or their choral singing. A few enjoy setting off fire alarms from time to time, requiring the evacuation of the entire building.[2]

Westside has all the normal institutional arrangements to control student movement and then some. A detachment of Chicago police officers is in the building at all times. Several aides are assigned primarily to hall control. Students are supposed to carry ID with their class schedules. A teacher is assigned to monitor every section of hallway and every stairwell virtually every minute when classes are in session. The guardians, though, are about as unpredictable as the guarded. Some issue half-hearted challenges, some ignore the chaos and try to catch up on their reading. Those who vigorously try to establish the rule of law are too few to make a difference. Defiance of the authorities becomes a sport for some students. The verbal exchanges with cops and hall guards become contests of wit and quick-mindedness. Being chased down the halls entails enough danger to give it zest, but hardly enough to be frightening.

In a school like Westside, getting students out of the halls and into the classrooms can be a complex and difficult matter, or so it is said. Revealingly, the school does not do much better with far simpler problems. If Westside does a poor job of getting its actors where they are supposed to be when they are supposed to be there, for example, it does an even worse job of getting them the information they need to play their various roles. No information is so simple that the institution cannot find a way to mistransmit it. Even so basic a matter as whether one is a member of the institution is not always clear.

I interviewed one freshman girl who was unable to compare her teachers because she had been going to only one class. For several months, she had been arriving at the building around 10:30, dutifully going to biology and then going home. At the beginning of the school year, she explained, her family had been in the midst of moving and she had expected to transfer to another school. The transfer did not work out, and she started Westside two weeks into the school year. Subsequently, a letter was sent to her home advising her that she had been dropped from all classes but biology. Her uncle came to the school to inquire about the problem, and left with the impression that there was nothing to be done about it. Her homeroom teacher gave no indication that he even knew of the situation, although he presumably was expected to keep records on both her attendance and her grades. Her counselor, eager to be of help, suggested that perhaps she should consider leaving school since her sixteenth birthday was coming up.

After the (brief) interview, the student and I went to speak to several members of the school staff about her situation, ending up with her counselor. The counselor explained that the whole thing was just a misunderstanding, that the letter that had been sent home had said only that she was failing most of her courses, not being dropped from them. The student vehemently denied this, but the counselor stood by his explanation, indicated very clearly that we were making too large a fuss over so small a matter and promised that he would have it all straightened out in short order.

Now, the interview in which I learned all this occurred in April; the letter had been sent in December. In all that time, the student had been allowed to just float along, acting on a false definition of the situation. In four months, neither her counselor nor her homeroom teacher could find the ten minutes it would have taken to straighten out her confusion. None of her classroom teachers managed to reach her, this despite the fact that Westside had aides specifically assigned to the task of calling the parents of missing students.

The incident surprised none of the staff members with whom I later discussed it, although perhaps they were merely disguising their true feelings. The institutional climate militates against showing surprise at bad news. In any case, the student had essentially lost a year out of her educational life, and the example is extreme only in its consequences. Just as it is not always clear who is a student at Westside, it is also not always clear who is going to graduate from it. Each June, a number of seniors find out that because of inaccurate information on their transcripts discovered at the last moment, they cannot graduate after all. In most cases, the anguish produced by that discovery could have been avoided with just a little attention to simple arithmetic. When I originally sampled student records at Westside, the total number of credits earned was inaccurate on about one card in five.

Records kept by teachers are hardly an improvement over those maintained by the central office. It is hard to know, for example, exactly what relationship teachers' records of student attendance bear to reality. One of the assistant principals told me that when auditors checked teachers' attendance books for the year prior to my coming to Westside, they determined that only 2 out of about 140 books had been done correctly. During the last several weeks of the school year, teachers' record books differed as to the total number of school days, largely because different teachers chose to stop taking attendance at different times, just as they decided to stop teaching at different times. During my first year at Westside, over half the teachers in the English Department marked students absent on Christmas Day, or during the teachers' strike or at some other time when school was not actually in session. That implies that the books were being filled in long after the fact, but what is interesting is the implication that teachers do not seem to make much effort to make the books even appear credible.

With urban schools we have to be even more cautious than we normally are about taking data drawn from official files at face value. If one looked only at school records, average class size at Westside would have been fairly large. The numbers of people actually showing up was ordinarily much smaller. Many classes had in fact between ten and fifteen students. What is interesting is how teachers responded to that. In the main, they did not adjust to the relatively small classes by shifting to teaching methods that would give students more individual attention. By and large, they continued with the kinds of class presentation that might have been designed for classes of forty.

In class, face-to-face communication could be as problematic as record-keeping. In the interviews, students mentioned some teachers with whom no relationship was established in which meaning, confused or otherwise, could be communicated:

He just sat in his chair, didn't do nothing, just wrote how many questions [we were supposed to do], like one to six or what page and he'll say do it Friday, and he don't explain. . . . When somebody ask him something, he act like he don't hear them, he'll just be sitting up there and keep on writing.

He's dumb. He'll daydream all day long. Don't nobody get no work done and half the time everybody be gone. . . . He probably knows what he doing, but he don't do it right whatever he supposed to be doing. . . . He got all the work up on the bulletin board. And you ask him when it's supposed to be turned in and he'll tell us, "Turn it in when you're ready to turn it in." And you ask him whether you failing or you got a passing grade and he say he don't know.

I had a problem with her in one of my marking periods. . . . It had something to do with the grade she gave me. I didn't like the grade she gave. And I tried to tell her about it but she just wouldn't listen to me. So what I did, I just stood there and looked out the window for about three weeks. Then she started telling me something that if I'd make a good grade this marking period I think she said she'd give me a good grade next time.

He come to his class, he do his work and that's it. He don't talk to you or nothing, he just give you the work and you do it, turn it in, grades you and all that.

In fifty-two interviews twenty-one students referred to at least one teacher who "doesn't listen," "doesn't talk to you," or "just comes in and sits there," all pointing to relationships so shallow that information is unlikely to be exchanged accurately. Similarly, of the thirty-six respondents who had been at Westside the previous year, fifteen forgot the name of at least one teacher they had had during that year.

Keeping attendance, keeping track of credits earned, letting students know where they stand, letting them know when the work is due—these are usually simple matters. The denial paradigm implies that Westside's failure to teach effectively or to control the halls results from the difficulty of these tasks, given the material with which the school must work; however, the same line of reasoning clearly cannot be applied to the school's failure in much simpler tasks. Westside consistently fails to do even those things that it very clearly could do.

The general disorder is so predictable that Westside's administrators have to plan around it, sometimes in humorous ways. Near the end of one marking period, a memo was distributed, detailing the procedures for handing in grades. There was grumbling at the end of each marking period because some faculty members were chronically late getting their grades in, which created difficulties for everyone else. In very strong terms, the memo stated that this time everyone had better have grades in by such and such a time on Tuesday afternoon. The very next paragraph said that any grades not turned in on Tuesday had sure better be in on Wednesday.

Another memo advised students that certain rules were going to be enforced more stringently than in the past. Male students were not to wear hats in the building, no radios were to be played in the building, and there was to be no more card playing. Two things are notable about the memo. First, it was dated January 28, which seems late in the game to be establishing ground rules. Second, the memo was accompanied by the following form:

Statement of Accomplishment

I certify that the following have been accomplished per the principal's instructions: Each student in my division has received a copy of the memo on student rules and a discussion of the memo has been held during division time.

Teacher's Name

The memos capture much of the essential administrative style at Westside. Administrators did not expect the cooperation of teachers even on routine matters, even when the teachers were substantially in agreement with administrative goals. Their distrust of teachers led the administration to adopt a quasi-threatening posture or to treat teachers like children, both of which techniques were ordinarily counterproductive. Even when trying vigorously to be taken seriously, the administration managed to convey its lack of self-confidence, its directives coming off as so much bluster. This was all the more likely because such attempts were inconsistent and untimely and often made much of fairly minor matters while granting teachers and students the freedom to do as they chose on larger matters. After a teacher has learned that it is possible to get away with not doing hall duty for a year, it is not easy to make that teacher think that something terrible is going to happen as punishment for failing to hold a discussion about playing radios in the building. To its credit, the administration frequently embarked on campaigns to reform this or that aspect of life at Westside, but the piecemeal and inconsistent nature of the campaigns sabotaged whatever chances of success there might have been and distracted attention from such underlying problems as the nature of administrative-teacher relationships. It was not so much that the administration did not want reform as that its reform efforts were always being undercut by its inability to take a holistic view of problems. It tried to approach this or that problem in isolation from its general context.

The above examples were chosen in part to suggest that even when teachers and the administration were substantially in agreement with one another, they could not work effectively together; however, one of the issues mentioned in the second memo was the source of a good deal of disagreement among faculty. It was the issue of prohibiting male students from wearing hats in the building. While some argued that the rule was absurd and unduly regimenting, others argued that it was a small but essential element in the process of teaching the students acceptable behavior. The split was racial, with Black teachers especially likely to fall in the latter group. Some regarded the white teachers' more permissive stand as an indication of a lack of concern for the students.

The administration's failure to be taken seriously shows up in the student assemblies, any one of which could provide the material for an entire seminar on social disorganization. From my field notes:

I didn't know that there was to be an assembly today. One of the cops told me that he didn't know either and neither did one of the assistant principals. I was in the main balcony. . . . The crowd was so noisy that I couldn't hear a coherent sentence the whole play. No effort was made to stop the noise and, except for the teacher who sponsored the play, I couldn't see any teachers or administrators around. There were two cops nearby, but they were trying to watch two floors and the nearby hallways. The crowd quieted down some, but never enough to make the dialogue hearable. The play was about the evils of drug use. . . . While they pretended to smoke pot on stage, two groups in my balcony were smoking the real thing.

Because of their special character, assemblies convey a special message. The failure to try to enforce school regulations in a school-wide gathering is clearly an institutional failure that cannot be written off as evidence of the laxity of a few teachers. If new students have not learned elsewhere that the institution does not take itself seriously, the very first assembly should drive the point home.

Certain school policies further complicate matters. One is the policy of scheduling extracurricular activities during the school day. Such activities seem to be very frequent, averaging perhaps two a week, prompting one teacher to claim that the school policy is to keep the niggers ignorant but happy. Dances are normally held during the last two or three class periods. For many teachers and students, they mean that all pretense of having school is dropped. Assemblies are normally held in the morning; while there is an assembly period in the schedule, assemblies usually mean that at least one class period will be disrupted. As occurs at the dances, students who are not even attending the assembly will gather around outside to see what's going on. Teachers' meetings are usually held during the last class period. They are not frequent, but they do mean that a few classes have to be called off, and always the same classes.

The confusion is compounded by the fact that students do not begin and end the school day at the same time. While this makes it easier for students to hold jobs, it naturally creates the impression among the relatively few students who have first- or last-period classes that they are laboring under a special burden. Table 1 presumably reflects in part

Table 1. Students Absent from English Classes, by Class Period

Period	Total Student Class - Days	Absentees	Percentage Absent
1	23,618	12,617	53.4
2	22,375	10,636	47.5
3	20,639	8,640	41.8
4-6	54,624	25,239	46.2
7-9	30,630	15,648	51.1
Total	151,886	72,780	47.9

Source: Attendance records from the Westside High School English Department, second and fourth marking periods, 1972-73. For some classes, data were not available.

the effects of such a policy. The data on which the table is based were taken from the 1972–73 record books of teachers in the English Department, using one ten-week period from November to January and another such period at the end of the school year.

It is clear from table 1 that absenteeism is highest during the first and the last three class periods.[3] Absenteeism is lowest during the third period, probably because, while it starts relatively near the middle of the day, it is not a lunch period (as are fourth through seventh). Of course, there are guards posted at all entrances to the cafeteria to make sure that students get in only when they are scheduled to, but students who want to skip classes always manage to get in anyway.

It can be as hard to get teachers to leave their lunchroom as to keep students out of theirs. The teachers' lunchroom is a popular spot for kibitzing, card playing, and generally whiling away the time, including some of the time that teachers are supposed to be in class. Some of the teachers are as casual about getting to class on time as some of the students are. For about three weeks, I counted the number of times teachers were late, taking late to mean not in the classroom within five minutes of the late bell. Ignoring situations in which I knew a teacher had a good reason to be late, I was able to check classrooms 126 times and teachers were late in 40 cases, which works out to slightly under a third.

Near the end of the school year or just before a long school holiday, the more dramatic kinds of disorder at Westside occur more frequently. The attendance of both teachers and students falls off. Those students who do come to school spend more time than usual in the halls. The frequency of fire alarms and actual fires—most of them small ones set in lockers or wastebaskets—increases. I once had a single interview interrupted three times by fire alarms. The number of teachers and administrators who leave the building early seems to go up. The police officer who remarked, just before Christmas vacation, that he'd like to catch a nap at his post but was afraid he'd be robbed, was only half joking.

It is clear enough that by the time they reach high school many of Westside's students are real hell-raisers, and that is the aspect of the situation that would be stressed from an attribute perspective. It is also clear that the characteristics of students do not by themselves explain Westside. The school reveals a pattern of disorder that is institutional in character, that is participated in by those who complain about it—including those who are paid to stop it—which means that disorder has perhaps as much to do with school policy as with individual weaknesses.

On the other side, Westside's disorder shows how cautious one must be in interpreting the large-sample surveys that support the attribute thesis. When one says that inner-city children do not do as well in school as other children, there is the assumption that both groups of children are in fact in something we might call "school." In the more demoralized institutions, though, even when children show up they may enter so irregularly into the web of relationships and activities that we mean by "school" that it is not always reasonable to think of them as being in school at all. Thus failing to consider school climate in an explanation for variations in achievement and problem behavior can be very misleading, and the attribute position has classically drawn much of its support from studies of that kind.

The hard-headed attribute retort would be that the distinctive social climate of the school is itself but a product of problems the kids bring with them from home. The minimal response to that is that whatever problems students may bring with them are clearly aggravated by the school, in part because the school consistently fails to do even many of the things that it certainly has the capability of doing. The school maintains that it does little because it has little with which to work, but that does not explain why a school does so much less than it might with what it does have.

The misbehavior of teachers and students constitutes a form of mutual exploitation. Both are trying to get by while only minimally living up to their respective responsibilities, trying to "get over," as the students put it, while still trying to retain whatever rewards their situations offer. The disorder at Westside grants everyone the consolation prize of being able to escape some of the strictures of institutional life. Hall duty, after all, is not the most pleasant aspect of teaching even under the best circumstances, and many teachers are quick to point out that they do not regard it as part of their professional duty. (As used by teachers, especially those in failing schools, the rhetoric of professionalism is another way of denying responsibility.) Teachers who spend every duty period over coffee in the lounge or who regularly dismiss students after the first period of a double-period class, like students who learn that they can exchange the monotony of the classroom for the excitement of the hall with little risk of failing, have learned to squeeze a few personal rewards from institutional failure. Virtually everyone has a stake in the freedom permitted by the disorder, even though virtually everyone complains daily about the collective manifestations of that freedom.

Some teachers not only put minimal effort into their jobs, they also try to define their jobs in ways that would legitimate minimal effort, or rather, they try to expand the definition of everyone else's job while restricting the definition of their own. I used to daydream about chiseling the words "It ain't my job!" over Westside's front entrance. Teachers frequently argued to me that keeping the students out of the halls was not their job, despite what their contract said; that was the job of the police and the hall guards. Nearly all of the police felt that it was not their job either. They saw themselves as responsible only for prohibiting explicitly criminal activities. When Westside got a new principal, he remarked that if the cops and hall guards did everything the teachers wanted them to do, the school could get by with fewer teachers. Two of the counselors told me they did not see why they should be calling the homes of students with attendance problems. That was the home-room teacher's responsibility. A number of the homeroom teachers said it couldn't be their job because they didn't have the time for it or the training, and besides, there were aides to do that.

Most of us, of course, try to define responsibility for unwelcome tasks so that it lies somewhere far from us. Westside's teachers are better able than many of us, though, to make it stick, to extract some privileges and rewards from their situation while refusing to accept any responsibility for their situation. The ability of both teachers and students to exploit their situation helps explain the tenacity of failure in the school and the seemingly elusive quality of success.

Reforms and the Ambiguity of Success

If one fails often enough, failure can become almost comforting. Failure at Westside is something like that. The place has been failing so long that it has become comfortable with failure. The pros-pect of success it finds somewhat unsettling. Remember that at West-side there are teachers who manage to do a good job in the classroom and get students to behave themselves, and there is a substantial con-sensus as to who these teachers are. People who are not successful at some enterprise often look at their more successful colleagues and learn from them and build on that learning. That does not often happen in a climate like Westside's, a climate in which people become predis-posed to ignore the very real instances of success around them and concentrate on the more comfortably familiar failures. The inability to learn from such successes as there were shows up particularly well in the various stabs at reform, particularly hallway reform.

We have already seen that Westside's teachers were more a part of the hall problem than of the solution. A handful of teachers made a practice of letting classes go early, knowing full well that students had no place to go but the halls. Study hall teachers seldom bothered to show up, so that most students who should have been in study hall wandered through the building. Those teachers who consistently started their classes late were effectively teaching their students that there was no reason to try to beat the late bell. These, however, were minor prob-lems in comparison to the high-handed attitude that many teachers took toward hall duty. Throughout most of my time at Westside, a substantial majority simply failed to occupy their hall posts. A minority made an outward show of fulfilling their responsibility by appearing at a post, but only to watch the mayhem without comment. The number fluctuated, but at any one time there were fewer than a dozen teachers who were consistently and actively discharging their duties as monitors, although a somewhat larger number were reputed to be able to make the students move along if and when they chose. Black teachers, 35 percent of the staff, were somewhat over-represented in both groups, which was attributed to their being less afraid of the students or to some vague special powers they were supposed to have over students.

Given a more active faculty, how difficult would it be to bring the halls under control? To let most of the teachers tell it, it would be difficult indeed. These are tough, unruly kids from one of the nation's toughest ghettoes. Nothing less than a detachment of Marines could bring a semblance of order to the place. In actual fact, despite the popular conception of what ghetto kids are like and despite what many teachers and even students said, bringing the corridors under control at Westside was really no trick at all. This was demonstrated by the periodic reforms, all of which succeeded for a time before they failed.

Prior to my coming to Westside, reform had come in the guise of the snatch-and-grab program. Teachers were to go out into the halls when the late bell rang and pull any students still out there into the nearest classroom, whether or not they belonged in that room. I was told that the program was quite successful while it lasted, but it gradually faded away, apparently without any official notice being taken of its demise. Sometime later, there were the hall sweeps, apparently begun in response to complaints from the district superintendent's office. Two groups of teachers, beginning simultaneously on the second and third floors, would begin to walk the halls, pushing students before them in a dragnet intended to herd all students toward the first-floor auditorium. Once there, first offenders would be given a warning and repeaters would be suspended for a few days. The corridors temporarily became so quiet that footsteps echoed. The program died just as quietly.

About midway through the next year, the sweeps were reinstituted. This time, they were conducted only during certain unannounced class periods. Even with the new format, the sweeps worked well until they faded out of existence again. Even this was not the end of the tale. Some months later, reassignments were made in the responsibilities of the assistant principals. The man in charge of the halls made several changes. He asked the police how they would be best utilized and they told him that they ought to be patrolling the halls rather than remaining at fixed posts. "Weak" teachers were taken off hall duty to be replaced by "strong" people wherever possible. Finally, he himself walked the halls a great deal, duty roster in hand. This behavior has to be contrasted with the Westside maxim that administrators will leave their offices for lunch and fires and very little else—a maxim that is probably unfair to the administrators but that accurately reflects the feeling on the part of the teachers that they were subject to very little supervision. Needless to say, the program worked while it lasted.

It may well be that the problems of inner-city education are so destructive of so much that we hold valuable that it is less disturbing to think of them as having intransigent and complex foundations. If bad things exist, it is some comfort to know that there are compelling reasons for them. Therefore, we may too readily picture the various failures of urban education as not easily amenable to change, and certainly not without the investigations of the learned and the infusion of vast outside resources. The implication here, however, is that with a bit of persistence the hallway disorder problem could have been ameliorated by just about any silly old thing that the staff dreamed up, including merely seeing that people did what they were supposed to do. It is almost a letdown.

How did the school, having discovered a number of alternative avenues to success, manage to avoid all of them? The answer seems to be partly a matter of self-fulfilling prophecy, but more finally a matter of institutional rewards and demands. One of the things left untouched by the temporarily successful reforms was the climate of opinion within the school. Students and teachers alike expected any innovation to fail. They seemed almost to take a grim pride in failure, as if to say, "Here is a school that *knows* how to fail, obstacles notwithstanding." When a new program was announced, the dominant opinion was that it couldn't possibly work. When it did work, the dominant opinion was that it couldn't possibly work very long. When that turned out indeed to be the case, the walls reverberated with "Didn't I tell you?" People sounded almost relieved to have been rescued once more from the nasty prospect of success.

The above remark is meant to echo the smug tone of voice often used to report failure at Westside. Such smugness is understandable. Success can be a much more ambiguous experience than we ordinarily take it to be, especially when people have learned to exploit a few advantages from failure. Success exacts a cost. Success at Westside would mean that teachers and students might have to give up the freedom from supervision to which they have become accustomed, a freedom that takes on a quasi-legitimate character, something that people feel entitled to. When a teacher makes demands on students, one often hears students remark, "No one else makes us do that." Teachers voice their claim to legitimacy somewhat more obliquely. Rather than saying outright that they have the right to goof off, they phrase it negatively, claiming that under the circumstances no one should ask them to do more than they are doing. Since the administration is so disorganized, they cannot be expected to reply to its directives; since the students are so ill trained, they cannot really be expected to teach high school material. Goofing off comes to have a normative character; teachers who do what teachers are supposed to do may come to feel a little like traitors to the group.

This is not to say the teachers' exploitation of disorder results from some rational calculation of self-interest. Self-serving ideologies normally involve both self-delusion and self-justification whereby we convince ourselves that our rewards are either clearly deserved or inevitable, or not really rewards at all. Many teachers at Westside were so consummately skilled at casting themselves in the role of the long-suffering servant that it would have been difficult for them to think of their illicit free time as a benefit. Moreover, since they generally thought of their failure to do hall duty as a result of the school's troubles, not a cause of it, their free time became, if not exactly something they had a right to, at least something that no fair-minded person could complain about.

These observations should not be taken to mean that Westside teachers just do not care about teaching, an idea about as useful as the notion that students do not want to learn. People who teach in inner-city schools are not so different from the common run of humanity that they would not choose, other things being equal, to be good at what they do. Give them their dream scenario and I do not doubt that they would turn the place into Harvard. But as it is, the path to even a much-diluted version of that ideal is far from clear; in the meantime, the current unpleasantness has its better side, enough so to create an inertia that pulls people back into failure even as they are learning, or could be learning, the way out. If trivial in comparison to the grand dream, the paradoxical rewards of failure are at least immediate and tangible, blunting the monotony and regimentation of school life.

Possibly the emotional rewards of failure are more important than the tangible benefits it makes possible. Mapping the road to success is accusatory. The claim that Westside does indeed have the resources to be a successful enterprise implies questions about who is responsible for preventing that success from happening. Institutional failure is comforting. It allows teachers to maintain an image of themselves as competent professionals even though there is little in their daily lives to support that image.

A climate in which people need to see failure as inevitable in order to justify themselves is hardly a climate in which people can learn from the successes they do encounter. Thus, what is remembered and discussed about the hall reforms, by and large, is their ultimate failure, not their temporary success and the potentially instructive implications of that success. In fact, I am convinced that Westside already has all the information it needs to have to become a successful school in the traditional sense. In its present climate, though, people cannot afford to look at it.

Working toward success requires change. Change is generally at least a little discomfiting and perhaps especially so to the alienated. Under the formal authority system of the school, teachers have rather little control over many aspects of their job situation, even if they may manage to carve out substantial concessions informally. That is, teachers are fairly alienated, if by alienation we understand the inability to control one's life or powerlessness.[4] Inner-city teachers presumably feel even more alienated than most, since they work in an environment that is unpredictable and potentially dangerous and they are unlikely to have the sense of personal efficacy that comes from being successful in the classroom. If innovation is threatening in general, it is even more threatening to those who feel they have little influence over their lives, a point James Comer (1980) discusses at some length. Comer implies that where teachers are more vitally a part of the planning and implementation of reform, teacher commitment to the success of reform will be more substantial.

The ambivalent quality of success and failure and the diffusely threatening character of change for the alienated cannot fully account for the tenacity with which Westside nurtures its failures. We have to look more closely at the structuring of institutional demand. Let us start with the ultimate failure of the various attempts at hallway reform. There seemed to be a fairly stable pattern of deterioration following each success. At first, teachers and aides would show up religiously. At some point, though, a few teachers, or perhaps the supervising administrator, would fail to show up. Often, they had valid reasons, or at least they gave me reasons that sounded valid. Possibly, too, some teachers stayed away just to see what administrators would do, a kind of testing behavior. In any case, the nonappearance of the few became the grounds for the nonappearance of others. Convinced that the program was destined to fall apart sooner or later, many teachers were quick to read its death knell into a few unexplained absences. Having reached that conclusion, they saw their own continued participation as futile.

The nature of administrative reaction is clear. The reasons for it are less so. Typically, administrators did not react in any way that meant anything to the teachers; in particular, they were unlikely to invoke any formal or informal sanctions against them. Administrators gave me no clear explanations for this. Two possibilities stand out. Reluctant cooperation shading into outright defiance was so much the norm among Westside teachers that the sheer magnitude of resistance may have inhibited administrative response. Rather than being a few isolated deviants, the teachers who don't appear for duty have the implicit approval of a substantial segment of the faculty. The quasi-legitimate character of noncompliance robs administrators of the chance to cast themselves as the righteous defenders of social order.

The second possibility has to do with the structuring of the relationships between teachers and their supervisors. Like guards in a maximum-security prison, administrators have few sanctions open to them and these few are fairly inflexible. The most important is the power to give a teacher a negative efficiency rating, which is considered a rather serious step, involving as it does formidable amounts of paperwork, justification, a good likelihood of trouble with the teachers' union, and legal expenses. In most Chicago schools, as in most urban school systems, positive ratings are normally pro forma affairs, except in cases where teachers commit out-and-out abominations. A poor efficiency rating is too large a cannon to turn on the teacher who just doesn't show up for hall duty.

In practice, the next step down is jawboning. If efficiency ratings are too heavy a threat, this one is too light. Any likelihood that administrators could successfully cajole teachers at Westside was normally precluded by the level of animosity among teachers toward their superiors. The hostility was deep and widespread, with neutrality on the issue sometimes treated as the equivalent of scabbing. In such an atmosphere, teachers were hardly likely to be talked into doing anything unpleasant. Overall, while the reasons for it are unclear, it is clear that the reforms failed in large part due to the unwillingness or inability of the institution to make demands on its employees.

When teachers were asked about why they refused to do hall duty, one of the most frequent responses was that hall duty was dangerous; the possibility of assault was always there. While I was at Westside, no teacher was actually assaulted doing hall duty, but the fear was there, nevertheless. I doubt that this will take us very close to an explanation. Fear might explain why a teacher won't go out in the halls, but it does not explain why that teacher comes to class late or lets the class go early. Then, too, even the staff members who gave the least indication of being afraid and who had the least reason to be afraid—the cops—eventually stopped doing anything in the halls. In addition, during the hall sweeps, teachers worked in groups, which should have reduced the worry about being attacked. Care was taken that at least one male teacher, and usually more than one, was in each group. Even so, teachers gradually just stopped showing up when the sweeps were scheduled. Fear may have played some role, but clearly something more important was involved in the noncompliance of teachers.

The teachers' most common explanation for not doing hall duty as well as a lot of other things was the futility of the attempt. No one could clear the halls anyway, so why knock yourself out over nothing? Nobody paid any attention to those record books, so there was no point in being very careful. These students can't be made to study, so don't even try to give homework.

In a few cases, I was able to see teacher behavior deteriorating, and always the teachers seemed to decide that there was just no point to fulfilling their obligations. There was one teacher who did her hall duty faithfully during a class period when only three or four other teachers in the building showed up regularly at their hall posts. Her post was at the intersection of two corridors that were generally unguarded. Still, she did her best for about three months. Obviously, it was not an easy job. Students have developed a whole array of tactics for dealing with the occasional hall guard. The most common is to claim a legitimate, if not urgent, errand. These Mrs. Moore just ignored, insisting that the student go back for a pass. (Of course, some teachers would send a student out in the halls without a pass, so students weren't always lying.) Other students would flash any scrap of paper, hoping that it would be taken for a pass. Mrs. Moore looked closely enough to be sure. Other students would argue that such and such a hall guard let them go past, so there was no reason she shouldn't, since they were going to get where they were going anyway. This kind of thing made no impression on Mrs. Moore. A few of the bolder students simply "Bogarted," trying to walk on past her as if they didn't hear her telling them to stop. In these cases, she wouldn't touch the student, but she would step in front of him or her so that she could not be ignored. As a rule, only students who broke into a dead run got by her post.

Mrs. Moore was serious about doing the job on her hall post. Nevertheless, after three months or so, she just stopped going, explaining that she was tired of it and it wasn't doing any good anyway. This was true; she really wasn't doing much good. The only immediate effect of all of her effort was that students had to route themselves around her.

The nonteaching staff went through similar changes. Near the beginning of my last year there, the police officers who had been assigned to the school were quite serious about clearing the halls and washrooms. As time went on, however, they began to complain that the school didn't do anything to punish even the most extreme offenders that they caught. I heard half a dozen versions of the following story: In the morning a cop takes a knife from a student and takes the student to the discipline office. The discipline office does nothing but talk to the student, and that afternoon the same cop takes another weapon from the same student. The details vary, but the pattern of the officer trying to do what he is supposed to do and being thwarted by the disciplinary procedures of the school remains constant.

The police officers had another similar complaint. They all felt that they would be more effective if they walked the halls rather than staying at fixed posts; if they remained stationary, students would just go someplace else. This was not to avoid work; walking the halls involves more work than just staying at a post. The administration decided, however, to keep them at fixed posts, so that teachers would always know where to find an officer when they needed one.

By the end of the school year, the police officers were virtually non-functional, except for sporadic activity or in the case of serious disturbances. Some spent much of the day reading the sports page and drinking coffee, while others went into the auditorium for naps. Despite their generally low opinion of Westside's teachers, they had begun to act pretty much like the worst of those teachers. Even if you are not lazy when you come to Westside, the institution is likely to make you act as if you are. Apparently, the police officers began to act that way because of the futility of their jobs. No matter how often they or people like Mrs. Moore rolled the rock to the top of the hill, it rolled back down. Eventually, they decided that it could stay down there.

Futility, or the Westside syndrome as one teacher called it, is a significant aspect of teacher misbehavior. Even so, I do not think it is the underlying factor. At the very least, there were conditions under which teachers really did put more effort into their jobs and those conditions seemed ultimately traceable to the level of demands placed on them. We had one example of that in the hall reforms. There were also others.

One of the themes that recurred in the conversation of veteran teachers is that under stricter administrations at Westside, they themselves worked harder and enjoyed it more. I don't recall ever hearing teachers discuss the fact they sometimes come to school late and leave early without hearing them mention that the administrators do the same. There has been nothing like systematic observation of teachers in the classroom by administrators for several years. The following field notes reflect both the absence of administrative pressure and teacher misbehavior as a response to it:

I went to see Mrs. Moore's tenth period today to pick up a copy of a memo she said she had. Mrs. Jones was there, too, filling out a crossword puzzle. We spent the entire period talking about the school and especially its lack of administration. They felt that the policies embodied in the memo, like so many others, would fade into the sunset. They said that the administration had several times started campaigns to make sure that various clerical duties of the teachers were done on time. Each time, the administration would huff and blow for a while, write nasty notes, then forget about it. Mrs. Jones said that she was observed for about "three minutes" once last year, but aside from that she hasn't been observed since this administration started. They said that teachers have to get an appointment to see the principal. They repeated the stuff about the principal being virtually invisible, noting that only one of the assistant principals had represented the administration at the morning assembly. Jones said that under other principals—the last good one being two or three principals ago—she made dead sure that nobody had to ask her for anything twice. Now she may get a form from the principal and forget where she put it. Said she enjoyed coming here more when there was more pressure on teachers to work. Now she dreads coming every morning. Both agreed that when Hampton was acting principal, he made a practice of coming into the lunchroom at eight o'clock with a copy of teacher's programs, asking teachers who were supposed to be in class to get there. The new principal, in contrast, has sat in the lunchroom and told Moore that there were teachers in there whom he knew should be in class, and having said it, would do nothing about it.

Previous administrations were seldom discussed without some reference to the greater pressure they put on teachers. One of the previous principals, for example, was described as being the first to come in every morning and the last to leave every afternoon. The current group of administrators were widely accused of coming late and leaving early. There was enough truth to this that it wasn't difficult for teachers to sign themselves out early from time to time, because relatively few administrators were around in the late afternoon. (Of course, on some occasions, the administrators must have had perfectly legitimate reasons for leaving early, but teachers were unlikely to interpret it that way.) Under more restrictive regimes, say the teachers, they were more careful about being where they were supposed to be themselves.[5]

Still, the best evidence for the importance of demands as a determinant of the level of exploitative behavior comes from a period after I had formally finished my research. Midway through the year after I left Westside, there was a shake-up of several high schools which had a reputation for producing chaos and not much else. The shake-up was relatively mild, amounting to transferring the principals involved to other schools, usually elementary schools.

It is not clear what led to this reorganization. Immediately prior to it, a group of local businessmen had issued a report which said that some Chicago high school graduates were so ignorant as to be nearly unemployable. That was followed by a series in the *Chicago Tribune* detailing the depth to which some of the city's schools had sunk. Westside was mentioned prominently in the series. Then came the shake-up. Whether it came as a response to the other events is an open question.

Be that as it may, the former principal, Mr. Barnard, was out, and Westside got a new principal, Mr. Walker, who proceeded to substantially reduce the level of exploitative behavior and the disorder associated with it. The hall problem was solved. Students seldom ventured into it without a pass and, if they did, teachers were doing hall duty and cops were patrolling again. Things reached a point where everybody assumed that teachers were going to show up for hall duty. Nonstudents were being stopped at the front door. Under the previous administration, guards were on the door and they were supposed to stop anyone without an ID card, but whether they would do so was anybody's guess. There were no more plate-throwing festivals in the lunchroom and almost no false fire alarms. Male students generally stopped violating the rules that prohibited their wearing hats in the building. Teachers stopped letting their classes go early. I first went back on records day—the day that teachers devote to preparing report cards and attendance data. At noon, most teachers had finished their records and were having a picnic. Under the old regime, records "day" normally dragged on through half the week.

There were other successes. Westside's commencement came off without any of the incidents that school officials find so embarrassing—that is, students acting at commencement just as they act in school. Before coming to Westside, Walker had established a reputation for being especially effective at community relations and that did prove to be the case. Parents filled the gym on Parents' Day. He also successfully brought off assemblies with the student body to explain his policies. In an atmosphere in which parents are widely seen as unconcerned with education or hostile to it, and students in a mass are regarded as being as unpredictable as a force of nature, such things can have a dramatic impact on expectations. Mr. Walker had not been there long enough to work any academic miracles, but he had made it clear that he was going to start. He had asked teachers to modify their materials to take student reading levels into account—the failure to do so is a pervasive problem in inner-city secondary schools—and teachers gave evidence of trying to respond.

In sum, the building was under control, staff morale was up, steps had been taken to encourage parents to take a more active role in their children's education, and teachers appeared to be putting more effort into some aspects of their jobs. The student population of Westside was much smaller by the time Mr. Walker came, which must have made it easier to bring the place under control. Still, the previous administration had not been able to do anything with the same population. The changes wrought by the new administration were real and substantial and teachers seemed to feel that this time they were going to last.

What made the changes possible? A large part of the answer seems to be that Walker was substantially more skilled and demanding than his predecessor. Teachers described him as "serious," as meaning whatever he says. He had some assistance in conveying that image from the manner of his appointment. Previously Westside placed no discernable limits on teacher behavior that went much beyond the requirement that teachers show up regularly. A teacher who chose to could work extremely hard. On the other hand, a teacher could regularly come late, leave early, and do next to nothing in between. The Board of Education gave no indication that what teachers did mattered a great deal; indeed, it gave rather loud indications of the opposite. For example, administrators at Westside, like their colleagues at many other schools, virtually ignored the board regulation that teachers must be observed and evaluated several times a year. This is not a difficult rule to enforce. By not enforcing it, the board announced to all who cared to listen that it was in some business other than that of inner-city education. The removal of Mr. Barnard, the former principal, countermanded the previous announcement, indicating that there were in fact some lower limits to what the board was going to (publicly) tolerate and it was going to appoint a principal to see that those limits were observed.

Aside from the manner of his appointment, there was much about Mr. Walker's behavior that made him appear serious. He walked the halls himself, shooing students. Of course, if a teacher failed to show up for hall duty, Walker would know it. He personally took hats from students. He did this although he himself probably did not care one way or the other about hat-wearing in the building. Teacher efficiency ratings were pretty much a matter of form. (Still, to my knowledge, Barnard did give a bad rating to at least three egregiously poor teachers; his problem was not that he did not care about the school.) Walker let it be known on his arrival that he wouldn't be able to give teachers any ratings at all because it would take some time before he could make a valid judgment. Presumably, that put everyone on notice that he or she was being watched.

Under the old regime, teachers who did duty above and beyond what was required of them might be allowed to take a day or two off with pay, a violation of regulations. Walker was more likely to give such teachers dinner tickets he had purchased himself. Politically, this was like the difference between night and day. The second gesture simultaneously rewarded desired behavior, announced the supervisor's personal interest in good performance and reinforced the idea that the rules would be upheld, period—an idea that previous administrators had never been able to get across, partly because they violated too many rules themselves. It is not that Walker governed by the book, which was probably not possible in any case. On substantive matters, though, he apparently did walk the straight and narrow, which helped legitimate his right to insist that others do so. The previous administrators exploited the school's lack of structure much as the teachers and students did, bending or ignoring rules when it was to their personal advantage. Much of it was petty and teachers certainly exaggerated in their reports, but there is no doubt that there was enough administrative misconduct to undermine the administration's authority. Administrators could not effectively make demands on teachers because they themselves had been caught so often with their fingers in the cookie jar that teachers could write off their demands as illegitimate. Since the formal power invested in the office of principal is so limited, a principal stripped of the air of legitimacy simply has little left with which to govern.

Some of the staff seemed particularly struck by the fact that if they took a question or a problem to Walker, they could be certain of getting a response. It might not be the response they wanted and they might not get it immediately—indeed, I suspect that Walker sometimes delayed for effect—but a response was certain. No doubt staff members remarked on this because it was so different from the old administration, but in these circumstances, more reliable administrative responsiveness means a somewhat less alienating environment.

Judging from teacher comments, the way in which Walker handled recalcitrant students may have been among the most important ways he made it appear that he was demanding. He expelled them or suspended them, consistently and in large numbers. (Even students who are skipping many classes do not like to be suspended.) Again, I think this announced that Walker was willing to invoke sanctions. Under an administration that showed that it was willing to take strong measures, the exploitative behavior of both teachers and students was sharply reduced. It is true that urban high school principals have very few formal sanctions, but informal sanctions can be quite severe. Actually, even their use against teachers was unnecessary. Just the threat of sanctions was enough. If it is clear that you will follow through, you probably will not have to.

No doubt an important part of Walker's success has to be attributed to his ability to make demands effectively. That comes through strongly in the comments about him made by aides, police officers, and teachers. (I am not so certain how students saw him.) He came very close to saying as much himself. Several times in an interview with me he said that people will ordinarily do just about what you expect them to, if they think you really expect it. Interpreting his success in terms of his ability to be demanding is also consistent with what happened in the temporarily successful attempts at hall reform and with what teachers said about their own behavior under previous administrations. Still, that may be a slightly misleading interpretation. It would probably come nearer the truth to regard his success as the product of a superior administrative style and his ability to make demands as a particularly important and visible component of that style. I did not spend enough time at the new Westside—less than a week—to be terribly confident of my ability to characterize the broader style, but I got a sense of style that included the ability to set and clarify goals, to mobilize resources, to be consistent, and to set an example of personal effectiveness. I also got the impression that Walker would score well on some test of social sensitivity. He seemed to be able to see simultaneously from the vantage points of actor and audience, to predict how various actions would be read by various constituencies, and to plan around their reactions. His approach was also much more holistic than that of the previous administration which had approached problems in a piecemeal fashion. Within a few months of his arrival, Walker had taken initiative on several different fronts. In any case, it would be simplistic just to equate demands with adequate supervision. Important as they are, if we separate them from the broader context in which they operate, we get a parody of leadership.

Mr. Barnard, the former principal, is not the villain of the piece, though a great many teachers would cast him that way. In fact, of the urban principals I have known, he was a couple of cuts above the average. He tried, for example, to untrack the English classes, over vigorous faculty objection, because he thought that students would get more out of heterogeneous groupings. No matter what one thinks of the idea, his pushing what he believed to be a reform suggests that he was looking for ways to make the school better serve its students and was willing to take a great deal of heat in the course of doing so. He was an activist willing to pay at least some of the price of activism, not a time-server.

That hardly changes the fact that he presided over an administration that was inept, internally disorganized, inconsistent, lacking in self-confidence and direction, and which undermined its own legitimacy by both participating in the minor corruptions it was supposed to prevent and by knowingly and publicly allowing others to do so. Barnard seldom seemed to fully realize how interlocked were the problems he was addressing and how piecemeal efforts at reform might make things worse. His people-handling skills were also questionable. Concerning the issue of abolishing tracking for English classes, he made cursory attempts to convince teachers that it would be a good idea and then proceeded to try to ram it down their throats, immediately generating a powerful reaction which obscured the issue of what was best for students. The reaction seems perfectly predictable, but Barnard either didn't predict it or didn't see that once he stirred it up, it guaranteed the failure of the idea even when it was nominally implemented. He did that sort of thing often, which probably accounts for what at first seemed to me a logical contradiction regarding his behavior. The dominant faculty opinion about him when I came to Westside seemed to be that he was wishy-washy and yet authoritarian; most teachers apparently held both images. What happened, I think, is that by pushing too hard and in inappropriate ways on some questions, he created pressures that led him to compensate by yielding too readily on other questions. Be that as it may, nice guy though he was, all of his good intentions came to naught.

To repeat some of the points from this discussion to which we will return later: First, during the time I was in contact with Westside, the institution changed—changed for the better, on the whole, and in some ways changed dramatically. An orderly school is hardly the same thing as an effective school, but some minimal degree of order is a precondition for effectiveness. The fact that it changed is more important than the reasons for the change, because it proves, in contrast to what many of the staff felt and in contrast to what is often implied by social science, that not all of Westside's problems were engraved in stone by some heavenly hand. It was possible, with the resources at hand, to eliminate much of the most destructive student misbehavior. Accomplishing this did not in this case require that the staff first understand the aboriginal causes of student misbehavior. The improvement in student behavior did not, you will notice, first require changes in the students' out-of-school cultural milieu, or their self-image, or a change in personnel. It required only that the school change the way it interacted with students.

Second, people at Westside were ambivalent about failure; all parties involved tended to develop vested interests in the status quo, vested interests which then frustrated attempts at change partly because they made it impossible for the institution to learn from the very real successes it did have every day. Given the institutional will to succeed, success in overcoming at least some of the problems vexing Westside is not so far beyond reach as it may appear.

My original conception of the problem—why were some teachers more successful than others—had built into it nearly all the problems I tried to catalogue in chapter 1. Trying to avoid an attribute approach, I proceeded to define the world in terms only slightly removed from the attribute approach. My approach was mystical in that it stressed the interpersonal, affective dimension of the teacher-student relationship in isolation from its context, from the school as an organization. It was also a version of the RAP thesis, since looking just at how classrooms vary is a good way to avoid looking at the central influence of institutional will. That student behavior varies from teacher to teacher is significant, but it does not come close to capturing what is most distinctive about Westside. To do that we have to consider the sheer level of disorder and how it varies from situation to situation; further, we cannot long talk about that without raising questions of how institutional power is employed or not employed.

However, what is primarily important here is not that teachers respond according to the quality of administrative leadership, but that teachers can respond at all. Much thinking about inner-city teachers—including much of my own—is hardly less stereotypical than most thinking about inner-city students. Possibly, the idea that inner-city students have untapped potential is more widely recognized than the fact that the same is true of their teachers. The teachers are resistant to change, the quality of their work is ordinarily criminally poor, but perhaps what is most remarkable is that teachers respond dramatically differently to different sets of circumstances.

It is interesting, given the way inner-city teachers think about their students, that the teachers here come off as being so very similar to their students. A good many members of both groups try to get away with what they can when they can. When someone insists on more appropriate behavior, they respond with more appropriate behavior. Teachers and students and administrators give exactly what they are asked to give. The next chapter, using the interview data, will make pretty much the same point.

Notes

1. Inter-rating coefficients of reliability for classroom observations are normally quite high (Leacock 1969). I am dubious. The behavior of many teachers did seem to change after they became accustomed to me. Moreover, there are limits to the validity of such observations even under the best circumstances. Few teachers will read a newspaper or give a class a free period with an observer present. I think we have to assume that observation generally yields data about teachers at their best.

2. For descriptions of hall problems similar to Westside's, see Lucey (1967) and Alan Jones (1972). The latter is more detailed and includes examples of how young teachers are socialized by veterans to avoid hall duty.

3. Given the large numbers of nonstudents carried on the books, the high degree of teacher error, and variation in the amount of cutting in different marking periods, the data are useful only as an indicator of relative absenteeism by period. My best guess is that an overall absentee rate of 30 to 40 percent might be close.

4. "Alienation" is used in such a variety of ways that it is especially important that readers fix this usage in their minds. Seeman (1971), commenting on several years of research on alienation, concludes that treating it as powerlessness, which is very close to the usage here, seems to be the most fruitful approach to a variety of problems.

5. In a study by Goldman and Larson (1971), four teachers were given a reduced class load and full discretion over how they would use their free time. Although teachers had intended to utilize the time to improve their teaching, in fact they did nothing related to that.

3

A World That Asks
Too Little

Asking why student behavior varies from teacher to teacher is a less powerful question than I had originally thought. It stresses teacher-student interaction to the exclusion of any consideration of the school as an organization. Nevertheless, looking at what students say about how and why their behavior differs with different teachers is another way to deepen our awareness of what is possible with supposedly incorrigible students. I began interviewing students about their attitudes toward teachers with two expectations. Specifically, I expected that students would be most likely to cooperate with those teachers who made the greatest effort to teach them. That is, I thought student cooperation would be positively and strongly related to the perceived *Quality of Teaching (QT)*. If some teachers got less than others in the way of student cooperation, perhaps it was because they gave less than others in the way of encouraging student growth. Second, I thought that student cooperation would be strongly related to the amount of perceived *Status-Degradation (SD)* in the teacher-student relationship. By status-degradation I mean teacher behavior experienced as insulting or humiliating or, as Max Weber might have put it, behavior that withdraws or denies social honor. The opposite of status-degradation will be referred to as *Status-Supportiveness (SS)*.

I expected that *QT* would be a more important determinant of student behavior than *SD-SS*. Still, I thought *SD* would be a significant determinant in its own right and would be a fairly pervasive phenomenon at Westside. Teachers in a ghetto school know that they are part of a failing institution and it is only normal that they externalize blame by finding the source of their failure in their students. That idea, once communicated to students, would constitute status-degradation.

These expectations were only partly borne out by the evidence, but there is a prior matter to take up before we look at it. What do students mean when they say that a teacher is a good one? A degrading one? How do students operationalize the concepts at issue here?

Student Interpretation of Teacher Characteristics

I asked students several open-ended questions about what they thought of their teachers and what teacher behavior led them to think that. The most important of these was, "What would a teacher have to be like before you said, 'That's a really good teacher'?" Respondents were then asked which of these characteristics they thought most important. The responses to that question are summarized in table 2. Most of the responses do seem to reflect the two dimensions of SS and QT, but there were so many references to the clarity with which a teacher explains things that those responses have been separated from other references to QT. The third category, teacher demands, was unanticipated when I began interviewing students; and in retrospect it seems short-sighted not to have expected it. The category refers to how demanding the teacher is, meaning by that the teacher's willingness to insist on some set of standards and to invoke sanctions to insure compliance with those standards. My respondents were about equally divided between those who saw the really good teacher as one who makes students toe the line and those suggesting that the really good teacher is one who will "give you some slack." The *Neutral* category refers to two cases where students said a teacher should maintain an appropriate level of demands, but gave no indication what they regarded as appropriate.

The composite picture of the ideal teacher as one who can definitely make students understand, be nice to them, and apply the appropriate amount of pressure as well, seems excessively modest. There is little suggestion in this picture that a teacher should be intellectually stimulating, personally involved with students, enthusiastic, or even interesting. It would appear that Westside's students don't expect too much of their teachers.

The responses summarized in table 2 suggest the categories of teacher behavior that are significant to students. However, we still need some idea of what kinds of teacher behavior indicate to students that a teacher belongs in a particular category. To answer this, I asked a more specific question about quality of teaching: "How can you tell if a teacher is really concerned about students learning something in the course?" Table 3 summarizes the distribution of responses.

A number of things are different in table 3. There is a new category, *Inspiration*, which refers to those cases where a student said that a teacher should talk to the class about the significance of the work or the signif-

Table 2.   Responses to "What Are the Characteristics of a Really Good Teacher?
(N = 52)

	Percent of All Responses	Number of Respondents	Percent of All Respondents
Quality of teaching (QT)			
Teacher clarity	24	24	47
General comments	26	21	41
Total (QT)	50	40	78
Status supportiveness (SS)	21	19	37
Teachers' demands on students			
High demands	11	12	23
Low demands	11	11	22
Neutral comments	2	2	4
Total Demands	24	23	45
Miscellaneous	5	3	6

Note: Respondents giving responses in more than one category are counted only once in the totals.

Table 3. Responses to "How Can You Tell if a Teacher Is Really
Concerned About Students Learning Something in the Course?" (N=52)

	Percent of All Responses	Number of Respondents	Percentage of All Respondents
Quality of teaching (QT)			
Teacher Clarity	33	31	60
General comments	14	12	24
Total	47	40	78
Teachers' demands on students			
High demands	35	26	51
Low demands	2	2	4
Total	37	27	53
Status supportiveness (SS)	5	4	8
Inspiration	6	6	12
Miscellaneous	5	4	8

Note: Responses falling in more than one category are counted only once in the totals.

icance of learning in general. Numerically, the category is insignificant, but it does suggest that pep talks are not totally wasted.

A more significant change in table 3 has to do with the increased strength of the *Teacher Clarity* Category. Where previously the clarity category accounted for about one-quarter of all responses, it now accounts for about one-third, coming from 13 percent more of the respondents. At the same time, references to clarity were much more specific than before. On the previous question, students generally just said a teacher should explain. Here, the comments were to the effect that teachers should check notebooks, ask questions, and encourage questions to find out who does and does not understand, provide students with some indication of their progress, and so on. Clarity, in short, seems to be primarily a matter of the extent to which the teacher elicits and provides feedback.

The most important point to be derived from this table concerns the demands categories, referred to here by about half of all respondents. Asked what characteristics they thought made a really good teacher, students as a group were undecided about whether they preferred relatively demanding or relatively undemanding teachers. In table 3, not only do more students refer to the dimension of demands, but they almost unanimously refer to the teacher who makes them walk the straight and narrow as the teacher who is concerned about teaching. The serious teacher is the one who stays on their backs about homework and attendance, keeps them working and doesn't let them fool around in class. Nothing here says that students like demanding teachers, but they generally see demands as stemming from highly legitimate motives. In the last chapter, we saw a tension between the desire of teachers to have order in the halls on the one hand and their desire to do what they wanted with their nonteaching time on the other. In the different distribution of responses to these first two questions (tables 2 and 3), we begin to see a similar tension among students, a tension between what they prefer and what they think best allows them to learn.

The greater emphasis placed on demands in table 3 is associated with an almost negligible emphasis on status-degradating or status-supportive behavior. Whether the teacher is nasty or nice seems to have negligible bearing on whether that teacher is generally perceived as being serious about teaching. The coding has been changed here. Previously, I coded references to teachers shouting and cursing as status-degrading behavior. In table 3 they are coded as demands. The change is justified by the way in which students elaborate on their remarks. In the context tapped by this question, hollering and cursing are not seen by students as insults so much as indications of the teachers' concern about students learning, provided of course that they curse at the right time and about the right things. What a particular action means to students depends upon the context in which it occurs. This means that we must change coding procedures as different questions get students thinking about different contexts if we are to avoid equating superficially similar responses.

These students, then, seem to determine who is seriously concerned with teaching largely on the basis of teacher clarity, which means largely on the basis of the extent to which feedback is sought and offered by the teacher. The serious teacher is also willing to make demands on students. For the moment, *SD-SS* seems of minimal significance. The sharp distinction here between nice people and good teachers reveals a more sophisticated approach than one might have looked for from high school students. Like the students Coles observed (1971:463), Westside students can distinguish between sympathy and "a determined businesslike effort to forge a working relationship." Notice again what students here do not say. Aside from the relatively weak *Inspiration* category, we still have virtually no indication that a good teacher is expected to be enthusiastic or interesting. The model of good teaching given in table 3 is remarkably spartan, asking nothing extra.

The distinction between nice people and good teachers may be clearer to the students than to many teachers. Some teachers come to see being "nice" as the most important aspect of their role, or come to feel that making demands is inconsistent with being nice, that all demands smack of authoritarianism or interfere with the rights of students (Comer 1980; Kozol 1972; Levy 1970; Ogbu 1974:163–64). One variant involves teachers who overidentify with students to the point of trying to imitate them, which at Westside usually translates into young white teachers trying to imitate the expressive idioms of the ghetto, which students generally find wondrously comic.

What does it mean when students say a teacher is status-degrading? Students were asked, "What would a teacher have to do before you said that teacher was acting snotty or acting superior?" Here it was more difficult to elicit descriptions of particular kinds of behavior. Many respondents said that a snotty teacher is one who "acts high-class" or one who "cops an attitude." Asked how one could tell when a teacher had an "attitude," a likely response was, "You can just tell." Such responses are not surprising, since the difference between degrading and supportive behavior often involves subtle dimensions of demeanor and tone.

When students did refer to discrete behaviors, by far the most frequent response—mentioned by 52 percent of all respondents and accounting for 45 percent of all responses—might be labeled outright disrespect. These were the references to yelling and cursing, snapping at students and hitting them, the crudest and most obvious ways to remind an individual of inferior status. When such things were done publicly, students found them especially obnoxious. Public degradation has its own argot. It is "fronting you off" or "loud-talking you."

The second most common type of response—given by 25 percent of all students and accounting for 23 percent of all responses—is not nearly so obvious. Again, it takes us back to the question of teacher clarity. Some students will see a put-down any time teachers refuse to make themselves clear, or react angrily to a student's lack of understanding, or put an assignment on the board without explaining it, or tell students that they should know something that they have asked about. When teachers make themselves clear, students take that as an indication that they are concerned about teaching. When they seem to deliberately interfere with clarity, some students seem to see in that, not merely unconcern about teaching, but an insult as well.

The third category is similar to the last, but different enough to be considered separately. In the last chapter, I referred to teachers who maintained a very shallow relationship with students. That kind of behavior is also regarded by some respondents as insulting. Teachers who ignore you, who put you off, who don't want to talk to you, are seen as "snotty." Of course, the same behavior must interfere with the clarity of teaching, but in their examples students did not refer to teachers who failed to talk to them about their work so much as to teachers who didn't want to talk to them about anything, period. Thus it seems reasonable to construct a different category, a category where the unifying thread is denial of relationship. This category comes to 19 percent of all responses from 23 percent of all respondents.

I said a moment ago that the meaning of a given action derives essentially from the context in which it occurs rather than from behavior in the abstract. Some of the clearest illustrations of that fact came while students were discussing the kind of teacher behavior they considered "snotty." There was a history teacher named Mrs. Ryan. When it came to deciding whether or not she was snotty, students hedged, saying both "Yes, she is," and "No, she isn't." It was difficult to categorize her; while she was a consistent screamer, probably yelling at students more than any other teacher that I observed, she was also among the school's most demanding teachers. She assigned homework by the bucketful. In a school where many students take four years of English without seeing a term paper, she assigned three long papers in a history course, and apparently gave all three a careful, critical reading. Because so much about her behavior indicated that she wanted students to learn, her yelling was seen as another aspect of that desire more than as an attempt to hurt anyone. Moreover, she tempered her screaming in various ways. She allowed students to make her the butt of jokes. She bantered with students about various subjects that had nothing to do with the class.

She sometimes rolled her eyes in mid-scream, as if to say, "You don't really suppose that I am as serious as I sound, do you?" As serious as she sounded, it was difficult for students to long maintain the idea that she disliked them or wanted to put them down. Although she seemed at first to be a perfect case of a status-degrading teacher, there was really very little status-degradation in her relationship with students. The point, again, is that the meaning of a particular kind of behavior is attached not to that behavior but to the context in which it occurs.

Teachers sometimes said two additional things that were widely regarded as insulting. Neither was mentioned often when I questioned students directly about status-degradation, but they were sprinkled around frequently enough to make them worth mentioning. First, teachers sometimes remarked to students, "I got mine. You got yours to get." There are several variations. All of them seem to be used mostly by Black teachers, and I have heard two of them describe this comment as a way of inspiring students. Students do not see it that way. With one exception, every student who referred to this remark regarded it as a put-down, and some students regarded it as a particularly sharp one. Most of these students are headed for rather uncertain futures and they see no need for anyone to remind them of it.

The other kind of comment that is likely to be read as a put-down is made by teachers of either race. Black teachers sometimes refer to the fact that they live on the South Side. White teachers may refer to their residences in the suburbs. If repeated often enough, such references are seen by some students as a sly way of coming down on the West Side and the people who live there.

Aside from these particular comments, students are likely to experience teacher behavior as status-degrading when the behavior involves yelling or cursing. To a lesser extent, judging by the relative frequency of comments, anything teachers do that interferes with clarity or seems to deny the relationship between themselves and students may also be regarded as status-degrading. When students in the aggregate say that a teacher is very much concerned that students learn something, they mean primarily that he or she insures clarity by eliciting and providing feedback, and is relatively demanding. They do not mean that such a teacher is nice.

Knowing something of what students mean when they say that teachers are nasty or that they are really teaching something, we can now turn to the key question. What factors determine whether or not students cooperate with various teachers?

The Conditionality of Student Response: Student Explanations for the Misbehavior of Other Students

Some of the questions I asked attempted to determine how the respondents explained variations in the misbehavior of students from one class to another. The first asked respondents if any of the teachers they had currently had more trouble making the class behave, and, if so, why. "Behave" here was taken to mean refraining from talking in class, and doing in-class assignments. To a somewhat lesser extent, it referred to staying awake in class and remaining in the classroom. Thirty-two respondents identified and explained fifty-five cases in which they thought a teacher's ability to control the classroom differed significantly from that of other teachers. (See table 4.)

Responses were very clearly dominated by the *Demands* categories. The diagonal from *Low Demand-More Trouble* cell to the *High Demands-Less Trouble* cell contains 55 percent of all explanations. No comparable diagonal comes anywhere close to that. Teachers have more trouble controlling the class, according to these explanations, when they are "too easy" or "too nice" or don't say anything to misbehaving students. "Too nice" is clearly explained as being reluctant to enforce the rules. What is important is the sanction, or at least the threat of it. Some illustrations:

Except for the ones with the paddles. I'd give them an "A" because the majority of kids are afraid of the paddle and they do right.

I guess she has a reputation so no one messes around in her class.

They don't play . . . they don't like people that fool around. Like if you fool around, they throw you out of class or send you to the office and kids don't want to get sent to the office.

Making demands of students, which seemed to be of secondary importance when students were asked what characteristics made a really good teacher, seems to be of primary significance in controlling the classroom. The extent to which students behave in class, like the extent to which teachers do hall duty, seems largely contingent upon the level of demands made on them. Even without recalculating the percentages on the table, one can see clearly (since all *Demand* responses fall on one diagonal) that the relationship here is quite substantial, as well as more significant than the other relationships reflected in the table.

None of the remaining categories accounts for much more than 10 percent of all responses. The responses in the quality of teaching category all take the form of saying that teachers have more trouble controlling the class because they teach badly, or have less trouble because they teach well or make the work interesting or enjoyable. One student, for example, explains why she gave her bookkeeping teacher a "D" for his ability to control the classroom:

They don't listen to him. He explains nothing. He be talking about something that nobody be interested in, that don't have nothing to do with that class. And he be talking and the students be talking over him.

Table 4. Explanations for Why Some Teachers Have More Trouble and Others
Have Less Trouble Controlling the Classroom (N=55)

	More Trouble		Less Trouble	
	No. of Responses	Percent of All Responses	No. of Responses	Percent of All Responses
Teachers' demands on students				
Low demands	23	42	0	0
High demands	0	0	7	13
Quality of teaching (QT)				
Low QT	2	4	0	0
High QT	0	0	5	9
Physical attributes				
"Wrong" attributes	6	11	0	0
"Right" attributes	0	0	0	0
Teachers' behavior toward students (SD-SS)				
Status degradation (SD)	2	4	0	0
Status supportiveness (SS)	0	0	2	4
Miscellaneous	5	9	3	5
Total	38	70	17	31

The third category, *SD-SS*, reveals that teachers have less trouble with the class because they are informal and friendly, or more trouble because they are "snotty":

She walk around, like she don't smile and she arguing over something all day long. I guess the students can tell if a teacher don't like them and so they mess with them just for the hell of it.

The direction of the correlation is precisely what I had predicted (*SD* with *More Trouble*, *SS* with *Less Trouble*). The correlation is perfect, but given that *SD-SS* accounts for a total of four cases, we will not make too much of it, nor of the similar patterns in the quality of teaching categories.

The last category is the new one having to do with the physical attributes of teachers—race, size, and sex. The explanations here indicate that white teachers have more trouble than Black ones, small teachers have more trouble than large ones, and females more trouble than males. However, this is difficult to take at face value. While it is probably true that at the beginning of a relationship students will be more careful about trying a teacher who is big, Black, and male, every teacher can expect to be tested sooner or later. Success in controlling the classroom over the long haul will be determined by factors other than physical attributes. Thus, when students are asked why one short white female teacher has more trouble making the class behave than another short white female teacher, either the respondent is not sure, or gives an answer that falls into one of the other categories, usually *Demands*. That, plus the fact that no one ever says that a large, Black male teacher has less trouble for those reasons alone, make me suspect that this entire category is a substitute for *Demands*.

Table 4 presents substantially more explanations for why teachers have trouble controlling the classroom as against why some have less trouble. This was true on several subsequent items as well. *Low Demands* is clearly the most probable explanation for *More Trouble*, but there is no one dominant factor accounting for *Less Trouble*. The difference between *High Demands* and *High QT* is negligible. Overall, good behavior appears to be more complicated than bad.

Demands being so important, it is worth considering in more detail just what kind of behavior is referred to as demanding. Just about half the comments put into this category are of the "He don't try" or "She doesn't say anything" variety. The statements should be taken literally. Just as some teachers observe rules being broken in the halls without responding, some completely ignore infractions in the classroom. When I first began observing in classes, I was surprised by the number of teachers who, knowing that an observer was present, would allow students to sleep in the classroom without saying anything about it. (It is true that a very large number of students at Westside have jobs outside of school and some teachers take the position that it is unfair to expect these, especially those with full-time jobs, to stay awake in every class.) Teachers might tell students to take notes or do a written assignment. In most classrooms, only part—although usually a majority—of the class would comply, while other students just did nothing. Some teachers would consistently ignore the students who did nothing, particularly if they did nothing quietly.

When students got noisy, it was altogether a different matter. I saw few teachers trying to compete with classroom conversations, unless the conversations were quiet ones. While talking seemed to be the in-class infraction most likely to draw a response from teachers, teachers differed a great deal in the type of response they made. The important distinction seemed to be between the teachers who said "Stop" and those who said "Stop" and meant it. The following notes describing two math teachers illustrate the difference:

While Mr. Carter is naming various types of triangles, three boys are talking about their grades. He speaks to them twice, just saying, "Matt," or "Cornell." The third time he just looks at them, but he goes back to his lecturing before they stop. They start fooling with a deck of cards and he has to speak to them a fourth time. They stop for a while. Three girls up front pass around a course book. No one takes notes. Most people seem to be listening, though, except that group of boys, which has now grown to five. He has to speak to them again . . . . He has to speak to them a sixth time. "Elbert, I have asked you to put them away several times. Would you do that, please?" . . . Mr. Carter finally stops talking and comes back and asks for the cards. Suddenly they can't find them and he says, "Why don't you go out into the halls until you do?" After they stand up, he goes on looking for the cards himself and then walks the two worst offenders out into the halls. . . . A student says, after the offenders have left, "They waste half our class time. We trying to learn something." Carter says, "Well, he took his cards down to Mr. Riley." [Riley was in charge of discipline. Actually, there is only a small chance that the boys went to Mr. Riley. Since they weren't escorted there, they probably took their cards down to the lunchroom.] Some boys in the back of the class are still talking quite loudly and Carter looks back at them several times, but only to glance at them. He doesn't say anything more. The bell rings while he is in mid-sentence and he stops right there. After class he tells me that those four or five boys do the same thing every day. They always come to class, but never bring a book or pencils, and never do any work.

I'm not certain how much Mr. Carter taught his students about congruent triangles that day, but he did teach them that he doesn't mean what he says. They learned that when he tells students to stop talking, he isn't going to invoke any sanctions if they don't, or if he finally does, they will not be serious. Most students seemed to dislike being sent to the discipline office, but that is not what he did. He set them free to go wherever they chose.

Mrs. Bell's classes were quite different:

She starts to tell the new people [those who have just been transferred in from another class] that she has a study sheet to help them catch up. [Notice that she assumes, probably correctly, that her class is ahead of whatever class they had been in.] She stops to go clear the halls, the noise from which is making it difficult to hear her. . . . When she comes back from clearing the halls, she tells them to stop the talking which started up and it does stop. I don't see much talking while she reviews, but one girl has her head down briefly. At one point, two girls start talking while Mrs. Bell is writing on the board, but she looks at them and they stop. . . . There is virtually no more talking until the bell rings.

This was a fairly typical class for Mrs. Bell. Students could get away with a little, but with very little. She communicated clearly that she intended that nothing would interfere with her teaching, even when the source of the interference came from outside the room. She seldom spoke above a conversational tone and she almost never told anybody to do anything more than twice. Certainly, if she has told a student to stop talking, she is not going back to her teaching until the talking has stopped. Although her students are firmly convinced that she would send them to the office, I have never known her to do so. In fact, she says she doesn't like the idea, since it implies that she needs help to run her own classroom.

The difference between Mrs. Bell and Mr. Carter is very much like the difference between the two principals we discussed in the last chapter. Like the former principal, most teachers at Westside were actively encouraging students to believe that the limits of tolerable behavior were broad. As students actually got away with more and more, some teachers became increasingly convinced of the futility of trying, so that student behavior got even worse. Mrs. Bell, like the new principal, made it clear that students didn't have to do very much to draw a reaction from her. Thus, students in her classes never even got around to doing anything as absurd as pulling out a deck of cards. Long before they ever got to that point, she had made it plain that she wouldn't stand for it by not allowing the milder forms of misbehavior. I doubt that her subordinates, any more than those of the new principal, had any clear idea of what she was going to do, but they knew she was going to do something. In both cases, it seems that not the actual use of strong sanctions but the unmistakable threat of sanctions made the difference.

So far as classroom misbehavior is concerned, the type of demanding behavior that seems most important is the determination to stop it, and if so, whether teachers do so in a manner that indicates that they are serious. Other types of demanding behavior, such as the amount of work given or grade pressure, are apparently more important for controlling other types of misbehavior, but they do not play a large role. I don't doubt that yelling works also (though that may be more subject to a law of diminishing returns), but even yelling appears unnecessary in enlisting the cooperation of students.

Mrs. Bell had to do a lot of work before she reached the point where she could just look at students and expect them to quiet down. She and others like her have to work very hard at the beginning of a relationship to create the kinds of expectations they want students to have. They then live off that preparation the rest of the year. I was never able to observe teachers at the beginning of the year, but I did see a number of cases where students were transferred to a class in midyear, which serves almost the same purpose. The first few weeks are probably critical in letting students know what is really expected of them. I asked my respondents how long it took them to figure out what a teacher is really like, and almost none of them said it took more than a month.

It is unlikely that much of the difference between a class like Mr. Carter's and a class like Mrs. Bell's is due to selectivity factors. The same students consistently behave one way in one class and another way in another class. Respondents said as much in the interviews, as we shall see in the next section.

Another question asked respondents how they thought other students could be made to behave: "If you were teaching here at Westside, what would you do to make sure that students studied and did their homework?" Eight students said they did not know. (This included two who gave "attribute" explanations, that is, the sources of behavior grow out of the character of the students: some students "just would" and some "just wouldn't" do their work.) Among the remaining students, the typical response was to make demands, particularly in reference to grade pressure. They would fail students or threaten to. They would let the parents know what was going on. Fifty-four percent of all responses were of this nature. On a question dealing more directly with academic behavior, more students referred directly to the teacher's ability to help them learn. They would have frequent quizzes, they would circulate around the room seeing who understood and who didn't. They would check the work carefully and explain things clearly. Thirty-eight percent of the respondents gave this sort of response. Less than 15 percent of all respondents gave answers dealing with SD-SS. Those who did said they'd make friends with students or wouldn't go around acting like kings or wouldn't embarrass people.[1]

This is familiar. The demanding teacher who taught clearly, irrespective of whether he or she were friendly and nice, was the composite picture of the teacher who was seen as being concerned about having students learn. It would seem from this that the teacher who makes the most convincing effort to get students to learn is also the teacher who will be most successful in getting kids to study.

Taken as a whole, these responses indicate strongly that students think that misbehavior is partly contingent upon the kind of relationship the teacher establishes with the class. What kinds of teacher behavior are most important depends upon the type of student misbehavior under consideration. Teaching carefully and clearly seems to help get students to study. Being demanding also seems to help in that regard, and it seems to reduce classroom cutting-up as well. Still, we must remember that students are saying that *other* students won't do right unless somebody makes them do right. We can now turn to what they say about their own misbehavior.

First, though, recall that chapter 2 makes the point that how demanding the principal is seems to be a chief determinant of how well teachers live up to their obligations. Here, how demanding the teacher is seems to determine the level of student obedience. Whatever differences may lie between an all-Black, lower-class student body and a largely white, middle-class faculty, students and teachers appear to react in a similar fashion to similar circumstances. It requires no great leap of imagination to see that the lack of demands made *on* teachers may help account for the lack of demands made *by* teachers, a point to which we return in the next chapter.

Student Explanations for Their Own Behavior

When I talked with students, part of the interview tried to elicit students' explanations for variations in their own behavior from teacher to teacher. One item asked whether they had some classes where they made a special effort to keep up with the work or any classes where they let themselves fall behind more than usual, and, in either case, why? Another question asked whether students skipped some classes more than others, and, if so, why?[2]

Almost half of the students said they worked just about as hard for one class as for another. The remaining twenty-eight students reported a total of fifty-one classes where they either slacked off more than usual or worked especially hard. (See table 5.) This time we have more cases where students reported making an effort, thus giving teachers less trouble, than the opposite. Whether this is due to phrasing of the questions or to the fact that now respondents are explaining their own behavior, I cannot say. The new category here refers to those cases where respondents say that which classes they work best in is determined by how much they like or dislike the subject matter.

Let us look first at the *Low Demand–Less Effort* (i.e., *MT*) and *High Demand–More Effort* (i.e., *LT*) diagonal. It now includes 32 percent of all

Table 5. Explanations for Why Students Work Harder in Some Classes Than in Others (N=52)

	Less Effort[a]		More Effort[b]	
	No. of Responses	Percent of All Responses	No. of Responses	Percent of All Responses
Teachers' demands on students				
Low demands	4	8	1	2
High demands	2	4	12	24
Attitude toward subject matter				
Like subject matter	0	0	11	21
Dislike subject matter	1	2	0	0
Quality of teacher (QT)				
Low (QT)	2	4	0	0
High (QT)	0	0	5	10
Teachers' behavior toward students (SD-SS)				
Status degradation (SD)	0	0	0	0
Status supportiveness (SS)	0	0	8	16
Miscellaneous	4	8	1	2
Total	13	26	38	75

a. Less Effort = More Trouble (MT)

b. More Effort = Less Trouble (LT)

explanations as compared to 55 percent in table 4. Nor is the correlation between demands and trouble with students as strong as it was; we now have three cases on the opposite diagonal. Nevertheless, treating these two diagonals as a fourfold table would yield a percent difference of more than 60 percent so the association is still substantial, though not quite what it had been.

The previous table left the impression that, relative to other factors, *Low Demand* was more closely related to *More Trouble* than *High Demands* was to *Less Trouble*. It seemed truer, that is, that undemanding teachers would catch hell than that demanding teachers would have an easy time of it. Table 5 has no such implications. Recalculating to the row marginals would show that *Low Demands* accounts for about a third of all the explanations for trouble with students, and *High Demands* accounts for about a third of all explanations for having less trouble.

Although the demands categories are less important, they are still slightly more frequent than either the *QT* or *SD-SS* categories. Now, describing their own reactions, students imply that supportive, encouraging behavior is slightly more important as a determinant of their responses to teachers, while degrading behavior seems to mean very little.

The second most frequent type of explanation, accounting for a little more than a fifth of all responses, was that students work better in those classes where they like the subject matter. I cannot say to what extent teacher characteristics help shape students' preference for subject matter or which teacher characteristics are most important.

Asking students why they skipped some classes more than others produced a different pattern of responses. The twenty-three students who offered explanations were most likely to skip a class because it met either very early or very late in the day, an explanation consistent with the attendance patterns discussed in chapter 2. Such explanations accounted for about 40 percent of the total. Another fifth of all explanations stressed low demands from teachers; that is, students were cutting where they thought they could get away with it. No other categories accounted for more than 10 percent of the explanations.

This is one point on which what students say can be checked against another source of information. Teachers' record books cannot tell us why students skip a class, but they can help determine whether a student really is skipping the classes he says he is skipping. I checked record books for the second ten-week marking period; by that time, the teacher-student relationship should be fairly well established. Four students had had their schedules juggled so much that their records had to be left out of my calculations. With four exceptions, the record books generally confirmed what students had said about variations in their skipping patterns. That is, if we take four days to constitute a significant difference, in fifteen of nineteen cases there was a significant difference between the class attendance record the student referred to in the interview and that of other classes, and always in the direction indicated by the student. In light of the uncertain quality of teachers' record books, we cannot assume that in all cases where there were discrepancies, the student was wrong.

Two interesting points turned up in the examination of the record books. The marking period had approximately forty-one class days. (The exact number varied from book to book.) When students said they skipped some class with greater frequency than others, they were recorded as being out of that class an average of sixteen days. The average in all other classes would be about eight days absent. Out of a total of forty-one days, I would regard the difference as quite large. This is particularly true if one remembers that classes taught by less demanding teachers are most likely to be skipped and one assumes that less demanding teachers keep less careful records, since they have less need of them. That would mean that the figure of sixteen days out underestimates the actual differences in classes missed. Still, even accepting the validity of the figure, it would seem that the interview tapped relatively gross differences. When a student says that he is skipping one class more than the others, that means a lot more. Similarly, Teachman (1979) finds inner city Detroit students averaging up to fifty absences a year in some classes and as few as ten in others.

If we combine the data from table 5 with the data on skipping, we can look at the distribution of explanations over a larger number of cases (see table 6). It does not change the analysis much. If we ignore the categories that do not refer to teacher characteristics, and consider the previous data, some generalizations seem reasonable.

First, teacher demands are inversely associated with the degree of student misbehavior. The association is there, irrespective of the type of misbehavior, so far as these data allow a judgment. The degree of the association is consistently substantial. Demands are more important than the other teacher characteristics examined, but how much more so varies with the question asked. Students feel that demands are important for everyone, including themselves, but they are absolutely critical for *other* students.

Both low QT and SD are associated with student misbehavior in the manner predicted, although this is not true on all questions. Nevertheless, they do not seem to account for as much misbehavior as demands do.

The numbers of students interviewed were very small. This, however, is partly countered by the consistency of the more significant patterns. The relatively great apparent influence of factors extraneous to the teacher-student relationship that we see in table 6 is not problematic. No one would think that teacher characteristics would account for all the vari-

Table 6. Explanations for Variations in Student Behavior: Skipping Classes and Effort Questions Combined (N=90)

	More Skipping and Less Effort[a]		More Skipping and More Effort[b]	
	No. of Responses	Percent of All Responses	No. of Responses	Percent of All Responses
Teachers' demands on students				
Low demands	12	14	1	1
High demands	4	4	14	16
Inconvenient class period	16	18	0	0
Like subject matter	0	0	11	12
Quality of teaching (QT)				
Low QT	7	8	0	0
High QT	0	0	5	6
Teachers' behavior toward students				
Status degradation (SD)	4	4	0	0
Status supportiveness (SS)	0	0	8	9
Miscellaneous	6	7	1	1
Total	50	55	40	45

a. More Skipping and Less Effort = More Trouble (MT).

b. Less Skipping and More Effort = Less Trouble (LT).

c. The category Dislikes Subject Matter has been eliminated, reducing the number of responses by one.

ations in student misbehavior. Then, too, the probability that these extraneous variables interact with the other variables is quite high.

Misbehavior among Transfer Students

Evidence of a slightly different sort supports the notion that teacher demands are an important determinant of student behavior. Among my respondents were six students who had attended schools that would generally be considered superior to Westside. Nearly all of them agreed that since coming to Westside, their behavior had changed in some respect for the worse, largely because there was a difference in the level of teacher demands. Such responses were interesting in light of the other data, so I interviewed a haphazard sample of ten more such students, giving me a total of sixteen. The sample was chosen by asking teachers and students if they knew anyone who had transferred to Westside from a Catholic high school, a school in the South, or a high school in Chicago that had a good reputation. This is a rather broad operational definition of "better" high school, but it wouldn't have been practical to restrict it much more.

The results were lopsided. Three students said their behavior had not changed one way or the other. One wasn't sure. No one said that his or her behavior had improved. The remaining twelve respondents all agreed that their behavior had got worse in at least one respect since coming to Westside. Nine of the twelve said that they had begun skipping more classes at Westside and seven that they did less work. It was generally agreed that they were given less work to do, but they still claimed to either do less of what was assigned or to do it more slowly. All of those who skipped more and three of the seven who were doing less work explained the behavioral change at least partly in terms of demands.

Last year [at a Catholic high school], you'd see me every night loaded down with books, books under both arms, books on down. Now, all I bring is a radio.

I probably cut more classes here [than in Louisiana]. You can't ditch classes at home. You can, but you get put out of school for it. Put out for a week. . . . I'm going to compare the two schools gradewise, like. At home, I'm an average student. I got Cs and some Bs. Here I'm slightly above. And I hear some of the kids around here saying the schools down South are inferior to the schools up North. I can't see how they can say that.

Yes [I skip some classes here] but at Steinmetz, I didn't. I did once in a while, but like they have this thing that if cut you be suspended. So I came to my classes all the time.

I don't have to work as hard. See, they don't give that much for you to do after class [as compared to Dumas, Arkansas] so you can take your time doing it. I can catch up before I get in too bad a trouble.

Demands made by teachers were not the only difference mentioned, of course. Four of the nine who skipped class more and five of the seven who said they worked less attributed the change either wholly or partly to differences in the teaching. Since the classes at Westside were more boring and they knew what was being taught anyway, they felt that there was no point in doing the work or coming to class.

Well, they try to teach you more [at Steinmetz] than they do over here. [Interviewer: Why do you say that?] Because of homework and things. Like, they give you a test every week over there to see if you've learned something and over here they give it to you when they feels like it.

There were a few references to differences in teacher behavior regarding their treatment of students—status-supportive versus degrading behavior—as well, but no one suggested that as a reason for behavioral change among transfer students.

A few students who had been to Catholic elementary schools painted the same kind of picture. When they were in situations where teachers were more demanding and teaching better, they themselves worked harder.

Them nuns was good, they was good. Those sisters were real strict. They believed in you learning. You wasn't going to leave that class until you knew something. . . .And the nuns were like big old men. Like the big old guards in prison. But at the public [elementary] school, you just do your work. They didn't care if you knew something or not.

Such comments add another reason to believe that student misbehavior is partly a response to the kinds of relationships students find themselves involved in. Again, particular emphasis is placed on teacher demands. Nevertheless, substantial emphasis is also placed here on the quality of the teaching. Certainly, there are plausible alternative explanations for the responses these students give. Nonetheless, taken in light of the previous data, they buttress the basic argument. Notice, though, that students are not necessarily saying that they *enjoy* public schools any better. Teachman (1979), asking similar questions of Detroit students, found that those who have had experiences in both kinds of environments frequently enjoy themselves more in the less strict environment of inner-city public schools. That is hardly surprising, but I note it here as a reminder that the disorder and looseness of the public schools is not, from a student viewpoint, entirely a bad thing.

The Significance of Factors Other Than Demands

The emphasis on teacher demands has been so consistent that it is easy to lose sight of the fact that the other dimensions of teacher behavior, while not so important as the level of demands they place on students, have not been altogether irrelevant. Some of the pertinent data have not been cited yet. In the items previously discussed, students identified some teachers with whom they misbehaved less than usual. As a measure of quality of teaching, students were also asked to grade their teachers "A" through "F" on their concern for students learning something in the class. It is possible to compare the grades of those teachers for whom students misbehaved more or less than average with the grades of all other teachers (table 7).[3] For the moment, "misbehave most" will mean that students said that they either worked less in that class or skipped it more. "Misbehaved least" means that students said that they either were especially careful not to cut that teacher's class or worked especially hard in it. Teachers for whom students misbehaved least received significantly higher grades than other teachers. Teachers for whom they misbehaved most received significantly lower grades than other teachers. Thus, student obedience and cooperation appear to be associated with the degree to which teachers are perceived to be serious about their teaching. This is not too surprising. We know that when students refer to teachers as high on concern, they mean partly that they are demanding. Because high teacher demands are associated with lower rates of misbehavior, this finding might be expected.

A similar analysis of status-degrading behavior is more ambiguous (table 8). Students were asked to grade their teachers on how "snotty" they were, with the higher grades representing the more friendly and agreeable teachers. Those teachers with whom students say they misbehave most do get significantly lower grades; that is, students do misbehave more for the more objectionable teachers. On the other hand, there is no significant difference between those teachers for whom students say they misbehave least and other teachers. It does seem that being nasty hurts a teacher's effectiveness, but it is not clear that being nice helps. This is consistent with what students said about skipping classes, but it contrasts with what they said about why they work harder in some classes than in others.

Exactly how the various dimensions of teacher behavior relate to one another is unclear. I would have too few cases in some cells to extend the analysis further. Still, while the interviews stressed the quality of teaching and how demanding the teacher was, these data remind us that status-degradation, while it may matter less, is not completely irrelevant.[4] Possibly, it plays a stronger role in the more dramatic forms of student misbehavior. Two people well acquainted with the school's

Table 7. Students' Evaluation of Teachers as to Their "Concern,"

by Degree of Student Misbehavior (N=51)

	Mean Grade on "Concern"	Standard Deviation	No. of Teachers Mentioned[a]
Teachers for whom students misbehave least	3.4[b]	0.90	37
All other teachers	2.9[b]	1.21	200
Teachers for whom students misbehave most	2.5[c]	1.28	48
All other teachers	3.1[c]	1.18	189
Total	2.9	1.20	237

a. Many teachers were graded more than once.

b. Difference between the means significant at .05; Z-obtained = 2.39.

c. Difference between the means significant at .001; Z-obtained = 3.62.

Table 8. Students' Evaluation of Teachers as to How "Snotty" They Are,

by Degree of Student Misbehavior (N=51)

	Mean Grade on "Snotty"	Standard Deviation	No. of Teachers Mentioned[a]
Teachers for whom students misbehave least	3.4[b]	0.80	37
All other teachers	3.2[b]	1.09	194
Teachers for whom students misbehave most	2.8[c]	1.35	48
All other teachers	3.3[c]	0.30	183
Total	3.2	1.09	231

a. Many teachers were graded more than once.

b. No significant difference at .05; Z-obtained = 0.83.

c. Difference between the means significant at .0001; Z-obtained = 11.49.

history claimed that teachers who got into fights with students and teachers who got their classrooms burned or vandalized conformed to the more status-degrading type. Judging from the burnings that occurred while I was there, this analysis seems reasonable, but the picture concerning vandalism and fighting seemed less clear.

"Our chief want in life," claimed Emerson, "is someone who will make us do what we can." The students I spoke to seem to feel much the same way. They respond to teachers who respond to them—to teachers, that is, who respect their potential as students and insist that students themselves do likewise. The teacher's sensitivity to the feelings of students matters to some degree, but much less than I expected. Clearly status-degradation is also a factor. I observed it frequently and students referred to it frequently. Nonetheless, it does not appear to be as important a determinant of the kinds of student behavior at issue here as how serious—that is, how clear and thorough in presentation, how insistent upon performance—the teacher appears to be.

Some caveats are needed. Nothing here ought to be construed as saying that it does not matter whether teachers try to be friendly, humane, and supportive. The point is that such behavior may not matter much for the responses among students that we have looked at and that being "nice" ought not to be equated with teaching. More pointedly, students may often hold a less saccharine definition of what constitutes being "nice" than other people. Methodologically, self-reports are limited under all circumstances, though I have no reason to think these students deliberately misled me in any significant way. Nevertheless, people are never fully aware of all of the reasons for their actions. At Westside the problem is all the more serious because the students have such a limited vocabulary of motive. That is, students may easily see that their peers are influenced by demanding teachers, but they may not see that they are also influenced by interesting teachers. Demanding teachers, while not common in their experience, are a great deal more common than interesting ones. They may not see some things often enough to have any idea how they would react to them if given the chance. I did not interview many students, but in this context, that is much less troubling than the fact that the sample is not so much taken from students officially enrolled as from those who come to school with some regularity.[5] What results we would get among the school's huge shadow population cannot even be guessed at and that is a critical question. Above all, we want to be particularly careful in the current political climate to avoid reading into these remarks the idea that all we need do is be more demanding of students. That again would be to confound all of teaching with what is only an element of teaching. It is more useful to say simply that the remarks of these students encourage us to think more carefully about the role of that part of teaching in urban education.

Still, there is little doubt that differences in teacher behavior can make substantial differences in student behavior, particularly judging from what students said about their patterns of class attendance and from what one may observe moving from classroom to classroom. If that is true for students in so troubled a school as Westside, it may be all the more so for schools that are less far gone. If that is true in a school where the teachers who insist on school-appropriate behavior do so merely as individuals, with virtually no support from colleagues or administration, it should be all the more true for schools that, as schools, insist that students take learning seriously.

The culture of Westside made it impossible for most teachers to see the full truth. They could certainly see that students were contributing mightily to their own miseducation. They could even see that the level of such behavior varied greatly from teacher to teacher. Everyone agreed that some teachers consistently got more cooperation from students than other teachers. That, though, was not seen as evidence of unrealized possibilities. Rather it was treated as the result of some vague, mystical power that some teachers just had. Thus the relative success of a few teachers was wasted on the others. They could not learn from such successes because, having defined them more or less as acts of God, they could not see them—perhaps could not afford to see them—as a potential model for change.

I said in the last chapter that much teacher behavior is usefully thought of as exploitative; that idea applies here as well. Certainly, it applies to the issue of teachers not being demanding. That people can be exploited by *not* having demands made on them is richly ironic. When teachers fail to insist upon reasonable performance from students, they fail to commit themselves, to put themselves at risk, to stand for something. More concretely, they reduce their own work load and take away a part of their obligatory contribution to the teacher-student relationship. In a situation like Westside, keeping the level of demands low is hardly doing students a favor over the long term, but, given the immaturity of students, it may seem like a favor over the short term. It means that students can go where they want to go, do what they want to do, giving them a stake in the mess. Every day can be a party.

In this respect, Westside students are probably very much like most others. I take it that it is ordinarily the case, irrespective of the educational setting, irrespective of issues of race and class, that one of the important determinants of how much work students get done is how serious the institution appears to be about insisting that it be done. In the end, it may well be that one of the most significant differences between Westside's students and others is that students at Westside are far less likely to meet someone who will insist that they do what they can.

The students he taught in the back country of Tennessee before the turn of the century, W.E.B. DuBois wrote, "found the world a puzzling thing: it asked little of them, and they answered with little, and yet it ridiculed their offering. Such a paradox they could not understand, and therefore sank into listless indifference, or shiftlessness, or reckless bravado." (1961:60).

Notes

1. Students were also asked why it seemed easier for teachers to clear the halls when they knew the students involved. Responses were about evenly divided between those saying in effect that teachers who knew them could "get them" and those suggesting students had more regard for teachers they knew personally.

2. Another question asked whether students had any classes in which they "cut up" more than usual or in which they made a special effort to behave. So little variation was reported that the item has been dropped from the analysis.

3. The average grades here are fairly high, certainly higher than one would have expected from the descriptions students offered of their teachers. This may have to do with the reference group to which the teachers are being compared— that is, with low expectations of students—and with the tendency of some students to minimize critical remarks.

4. How to explain the difference in the importance of status-degradation here and at the street academy where it seemed to matter more? The population of the street academy had much more troubled school histories. Then, too, the egalitarian practices of the street academy may have focused student attention more forcefully on teachers' behavior toward students, either status-supportive or status-degrading.

5. The sampling here involves an ill-defined universe, given the margin of error in school records. I sampled 142 names, expecting that to yield 70–75 interviews. The administrative reshuffling that year, though, meant that the records were more in error than usual. Using the 50-odd interviews done the previous year would have allowed me to make a marginally stronger case for the salience of status-degrading behavior, but would not otherwise change the analysis here.

4

Alienation and the Failure to Teach

The two final chapters of this book examine the academic performance of urban schools along lines that parallel the examination of disorder at Westside. Perhaps no educational problem has attracted as much attention from researchers over the past two decades as the problem of explaining how social status comes to be so closely tied to educational achievement. Much of that discussion was flawed primarily by the characteristic dangers of the denial paradigm—those theories that deny or minimize any relationship between the Haves and what happens to the Have-nots—and secondarily by problems more typical of the more simplistic versions of progressive theorizing. For a long time, for example, discussions of educational achievement simply ignored questions of process, questions about what was going on inside the school. That is, achievement was discussed separately from its real-world context. Minimizing context and process meant that behavioral problems such as those of Westside got placed in a box to themselves, artificially separated from achievement problems, which, of course, is not the way teachers and students experience the world. For an even longer time, questions of power and of vested interests were largely ignored. Stanfield (1982) suggests that the tendency to define inequality problems in terms of educational achievement should itself be understood as a means of avoiding questions about who has power over whom. Discussions of the achievement problem in inner-city schools have also continued the long tradition of defining inequality strictly in terms of interpersonal relationships, this time in the guise of an unreasonable concentration on the relationships between individual students and individual teachers or stressing the affective dimension of classroom relationships to the virtual exclusion of all else. Notice that with either definition of the problem, reform does not require that anyone give up anything tangible, let alone any power. In this respect, these approaches to the problem are typical of mystical thinking. Until just the last few years, all but a handful of those studying and commenting on inner-city schools were hypnotized by the typical, so concerned with explaining failure as to be insensitive to such limited successes as there were.

If we examine some of the most provocative recent research—and some of the work done lately is incomparably more useful than the kinds of work that used to dominate the field—we find not so much deprived students and teachers who are not "dedicated" as students and teachers who respond to an alienating social structure by striking out at one another, thereby helping to perpetuate that structure. We find too that the failure of teachers and students is predicated upon the absence of an effective governing structure, or, better, upon the distortion of that structure by the vested interests of those who staff it. One of the generalizable lessons of Westside is that teachers will do pretty much what they are asked to do. The dilemma facing inner-city parents is that they are ordinarily not in any position to ask for effective teaching in a manner that would be politically meaningful and those who are so positioned have nothing to gain by doing so.

By a wide margin, the most common approach to explaining the problems of learning in the inner city has been the attribute approach. By this I mean the various theories holding that racial and class disparities in achievement result essentially from processes that have stunted the educational growth of children before the schools can get a fair crack at them. With substantial differences in language and formulation, this view has been expressed any number of times (as, for example, by Jencks et al. 1972; Coleman et al. 1966; Reissman 1962; Bernstein 1960; Passow 1963; Deutsch 1963; Heath and Nelson 1974; Ausubel and Ausubel 1963; Burkhead 1967; Schwartz 1970; Justin 1974; Scott and Walberg 1979). The variables held to be critical variously include lack of stimulation at home and resulting cognitive underdevelopment, overstimulation at home, lack of familiarity with educational materials, nonexistent or inadequate verbal skills, lack of capacity for abstract thinking, authoritarian discipline in the home, lack of any discipline in the home, lack of respect for the value of education or for teachers and other authority figures, present-time orientation (that is, no incentive to defer gratification), perceptual difficulties, and disorganized home life. This is hardly an exhaustive list. For present purposes, it can be regarded as all of a piece. All of these approaches virtually ignore the transaction between schools and children, focusing instead on the attributes children bring to school.

It is not a very persuasive body of literature, even if one is inclined to be generous. I have pointed out earlier that the most influential studies have focused on central tendencies within large aggregates of data. James Coleman's work involved 645,000 students, 60,000 teachers, and 4,000 schools. At the time, it was the second largest social science research project ever undertaken. The huge numbers involved, I think, give the conclusions of the work an undeserved air of credibility. Such an approach does yield generalizable results, but often at the cost of obscuring significant variation within aggregates. Nor is it a particularly good way to understand patterns of influence; it ordinarily infers causation from static correlations, leaving the floor open to all manner of logically possible alternative explanations, most important, the argument that the crucial difference is the difference in the way inner-city students are taught. So thoroughly does most of this work ignore what goes on inside the school, for example, that the possible significance of the kinds of disorganization and outright refusal to teach that I observed at Westside is artificially eliminated from consideration. The implicit assumption has always been that inner-city students have access to much the same kind of schooling as everyone else, but it does not work for them because they don't have the same kind of intellectual and social equipment that other students have.

Some of the supportive research for the attribute positions comes from small-group laboratory studies, studies that hardly approximate real-world conditions. Referring to this literature, Urie Bronfennbrenner (quoted in Delone 1979) claims that so much of it involves placing children in strange situations, with strange adults asking them to do strange things, as to cast doubt on the value of the entire body of work.

There is particular reason to doubt the argument that the crucial factor is the lack of home-nurtured skills. Entwistle (1966; 1968) has demonstrated that in some respects the language skills of Black slum children when they enter school are more sophisticated than those of white suburban children.[1] Better still, it is well known that a variety of compensatory education programs, programs that are the political embodiment of attribute theory, are quite successful in developing testable skills in young slum children. When the same children are returned to a normal school environment, however, the gains are frequently washed out after a few years, as if students who had been given the theoretically critical skills were rapidly being deskilled by the school environment. Similarly, Mackler (1969) finds in a study of Black and Puerto Rican school children that of every hundred children with the tested ability to work at or above grade level in the first grade, only three will actually be working at grade level two years later. Something more than unsuitable home backgrounds must be operating here. Finally, it has long been known that measurable skill differences between inner-city children and others are quite small at the point of school entry but grow significantly and rapidly after that time.

Weak though the evidence is, we must suppose that inner-city children do in fact begin school with certain disadvantages stemming from their background. It is not unusual for low-income families to have to move several times within the space of a year or two, which can have disastrous effects educationally. In some neighborhoods, physical safety is an issue even for very young children, which presumably does not help them concentrate on school work. Some families have so many of the problems associated with poverty as to create emotional problems for children that carry over into their school life. However, hackneyed the idea, it is plausible that less exposure to formal educational materials at an early age constitutes something of a handicap. Without worrying too much about the quality of the evidence or the precise nature of the burdens, therefore, we can assume that slum children carry with them some extra burdens that are educationally relevant. As we go through the evidence, however, I think it will become clear that schools create a great many problems themselves and that when schools are well run the disadvantages of home background, whatever they may be, can be largely overcome. The problem with the attribute position has been less the idea that slum children have problematic attributes than the associated assumption that schools cannot, without a major overhaul, respond effectively to them.

One of the more plausible approaches to specifying the nature of disadvantage is the approach that centers on verbal skills, an issue pointed to by much of the attribute literature. I do not mean that inner-city children are nonverbal, a position which is just absurd (and which again illustrates the danger of ignoring situational context by assuming that behavior seen in one situation carries over into others). Nor is it that the types of verbal skills developed within slums interfere with logical thought or the capacity for abstract thinking. Nor can it be argued that children who speak one dialect have difficulty understanding teachers who speak another. Baratz (1969) has demonstrated that oral code-switching is virtually automatic.

Still, one certain difference between slum children and others is that slum children enter school displaying language which in its grammar, its syntax, its vocabulary, and its idioms is different from the language the school prefers, especially so for children from nonwhite slums. The language problem has two dimensions, intellectual and social. The first just means that the slum child first trying to learn school English may find certain vowel sounds difficult, will have to remember new rules governing tense, subject-verb agreement, possession, and so forth. Thus, the real curriculum of the slum child is somewhat larger than the formal curriculum. Intellectually, it is not a very formidable task. Socially, it is a different matter. Fairly small differences in speech patterns, as Jane Torrey says (1970), can take on major symbolic importance. Language stigmatizes. Thus, Seligman, Tucker, and Lambert (1972) find that a tape-recorded sample of speech patterns had more influence on how third-grade teachers rated students' intelligence than the quality of the students' written composition or drawing, even though the latter almost certainly reveal more about a student's creativity and capacity for expression than a speech sample. Language stigmatizes directly, but it may also do so indirectly. Some children may appear slow to the teacher because they are trying to do a bit more than the teacher's judgments take into account.

The primary disadvantage of the low-status child is low status itself, and language is one of the obvious ways in which low social status gets announced. Not the only way, though, as Helen Gouldner's *Teacher's Pets, Troublemakers and Nobodies* (1978) shows. Gouldner goes a long way toward explaining how slum schools transform a minor handicap into a major social problem. (Ray Rist [1977] draws largely from the same body of research.) Gouldner's work involved having a team of observers follow pupils in four all-Black city schools as they progressed from kindergarten through the end of second grade. Researchers also visited the pupils' homes periodically. All of the schools included some pupils from middle-income homes, but the majority of students in each school came from either the working poor or families dependent on welfare. Hers is a particularly valuable work partly because it is longitudinal, partly because it looks at both home and school, but also because it examines the critical first few years of schooling. The great bulk of research on inner-city education looks at the later years in the process. By that time, the consequences of prior interaction between school and child may show up as "attributes" of the child.

Despite variations among teachers, the team of observers described in Gouldner's study found the general atmosphere of the classrooms quiet and orderly, yet harsh. Teachers made insensitive retorts to students, ignored students' contributions to discussion, ignored requests for materials or for clarification of instruction. Teachers seemed reluctant to be physically close to students. Bodily contact—hugging or petting—was seldom used to console students. If a teacher touched a child for any reason, it was ordinarily to hit the child. Teacher-student interaction was quite different in the two suburban schools chosen as comparisons. "In sharp contrast with this drill-sergeant behavior, the teachers in the upper-middle class schools acted as if they were almost afraid of hurting a young child's feelings. They seemed to think that a child's self-image was fragile" (Helen Gouldner 1978:37).

The punitive stance of the teachers in the ghetto schools was not simply a response to disruptive behavior, though teachers thought of it that way. Remember, the rooms were generally quiet, the students "overtly docile." Such misbehavior as occurred was of a relatively mild sort. Students were not fighting, being defiant or abusive. Rather, teachers saw as disruptive the student who spoke without permission, even if in response to a teacher's question, or the student who got out of his seat, touched another child, opened a desk drawer and so forth, much of this happening when students were unoccupied, making the transition from one activity to another, or during long recitation sessions. Unfortunately, Gouldner does not tell us whether these minor forms of misbehavior were equally common in the suburban schools or how teachers there defined them. She does make it clear that when they did occur, teachers responded in a less punitive manner. Still, it is interesting that while at Westside I observed teachers ignoring or underreacting to very serious transgressions, at the other end of the process—at least in Gouldner's work—other teachers seem to consistently overreact to minor failings. It is not too much to suppose that they overreact largely because, having prejudged the students to be unmanageable hoodlums, they read that potentiality into minor misbehavior and react accordingly.

Gouldner is not the only researcher to describe the tone of the inner-city school classroom. More or less the same portrait comes from several other sources. Gerry Rosenfeld's *Shut Those Thick Lips* (1971), for example, describes a Harlem elementary school where teachers are much more status-degrading than those in Gouldner's study, much less concerned about teaching at all. What is distinctive, however, is Gouldner's detailed attempt to sketch the process by which the school decides which children will be taught. What is most striking about that process is how quickly teachers can begin weeding out the "dummies." In one kindergarten, the teacher had by the eighth day placed students at three tables based on their abilities. At that point, of course, the teacher is judging ability without any "objective" data and without having had much time for observing the children. How then is the division made? Gouldner found that the teachers she questioned typically gave unclear answers to that. She also found that the division was patterned, and patterned according to cues of social status. The "bright" students, who were seated at the table nearest the teacher and the blackboard, tended to be better-dressed than the others (who were, of course, seated at the back of the room), tended to have lighter complexions, tended to have no body odor—some of the children in the lower groups sometimes smelled of urine—were more assertive, spoke more standard English, and came from the more well-to-do families. (Since all of the teachers were Black, the significance of the students' complexions may be related to the history of ambivalence about skin color among Blacks.)

Having divided the children into the hoped-for and hopeless, teachers then proceeded, logically enough, to teach those children for whom they had hope and only those children. High achievers got more attention, more praise, and more support. In almost all classrooms observed, teachers tended to interact more frequently and more favorably with "high" students. "In fact, the teachers tended to make the lessons revolve around a very few students, concentrating largely on those who could give the correct answers" (Helen Gouldner, 1978:53). The "low" students eventually removed themselves socially and physically to the periphery of classroom activities. By late spring they had little communication with the teacher and almost no involvement in classroom activity (p. 51). "The 'low' students tended to tune out of classroom activities a good deal of the time. When they were not looking out the window or talking among themselves in almost imperceptible whispers, they were writing, drawing, and erasing, and then writing, drawing and erasing again" (p. 56).

Not at all surprisingly, grades and test scores at the end of the kindergarten year tended to confirm the judgments teachers had made at the beginning of the year. With few exceptions, students were subsequently classified by their first-grade and second-grade teachers just as their kindergarten teacher had done, using no discernible rational basis beyond status cues. The later teachers, though, could point to "objective" data to justify their placements. Teacher-student interaction in one year becomes objectified in later years as apparent attributes of the children. Even when test scores at the end of the kindergarten year did diverge from the teacher's initial judgment, ability grouping in first grade tended to replicate that of kindergarten. "Objective" data here are taken seriously only when they support judgments that teachers have already made.

The rigidity of track placement, which has been repeatedly confirmed in other studies, facilitated differential teaching. Teachers ordinarily proceeded as if a student's abilities were identical in all curricular areas, so that there was no chance of a student being labeled smart in one area and mediocre in another. The judgment was a generalized one lending itself to generalized styles of teaching. Students were kept to the pace of their group, leaving little possibility for a student to demonstrate by forging ahead that he or she had been misplaced. It did sometimes appear that students in the low group had learned more material than the teacher had presented to them by listening in on the presentations to the high group, but the structure of the formal lessons gave them no way to demonstrate that to the teacher.

Could it not be argued that this weeding-out process is more rational than it first seems? It is reasonable to suppose that, say, children who come to school smelling of urine come on the whole from the most disorganized families in the community, and that children from such families do indeed on the whole have more trouble learning. Over time, teachers learn, perhaps without being fully aware of it, to respond to this cue and others like it, cues that in fact correlate with how well children are likely to do in school.

The trouble with that stance is that kindergarten teachers do not teach students "on the whole"; they teach individual pupils. Even if it were the case that these status cues correspond in the aggregate to real differences in ability, treating individual cases as if they must necessarily reflect the character of the aggregate is egregiously poor pedagogy, all the more so given the permanence of the initial judgment. Worse still, the typical response to the initial judgment—putting the least teaching effort into teaching those deemed least prepared—of necessity amplifies any real differences that might have been reflected in the original ranking and over time creates real differences where there originally were none.

Gouldner's portrait of the initial contact between the slum child and the slum school is one of a relationship that gets off on the wrong foot and slides downhill so rapidly that the original problems are lost under a heap of secondary ones. School, for a good many children, is initially a harsh, unrewarding environment in which they find themselves judged too quickly and too permanently, setting in motion a chain of institutional responses that virtually guarantees that some children will be taught and some will not be taught. As Rist points out, it is not so much that the teaching is incompetent, although no one denies an overabundance of that, as that different children have different access to whatever teaching is going on. Gouldner's methodology is not generalizable, but on two points—the general tone of the classroom in the elementary grades and the poor teaching offered to many children in those grades— we have every reason to think that Gouldner's portrait is widely applicable to slum schools (Leacock 1969; Levy 1970; Rosenfeld 1971; Herndon 1965; Silberman 1970; Kozol 1967). Indeed, "poor teaching" hardly says enough. Much of the teaching described in the literature on inner-city schools and much of what we saw at Westside is not so much a matter of teachers inadequately or infrequently doing those things that lead to intellectual growth as teachers doing those things that positively contribute to intellectual retardation, a kind of unteaching.

One of the reasons it is unfortunate that so much research has considered later stages in the academic process without trying to connect them to the initial stage is that the initial years are a key to the manner in which educational retardation becomes *rationalized*, using that term as it was used in the first chapter. That is, the process is so fragmented that whatever was done to the child at the point of first contact is socially invisible to those who have contact with the child at later stages of the process. The fragmentation itself makes an attribute interpretation more plausible. Methodologically, this means that cross-sectional studies, unless interpreted with care, will consistently underestimate the school's impact. Haller and Davis (1980), for example, test the argument that the social status of children affects their assignment to reading groups by looking at fourth, fifth, and sixth graders, which is coming in on the middle of the movie—a persistent problem among denial theorists. It follows from the Gouldner-Rist argument that by the time students are that old, teachers will have plenty of "objective" evidence to justify group placement, even those placements which in fact were based on educationally irrelevant criteria. Haller and Davis cite several other works which are similarly ahistorical, some of them looking at high schools.

The point, again, is not that the school creates problems out of whole cloth. One of the more encouraging signs in recent research is a tendency to cast the problem in terms of home-school interactions (Comer 1980; Lightfoot 1978) rather than trying to maintain that either one or the other is entirely at fault. Helen Gouldner is at some pains to show that in-school peformance is affected by the irregularity of home life for some children, or by frequent moving for others, or by the inability of the home to provide adequately for the physical needs of children. Some students who had a low frequency of interaction with their parents had a low frequency of interaction with their teachers. Students who learned to manipulate adults at home had the advantage of being able to do so in school. Home and school do interact, and some of the problems that show up in school carry over from home. The school's error is to make ineffective and counterproductive responses to problems that are real in some cases and imaginary in others, although in the latter cases the school's responses will ultimately make them real as well. Much of the point of chapter 5 will be to demonstrate that whatever the real home-linked problems may be, schools, if they choose, are quite capable of effectively overcoming them.

Briefly, we can support that point here. The central implication of this discussion of the initial contact between child and school is that inner-city children do not learn because a great many of them just are not taught; Kenneth Clark (1965), among others, has been saying this for a long time. Some of the most significant support for that argument comes from a series of studies done by the methodology freaks at Educational Testing Services to evaluate the *Sesame Street* television program (Averch et al. 1974). The studies concluded that when disadvantaged children view the program as frequently as middle-class children, they learn about as much. On its face, this is very hard to reconcile with the idea that poor children begin school with deeply rooted intellectual deficiencies that make it impossible to teach them.[2] More important, this is the opposite of what Gouldner is describing. This is about as close as we can come to a situation where we have adequte samples and where we can be certain that children from different social backgrounds are receiving the same teaching treatment. Given comparable teaching, we find comparable rates of learning, suggesting again that despite the burdens under which they labor, poor families in general send their children to school quite adequately prepared for learning (which is different, of course, from saying that poor families do all that they might do or should do).

In the early years of schooling, the expectations of teachers appear to play a significant role in starting the process of miseducation. Indeed, works emphasizing teacher expectation are probably the most popular alternative to attribute explanations of inner-city educational failure. What, in general, do we know about teacher expectations?

It is no longer necessary to argue that inner-city teachers typically hold very low expectations for their students. The fact is widely acknowledged. It may be worth repeating, though, that such expectations take on a normative cast. At Westside, this could clearly be seen in the discussions in the teachers' lunchrooms, discussions which could be as stereotyped as if everyone had been handed a script to follow. At one of the primarily Black lunch tables, the script went something like this: a teacher would complain about some problem with students. Other teachers would then contribute similar complaints, with the students coming off worse in each successive account. Nothing can be done, one would say, until they get rid of mandatory school attendance. Most of these kids don't want to be in school, so they spend their time making school miserable for the few who do. At an adjoining white table, similar conversations were more likely to be punctuated by a discourse on the necessity of educating parents. Until that was done, nothing else was going to make a difference. One of the teachers at that table was fond of saying that they should make a film about Westside. Set up cameras in the halls and make a film about it. She would suggest it and then she would correct herself. "No," she would say, always as if the thought had just occurred to her, "nobody would believe it. Nobody would believe it if they could see it." This competitive admission of failure, to use Levy's phrase (1970:68), not only reflects the fact that teachers have low expectations for students and reinforce them to the point of group-think, but it also suggests something of the normative character of such expectations. One is expected to have them and to wear them on one's sleeve. The deviant in such a climate is the person who defends students' capacity for and interest in learning.

The best-known attempt to assess the impact of teacher expectations on learning is Robert Rosenthal's and Lenore Jacobsen's *Pygmalion in the Classroom* (1968). Briefly, the researchers told teachers in an elementary school that they had developed a test to identify late-blooming students. Teachers were then given the names of students that in fact had been drawn randomly and were told that these students were about to "spurt ahead." At the end of the year it turned out that those students for whom teachers' expectations had been artificially raised did in fact make more progress than a control group, with younger students and the more ethnic-looking students gaining most from heightened expectations.

There is nothing surprising about the finding. That much social behavior is shaped, in ways subtle and dramatic, by the expectations of significant others is an idea with a long and fruitful history in social psychology, undergirding our understanding of how self-concept is formed, how placebo effects operate in medical research, how workers set productivity levels among themselves, and how racial stereotypes are sustained. While *Pygmalion* itself was the center of much controversy, certain points concerning the implications of teacher expectations are now reasonably well established. Two reviews of the literature proceeding from quite different ideological viewpoints, one by Caroline Persell (1977) the other by Christopher Hurn (1978), agree that teacher expectations are shaped in part by ascribed and status-related characteristics of students, just as one would expect from Helen Gouldner's work. Persell finds, for example, that seven of nine studies on the subject conclude that the race of a student, particularly when there are few other cues to go on, affects teachers' assessments of intellectual capacity. A number of other studies support the idea that a student's language similarly affects teachers' assessments. As one would expect, the effect of expectations of student learning show up most clearly when the expectations are ingrained rather than experimentally induced.

Hurn and Persell also agree fairly well on the kinds of factors that may mediate the impact of teacher expectations on student learning, although this is still a more difficult point to address with confidence. Available evidence suggests that expectations influence both the quantity and the quality of teaching. When teachers are given arbitrary labels about the abilities of their students, they tend to praise the supposedly brighter students more and to ask them more questions (Rubovits and Maehr, 1971). Good (1975) finds that teachers tend to call most on those students who are achieving most, although his work is particularly subject to reactivity effects. Beez (1970) suggests that how demanding teachers are about the amount of work to be covered will be partly determined by their expectations. He had his subjects teach nonsense words to preschoolers, telling one group of subjects that their students were bright and telling another group the opposite. Again, students in the high-expectation group learned more. More to the point, teachers in the two groups did not try to teach the same number of words. Where teacher expectations were low, only 13 percent of the teachers tried to teach eight or more words; where expectations were high, 87 percent tried to teach at least eight words. Persell cites about a dozen works indicating that teachers ordinarily spend more time interacting with pupils for whom they have higher expectations and several others concluding that the tone of interaction is more encouraging, warmer, and more supportive with those students expected to do well.

If expectations tend to affect teaching style and tend to be lowest for nonwhite or non–middle class populations, we would expect to find significant variations in teaching style across racial and class lines. A study mentioned earlier found that, as compared to Anglo students in the same classroom, Mexican-American students were significantly less likely to be praised by the teacher, to be asked questions, or to have their contributions to class discussions elaborated on by the teacher (U.S. Commission on Civil Rights 1973). King et al. (1973) find that Black male students have less interaction with their teachers than white students of either sex. (In a triumph of attribute theorizing, they proceed to interpret that finding in terms of the heritage of slavery.) Richer (1974) finds that working-class children receive less than their share of teacher interaction in teacher-centered classrooms, but more than their share in student-centered classrooms. The conventional wisdom, of course, holds that most classrooms are teacher-centered. In her comparison of four schools, Leacock (1969) found that the fifth-grade teacher in the Black, low-income school made the fewest remarks about curriculum, both in total and per child, and was the only teacher who made more nonsupportive responses about curriculum than supportive ones; that is, she taught less and degraded students more. Another experiment by Rubovits and Maehr (1975) finds that Black students, even when the teacher has been led to think of them as gifted, receive less teacher attention, less praise, and more criticism than white students.[3] Good (1981) summarizes the decade of research since *Pygmalion* as follows: As compared to high-achieving students, low-achieving students are more likely to be seated away from the teacher, less likely to be called on, more likely to be interrupted if called on, praised less for good work and, interestingly, praised more for marginal or inadequate work. They receive less feedback overall and have less work and effort demanded of them.

As suggested by the Beez experiment, it seems especially plausible that low expectations should be expressed as low demands from the teacher. Johnson (1970:87) claims that teachers' main adjustment to lower-track classes is simply to give them less work. Leacock (1969:94) finds that the Black, low-income fifth grade was the only fifth grade in which the students interviewed did not refer to low grades or nonpromotion as a form of punishment used by the teacher. Dornbusch et al. (1975) claim that their study of four ethnic groups of high school students in San Francisco shows that Black students encounter the lowest level of academic demands. Acuna (1975:13) refers to the tendency of teachers to use grades as tranquilizers for minority students. Alan Wilson (1963) supports that. Comparing three schools of differing racial and socioeconomic mix, he finds that the fewest high grades are given in the working-class Black school. However, when student performance on tests and other measures are taken into account, teachers at that school were giving high grades more readily than teachers at two academically superior schools.

Some of the Westside data are relevant here. All respondents were asked how much homework they were given by each teacher and which teachers they thought were giving either too much or too little homework. Two dozen respondents chose neutral ground, saying that all of their teachers were giving just the right amount of homework. The distribution of response among the others was striking. The students identified only eight cases where they thought a teacher was giving too much homework, with one teacher accounting for three of the eight remarks. And thirty-nine times a student said a teacher was giving too little homework. This is a far larger number than I would have expected, considering that these students, like most, are not especially fond of homework. As a rule, when a teacher was described as giving too little homework (and frequently when a teacher was described as giving just the right amount), the teacher in question was giving no homework at all. By far, the most common homework policy is to give either none at all or to assign as homework whatever cannot be finished in class time. In this Westside students seem typical. According to the 1980 Gallup poll on education, two out of three Black high school students consider their course requirements too easy.

If schools for the least privileged among us tend to be the least demanding, schools for the most privileged have tended to be the most demanding, which might be thought a curious way for privilege to express itself. (It is also true that experiments with the most permissive models of education have been particularly attractive to the upper middle classes.) Part of what makes Harvard Harvard, quite apart from whatever talents people may bring there, is an institutional environment that demands that all those who wish to stay there stretch such talents as they have. By the same token, part of what makes Westside Westside, all apart from any questions about real deficits, is the institutionalized habit of asking too little, of failing to encourage people to use the talents they do have.

Taken as a whole, what can we say about the implications of teacher expectations? First, the expectations of teachers vary with the social status of students, and, independently of student ability, these expectations affect student learning. Exactly how this happens is not so clear, but we can say broadly that expectations affect both the quantity and the quality of teaching, or if you will, just the amount of plain effort that a teacher is disposed to put into the job, which includes the question of how demanding a teacher is likely to be. The effect of expectations is likely to be greatest with students who are younger, lower-class or products of minority groups. (On the later point, see Persell 1977:132. She also cites evidence to the effect that negative information may shape teacher thought more readily than positive.)

This has to be taken with due caution. Allowing that expectations influence achievement does not, as the admirably hard-headed Mr. Hurn reminds us, say anything about the ordinary magnitude of influence. Even allowing for work done since Hurn's, it is not clear that we know much about the degree of difference made by teacher expectations and associated changes in the relationship between teaching and learning behavior, especially if we are thinking of older students. What can be said, particularly in light of what we know about inner-city schools that do work, is that expectations and the associated behavioral changes *can* make significant differences. That is different from saying they always or ordinarily do, but for purposes of policy, just about as important.

We also want to be careful about thinking of the relationship between expectations and learning as necessarily linear. Leaving aside teachers of ritualistic bent and cases of students whose progress is largely independent of the teacher, sufficiently low expectations probably guarantee less learning, unless teacher behavior is very tightly controlled by a supervisory system. The latter is doubtless a rare circumstance, but the basic skills system marketed as Distar comes close, prescribing quite minute sorts of teacher behavior. High expectations, if ordinarily a precondition or a spur to effective teaching, cannot guarantee it. Indeed, where expectations are so high that students are being asked to do things which really are beyond their grasp or where high expectations are combined with confusing styles of explanation—that is bad teaching—high expectations may be counterproductive.

Part of the reason that work on the precise nature of the intervening variables must be treated with particular suspicion is that few of the studies do the kind of context-setting that Helen Gouldner, for example, was doing. We have already seen that praise and criticism can mean one thing coming from one teacher and something entirely different coming from another teacher. Then, too, it would sometimes be useful to know just what students are being praised for. One of the problems with teaching in poor schools noted by Dornbusch et al. (1975) in a study of San Francisco students and by Brookover et al. (1978) in a study of Michigan fourth and fifth grades was the tendency to praise students for incorrect responses (that is, unteaching) or to respond in the same fashion to correct and incorrect responses from students.

The most troubling aspect of framing the issue overmuch in terms of teacher expectations is the conceptual one. It can easily make us forget that in an inner-city school nearly everyone has low expectations of everyone else. Then, too, the imagery the phrase seems to evoke, one where we picture a particular teacher working with a particular group of students at a particular time, can turn attention away from the cumulative effects of miseducation. We do not want to be in the position of encouraging high school teachers, say, to think that *the* problem with urban schools is the problem of low teacher expectation. By the time students have reached high school, things have become more complex. Then, too, if formulated simplistically, the idea becomes another version of subjective mysticism; that is, it can lead to inappropriate emphasis on interpersonal relationships and feelings, akin to the tradition of isolating race prejudice alone as the cause of racial inequality. It is also a version of the RAP thesis, distracting us from the significance of higher levels of power. Teachers' sense of futility, here as in the halls at Westside, has to be understood within an institutional context if we are to avoid the distortions of misplaced emphasis.

One way to do that would be to speak of teacher alienation rather than of teacher expectations. That is, if alienation results from the sense of one's inability to affect one's environment, the sense of professional futility among urban teachers can be treated as an indication of perceived alienation. Volumes of research attest to the fact that within industrial settings greater alienation of workers is associated with diminished productivity. The same should be true even more powerfully of teachers whose work is often more complex, less measurable, and less closely supervised. Treating the literature on teacher expectations as a continuation of the tradition of research on worker alienation may help us focus on the alienating institutional context rather than on teacher attitudes taken in isolation from their context.

Students as Accomplices

The next section will take up the institutional structuring of expectations. Right now, I want to look at some of the ways in which inner-city children come to contribute to their own miseducation, a theme that does not always emerge as clearly as it might from the teacher expectation literature, even in so thorough a treatment as Persell's. The dynamics differ for different children and at different stages in the school career of any one child, but a critical number of poor children adapt to the problematics of schooling by withdrawing positive effort and substituting negative interference.

Like their teachers, students will withdraw effort when making an effort seems futile; we have good reason to think that one of the genuinely problematic elements in the lives of inner-city children is frequently their inability to convince themselves that they can in fact exert some positive influence on what happens to them. One of the more interesting sections in the Coleman report is the discussion of what he calls "fate control" or what some others refer to as "locus of control."

For Coleman, "fate control" refers to the extent to which students feel they are controlling the immediate environment rather than being controlled by it. He measures it by asking whether they think hard work is more important than luck in getting ahead, whether they feel that somebody or something tries to stop them when they try to get ahead, and whether they feel that people like them have much chance to get ahead in life. Again, if we understand "alienation" to refer to the inability to control one's life and activities, to personal impotence and inadequacy, Coleman is measuring perceived academic alienation.

Coleman finds, first, that a sense of controlling their own fates relates to academic achievement more strongly among Black students than among whites. Secondly, he finds that of all variables considered, *family background included*, fate control relates most strongly to achievement for Black children. St. John (1971) replicates his findings about the significance of fate control, using a slightly less ambiguous set of questions. So do Brookover and associates (cited in Brookover and Erickson 1975:370–76), again using a slightly different index they call Student's Reported Sense of Futility. Using a sample of twenty-four elementary schools matched for racial and socioeconomic composition but differing significantly in academic achievement, they found that of ten social-psychological variables considered, Student's Reported Sense of Futility was the most important, accounting for about 45 percent of the variance in achievement. Moreover, they found that teacher expectations were the most important of the variables considered as determinants of students' sense of futility, followed by the extent to which students felt school norms stressed academic achievement and saw significant others aside from teachers as having high expectations for them. Teacher expectations accounted for 25 percent of the variance in students' sense of futility with each of the other two variables accounting for 8 percent.

The study does not allow causal inference and we can be almost certain that there is some circular influence. Still, taken with the other works, it makes the interesting suggestion that the feeling of alienation is an important determinant of achievement and that teacher expectations may have an important influence on how alienated students feel. Giving up on students encourages them to give up on themselves.

Whatever teachers do, inner-city life itself is, of course, often not conducive to a sense of personal efficacy. For those with the personal resources or the luck, growing up with economic deprivation may mean that large challenges are met and mastered early. For others, daily life will appear to be a constant fight against a stacked deck. The school, through poor teaching, an unsupportive atmosphere, and the division of students into the favored few versus the nobodies aggravates whatever problems may already be there, turning the first few years of schooling for many poor children into an alienating assault on the self.

That would be true for many children even where the teacher's interpersonal style is relatively supportive. Beyond that, though, we do have the grosser, uglier forms of status-degradation which may make more difference to younger students than it seemed to make at Westside. Descriptions of inner-city grade schools are replete with examples of status-degradation (Asbell 1968; Kenneth Clark 1965:148; Leacock 1969; Silberman 1970; Herndon 1965; Kozol 1967; Rosenfeld 1971). These works describe the more extreme forms of degradation—teachers who discuss the shortcomings of their students within hearing of the students being discussed, teachers who tell their students that they'll never amount to anything, teachers who call students animals.

It is not difficult to see what effect such humiliation might have on the children's feelings toward themselves. On the other hand, because they are so extreme it may be unwise to take anecdotal reports as being representative on this point. Then, too, children are not without defenses against these and other assaults. Where the source of a hurt is obvious, that source can be written off as unimportant, invalid, foolish, though this may be more a tack for older students to take. If, as Gerald Levy (1970) says, four-fifths of the students in a ghetto school discover that they are "dumb" by the fourth grade, it is at least a shared stupidity, which has to take some of the edge off. In addition, teachers are not wholly wrong when they say low standards are a buffer for students. They allow students to take home passable grades, even for inferior work, which can serve as a source of some pride in their academic ability, regardless of how they would measure up in a different context. Students also have ways of proving worth over which the school exercises no control—games of verbal facility or athletic ability, musical talent, success with the opposite sex and so forth. Certainly the peer groups formed among students operate as a defense as well.[4]

We have to be very careful, then, not to draw a picture that revives the once-traditional image of the torn and tattered self-image of the inner-city child. In all probability, most such children feel pretty good about themselves when they start school (Baughman 1971) and retain, at least in some respects, a positive regard for themselves as they grow older. What they feel about their intellectual potential is another matter. On that score they do face threats connected with the meaning of their race, poverty, language, and with the peculiar nature of their schooling. It is dangerous to talk too generally about self-image, but it is safe to say that a good many inner-city children come to feel ambivalent about their intellectual abilities, at least in situations where their defenses are not operative. When the message that one is stupid comes from a "nice" teacher, fewer defenses are likely to come to one's aid. The most difficult situations may be those where the message is conveyed impersonally, through test scores or through the baffled feeling that comes when students do not understand material known to be at their grade level.

Where defenses do work, of course, they are likely to interfere with the educational process. Where one writes off the teacher, the result is likely to be a nonworking relationship. Alternatively, one can negotiate labels, choosing to be a "bad" child rather than a "dumb" one. The one predictable power students do have over their school environment is the power to disrupt it and some students will learn early to defend themselves by taking the offensive. Something of this connection between what students think about themselves and their misbehavior is suggested by the experience of New York's Higher Horizons program. It was found there, according to Asbell (1968) that as reading scores improved, incidents of vandalism and disruptions dropped off, an association which might be taken to suggest that as students come to feel competent in dealing with their environment, they feel less need to destroy it.

Striking back at an environment that one finds to be largely an assualt on oneself is, I would suppose, a good, normal healthy reaction. Perhaps the students we should be most worried about are not those who strike back, but those who withdraw, protecting themselves by minimizing interaction with the teacher or other students or the material. It is my impression that this adaptation is more common than sustained troublemaking, but since those who withdraw are a problem only to themselves, they may be even less likely than their more rebellious peers to attract any helpful attention.

One of the insidious side effects of teacher harshness is that it poisons relations among students themselves. There is substantial evidence to the effect that the teacher's warmth or lack of it helps determine how well students get along with each other, and, specifically, the degree of scapegoating and aggressiveness among them (Sexton 1967; Anderson 1959). In the Gouldner study students in the highly ranked groups internalized the attitudes of teachers toward the students in the slow group and treated them in much the same disparaging way, a pattern allowed and even encouraged by teachers. High-group students were much more likely to put down low-group students than vice versa, although we might suppose the pattern would be different with older students. "Low" students often capitulated to the prevailing definitions altogether, reminding one another of their stupidity.

Internalization of the school's attitude toward them may, as Gouldner says, erode the bonds of solidarity among the academically unsuccessful, but the bonds remain, serving a protective function partly made necessary by the school itself. Stinchcombe (1964) makes essentially that point in his work on high school students. Much misbehavior among working-class youth, he argues, results from their ritual poverty; that is, since the school gives them little to symbolize their worth, they create symbols of their own, a process of creation experienced by the school as misbehavior. Sennett and Cobb (1972:84), referring to a white working-class elementary school, come to a similar conclusion:

Breaking the rules is an act "nobodies" can share with each other. This counterculture does not come to grips with the labels their teachers have imposed on these kids; it is rather an attempt to create among themselves badges of dignity that those in authority can't destroy.

In making nobodies of students, schools encourage the growth of peer groups antagonistic to education. Another study by Brookover and associates (1978) gives a sense of how much negative influence these peer groups, in combination with some of the other factors we've discussed, may have. Using a sizeable and random sampling of Michigan fourth and fifth grades, they examined the effect of several aspects of school climate on achievement. School climate meant three things, essentially. The first was (again) student's sense of academic futility, or perceived alienation, if you will. The second was teacher commitment to doing a good job and the third was the degree to which students see fellow students as hostile to achievement. All three were measured by questionnaire. As you would expect, school climates were most negative in majority-Black schools or low-income white schools. The factor that mattered most, especially so for Black schools, was the students' sense of futility. Whether teachers were seen as being committed to doing a good job also mattered more in Black schools. With socioeconomic composition of the schools held constant, the climate variables explained 44 percent of the variance in achievement for white schools but 72 percent for Black schools. With the effect of climate variables statistically removed, socioeconomic composition accounted for no more than 5 percent of the variance in any of the subsamples. This is not causal analysis, but it does tell us that the possible combined influence of peer groups that reject school values, low teacher commitment, and students' feelings of academic futility is quite large, a potentially large enough influence to render the significance of family background negligible.

We have already noted that schools inadvertently encourage the growth of peer values hostile to schooling. Teachers lead students to become accomplices in their own miseducation in other ways. Levy (1970) describes a pattern that seems fairly common among younger teachers. Some teachers are so anxious to avoid an authoritarian stance that they are uncomfortable about exercising any authority at all (Comer 1980; Copperman 1978). That, according to Levy, can lead inexperienced teachers to try to get on the children's good side early in the year by allowing students to ignore some rules. As a reward for the teacher who takes the soft line, students promptly proceed to trample all rules into the dust. Feeling betrayed, the teacher then tries the neat trick of trying to enforce rules previously ignored and, failing in the attempt, becomes angry. Students, aware that the ensuing threats and shouts are not part of any rational disciplinary scheme but merely an emotional response, treat the teacher's loss of self-control as a moment of victory. "The more the teacher screams at the children, pounds his fist on the table and chases them around the room, the greater their delight in the victory" (Levy 1970:42). Levy claims he saw several teachers at his Harlem elementary school go through this pattern of behavior. In some cases, frustrated teachers escalated their threats and punishments until they became quite extreme, so that the very teachers who came in most determined to be "nice" ended up smacking the students around more than anyone else. The moral of the piece is not that all rules, even the silliest and most irrelevant, must be enforced, but that teachers who are inconsistent or who fail to make clear to students the rationale for ignoring some rules may create problems for themselves.

Even when misbehavior begins primarily as a defense against the alienating aspect of schooling, it is likely to be sustained by other factors. The rebel leaders, as Levy calls them, are going to quickly learn that their misbehavior brings them a measure of respect from the other children and that to maintain that respect they must go on defying the teacher. Moreover, misbehavior has the happy side effect of allowing children to avoid doing even that part of the work they are perfectly capable of doing. Rebellion may often be just more fun than schoolwork. An adaptation that begins for one reason may be continued for quite different reasons.

The rebel leaders also change the situation for everyone else. They expose for the rest of the class the rather limited range of negative sanctions available to a teacher, enabling other students to see how easy it is to get away with breaking the rules, especially when the misbehavior is massive. Even "good" students will occasionally be drawn into the excitement. The leaders also help the less adventurous define the allowable limits of transgression. "If the rebel leader screams at the teacher and gets away with it, the other children feel they can talk to one another without consequence. If he runs around the room, they get out of their seats and walk around. If he starts a fight, they run around the room" (Levy 1970:42). At the elementary school level, a relatively small number of students who have learned to be consistent troublemakers qualitatively alter the tone of the classroom for everyone, reinforcing, of course, the teacher's sense of futility.

Once the problems reach a certain point, parents are, in the main, ill equipped to deal with them. Many parents waver between blind faith in the professionals who run schools and quick, sometimes overly quick, distrust of these selfsame professionals (Ogbu 1974; Comer 1980). Many parents tell their children to work hard in school, do what the teacher says or else. A good many parents, if they have even the slightest faith in the teacher, will invite the teacher to feel free to smack their child at the first sign of trouble. For many nonwhite or ethnic parents, that was the posture their parents had taken toward their own schooling. That, however, was under a very different set of circumstances. For nonwhites of a generation ago, educational inequality manifested itself as severely restricted access to formal educational resources. Today, nonwhite children contend with formally free access to educational enterprises that proceed from the assumption that failure is inevitable for many students. Partly for that reason, the schools themselves are counterproductively organized, a pattern quite beyond the experience of their parents. Much of the misbehavior and minimal effort of students today is a reaction to an environment which is in fact attacking them. Parents may often fail to understand that misbehavior so grounded cannot be whipped out of children, nor threatened out, nor cajoled out. Changes in the way in which inequality manifests itself makes it more difficult for one generation to pass on to its heirs the kinds of advice that make for more effective coping, and more difficult for one generation even to understand the next. I often get the impression that inner-city parents can be as bewildered by the failure of their young to "act right" as inner-city teachers.

Precise information on how inner-city parenting has been changing is scarce. For Blacks and most Hispanics, there is no doubt that the parental generation of 1960 was much closer to their respective traditional cultures than is the case now. Contemporary inner-city parents participate much more fully in a version of American mass culture. Indeed, a key difference between them and the groups that previously occupied the bottom rungs of the social ladder may be that they are looking for mobility at a time when media influence has given mass culture a pervasiveness it has not previously had. The severance from traditional culture means the loss of sources of self-discipline and self-denial, of certain moral and communal orientations; presumably it also means the development of inner-city populations more easily manipulated by the cultural apparatus, more easily distracted from the kinds of orientations and institutions that foster effective child-rearing. Ultimately, we may see such cretinization of the inner-city population, to use Adolph Reed's term (1979) that the cultural deprivation hypothesis will come to be true, after a fashion.

In the meantime, the mistrust that sometimes characterizes parent-school relations in the inner-city encourages some parents to adopt a hostile and aggressive stance toward schools. (It is probably fair to say that people in low-income urban areas frequently compensate for the absence of other resources by adopting an aggressive interpersonal demeanor.) Schools are typically uncomfortable with outside scrutiny even under the best circumstances (for example, Lightfoot 1978) and the type of parental involvement they prefer is the type they can control, which usually means diverting parental energy into trivial activities. Confronted with parents they cannot control, urban schools are likely to respond by presenting a unified front against parental "intrusion," a tendency reinforced by the norm, often a very powerful norm, which says that the good principal is the one who backs up his or her teachers. The more aggressive the parent, the stronger the tendency to "stonewall." The resulting frustration, if communicated to the child, even inadvertently, can encourage the child to adapt to school in negative ways.

Study after study have confirmed the high regard in which poor parents hold education. The 1980 Gallup poll of education, for example, found that most parents approved of the idea, modeled on a Houston program, of having school officials develop a work schedule for students to be followed both in school and at home. The highest levels of approval, though, came from northern Black parents, who endorsed the idea at a rate of 95 to 1. (They were also the group most critical of schools.) Nonetheless, their lack of confidence in their ability to deal with professional people, their limited expertise with bureaucratic roadblocks and with schools as experienced by their children, the poor feedback they get from schools, their lack of either political clout or easy interaction with teachers mean that many inner-city parents make ineffectual advocates for their children.

Some parents are simply drained by some of the other problems they face. In many neighborhoods they have to protect their children from the dangers, pressures, and temptations of the street and its culture, a culture that encourages aggressiveness as well as cynicism about and resistance to formal authority. It is hard to say at what age it typically becomes important, but certainly by junior high school age, large numbers of children, particularly boys, are likely to be acting out in the classroom lessons learned on the street corner. Usually such behavior is in defiance of the best efforts of the home, but in the most demoralized families the negative lessons of the street are constantly reinforced by the home.

John Ogbu (1974; 1978) has made significant contributions to our understanding of how older students become accomplices in the processes that make them "dumb." Drawing largely from his ethnographic work in a racially mixed working-class community in California, he tries to explain why minority students put so little effort into their school work. His interviews with Mexican-American and Black students found them to be generally pretty satisfied with their grades, though many of them were taking dead-end courses or remedial work. They were satisfied because they judged themselves by the standard of their neighborhood and by those standards felt they were doing well and so felt little inclined to push themselves harder, despite substantial pressure from their parents to take school seriously.

This does not mean that they were not aware that they were doing less well than Anglo students. They knew it and talking about it made some of them uncomfortable. Asked why Anglo students learned more, Ogbu's respondents most typically attributed that to the fact that Anglos worked harder. The Anglos worked harder, it was added, because they knew that if they did well in school they were going to get good jobs after graduation. They saw their own futures as less rosy and thus extending themselves in school was seen as less relevant. Here again, low-income parents are handicapped. Parents who have achieved a comfortable economic status are much better prepared to accurately and convincingly articulate for their children the links between education now and jobs later.

Ogbu reverses common thinking about the relationship between the schooling of the poor and their later economic status. Rather than attributing poverty to educational inadequacies, he attributes educational retardation to the perception of limited economic opportunity. The relative lack of seriousness and perseverance with which many minority students approach schooling stems from their perception that, for them, schooling has minimal payoff. Not only is this true for Blacks, Hispanics, and native Americans in this country, Ogbu contends, but also we find similar patterns wherever minorities occupy a caste-like position in their national economies. In the American case, opportunities for minorities have improved markedly over the last three decades, but the students to whom Ogbu spoke presumably know that they are not the types of minority individuals likely to cash in.

It is clear that academic retardation sets in well before the age at which students begin to think seriously about their future position in the job market and that even after they have reached that age, academic growth is interfered with by an array of factors. Even so, the idea that students who expect little to come of their labor find it that much harder to take school seriously is perfectly plausible.

Stinchcombe's *Rebellion in a High School* (1964) makes an interesting parallel to Ogbu. Studying a rural California high school, he finds that what appears to be merely social class differences in rates of rebellious behavior (skipping class, flunking a noncollege course, being sent out of the classroom) can better be explained by the articulation—that is, the degree of fit—between school curriculum and expected future employment. Stinchcombe's data, partly from school records and student self-reports, suggest that it is not so much that middle-class children have been socialized to behave well as that they are more likely to see a connection between their high school work and their envisioned futures. When that is not true, class differences fail to follow the expected patterns. Thus, middle-class boys in noncollege programs are among the most rebellious of the subgroups in his sample.

What Helen Gouldner and Ray Rist and some of the other works we've looked at say about the beginning of school, Stinchcombe says about the end. Those for whom school answers no future purpose are failures by the school's standard and from them the formal organization of school withholds symbols of worth. Such students respond by insisting more than other students on claiming adult status and its privileges which gives them an alternative means of establishing self-worth but which also throws them into conflict with school authorities whose conception of order requires that students see themselves as adolescents.

Although he is not looking at an inner-city school, Stinchcombe's analysis dovetails pretty well with Ogbu's. Given school experiences that articulate poorly with students' expectations for the future, we can expect more misbehavior and less serious investment of themselves in their work. That is, many such students do not see high school as a tool that they can effectively use to shape their environment, which contributes to their sense of alienation. Convinced that they are powerless to use school to make a positive difference in their lives, students respond in ways that help assure the fulfillment of this negative expectation.

These studies warn implicitly against trying to understand all the ills of urban education as caused in some simple fashion by either the home or the school. The position of the poor and of minorities in the broader society plays a role beyond whatever roles are played by home and school. Schools, though, do teach children directly and indirectly to behave in educationally counterproductive ways. Moreover, even forms of acting out whose roots lie outside the school are much less likely to manifest themselves in a well-organized school environment, a point James Comer (1980) draws from his extensive involvement with the New Haven, Connecticut, public schools. Those forms of acting out that do manifest themselves are likely to be severe, but the staff in such schools are better positioned to respond. Comer is thinking of elementary schools, but as nearly as we can tell from the experience of Westside or from some of the other cases discussed in chapter 5, even for older students a well-run school can make dramatic differences in the degree to which students are not allowed to hurt themselves.

Through disruption, lack of perseverance and application, disobedience, and withdrawal, many urban students come to be junior partners in the process of their own intellectual destruction. They cannot make the system work for them, so they work the system for what they can, which applies with equal force to their teachers. The kinds of self-destructive attributes the denial paradigm centers on come to be there, although they are not so much the whole problem as that paradigm supposes, nor do they stem primarily from the kinds of sources that paradigm points to, nor are they so difficult for the school to counteract as that paradigm implies.

The sources of the problem are multiple, including (but not limited to) peer group norms, the culture of the street, poor and repressive teaching, ambivalent feelings about oneself, and parental inadequacies, most of these feeding a sense of alienation. Any one element in this constellation of forces interacts in complex ways with several other elements and in different ways at different points in the school history of any one child, all of which warns against single-factor, static interpretations.

Each class of participants is engaged in a massive negative feedback loop with all other classes of participants. Each turns to the others its least attractive aspect. Each reinforces in the others the attitudes and practices and values that are most threatening and demoralizing. Parents, teachers, and students respond to their respective kinds of alienation similarly. They all tend to respond in ways that increase the alienation of all others involved and the response frequently takes the form of investing too little of themselves into their formal responsibilities.

The role that students play in this is important partly because it shows that teacher expectations are low not just because teachers are malicious or too undiscerning to see the real potential in children. Their expectations are founded on the hard rock of what they see every day, all day. Certainly from junior high school on, many urban teachers are seeing a great number of students who are ill-humored, foul-mouthed, to all appearances lazy and dishonest, not only uninterested in learning but actively involved in trying to sabotage it. As students grow older, low teacher expectations are increasingly an adjustment to reality, or to that segment of reality most apparent from the vantage point of the teacher. Even so, I think it is certain that even with older students teachers consistently expect less than what is possible.[5] Certainly, this was the case at Westside.

As has been traditional among rednecks, many teachers adopt a stance of nobody-can-understand-us-but-us, a way of circling up the wagons against attack. That teachers are the rednecks of the piece also means that their contributions to a pernicious educational system are relatively obvious, once one looks beyond the inadequacies of parents and children. Indeed, the numberless inadequacies of urban teachers are so obvious as to obscure the workings of more powerful forces, including the ways in which unteaching and nonteaching are fostered by patterns of school governance, a point to which we now return.

The Institutional Roots of Teacher Exploitation

Pygmalion in the Classroom ends with the following thought:

> If further research shows that it is possible to select teachers whose untrained interactional style does for most of her [*sic*] pupils what our teachers did for the special children, it may be possible to combine sophisticated teacher selection and placement with teacher training to optimize the learning of all pupils. (Rosenthal and Jacobsen 1968:179).

To the extent that expectations are a part of the baggage teachers bring with them to school, the emphasis on selection and placement may be a helpful recommendation. If, however, the school itself creates and sustains low expectations—or rather the syndrome of low expectations and poor, undemanding teaching—it is a case of misplaced emphasis. We have to know more about the role played by schools themselves in creating and sustaining expectations. Beyond that, what characteristics of the institutions make it possible for teachers to act on low expectations? In his classic essay on the self-fulfilling prophecy, Robert Merton (1957) pointed out that the prophecy operates only in the absence of deliberate institutional controls. Where are the controls on teacher behavior?

We can start with what passes for the training of teachers. Teachers' colleges annually certify a number of inadequately prepared teachers. As of 1980, at least fourteen states had responded to worries about teacher competence by instituting tests for new teachers. Johnny can't write, claims William Lambdin (1980), because too many English teachers can't either. He cites a report from the Educational Research and Information Center claiming that only about 5 percent of the preparation of new English teachers is devoted to writing with the bulk of their time going into the study of literature. He also cites the case of a Florida county where 30 percent of the newly trained teachers applying for jobs between 1976 and 1980 flunked a district literacy test, including several English majors.

While I was at Westside, 63 percent of the education graduates of Chicago State University, at that time the city's largest supplier of teachers, failed the National Teacher's Examination, up from a failure rate of 20 percent in 1967. In a more widely publicized case, over half the first-year teachers in Dallas in 1978 failed to achieve minimally acceptable scores on a rather easy test of general knowledge (Lyons 1980). In fact, they were considerably outperformed by students from a good high school. Of greater significance, of the seventy-seven administrators who took the test during a trial run, 57 percent would have failed. Of the teachers hired in the next three years, one-third would have failed had not the system abolished failing grades and at least a few of those hired were functioning around the fourth-grade level (Linda Austin 1981). It is not surprising that we get stories (Copperman 1978:237) of reading teachers who cannot distinguish between a vowel and a consonant. Too often we are entrusting the uneducated to the ignorant and it is a safe bet that a disproportionate number of the most poorly trained teachers end up teaching poor children.

On most college campuses, teacher education has long been regarded as a "gut" major, but in the general decline of academic standards over the last ten years, it has become, as Lyons puts it (1980:108), "a sham, a mammoth and very expensive swindle of the public interest, a hoax, an intellectual disgrace." This, too, is failure with a saving grace, at least from the perspective of those who train teachers. Schools of education have never found it easy to compete for the best students, but for the last decade job market conditions have been so poor that it is difficult for them to attract any students at all. The laxity of standards helps keep the warm bodies coming through and the faculty employed. The chancellor of the New Jersey Department of Education is quoted as saying that too many programs have supported their tenured faculty by accepting unprepared students (Cooke and Moss 1980:29). More reasonable standards would mean, over the short run, more arduous workloads, longer hours, and a less competitive position in the intra-university scramble for funds normally allocated partly on the basis of the number of majors enrolled. Similarly, teaching prospective English teachers literature rather than writing skills is teaching them what most members of college English departments are interested in. Vested interests may not be the prime cause of inadequate teacher preparation, but I don't doubt they interfere with the search for a solution.

This is another case where responsibility is elusive, in part because people duck so fast. Teachers' colleges, like universities generally, are quick to claim that the products they are being sent from the high school are so ill-prepared that there is little the colleges can do with them (which might explain how semiliterate students get into college but not how they get out). Secondary schools say that given the products they get from the grade schools and the poor teachers they get from the colleges, the colleges should hardly expect much more. Some schools, notably the University of California, have taken steps to improve the quality of high school education by working directly with high schools and their teachers, a welcome change from the usual buck-passing.

The largely self-serving character of teachers' unions has long been common knowledge, but it is important that we take notice of the willingness of members of the professoriate to participate knowingly—knowingly—in the certification of incompetents so long as the interests of the professoriate are served or at least not jeopardized. The ideology of educational credentialism—the idea that the more education courses teachers take, the better teachers they will be—is an even better example. The number of education courses taken by school teachers demonstrably bears a much closer relationship to the well-being of education professors than to the learning of schoolchildren, which is at least part of the reason for the proliferation of intellectually vacuous courses in schools of education, of inflated masters' degrees, and—Lord preserve us—the proliferation of educational specialties. Why does a profession that has yet to demonstrate that it knows in general what it is doing need specialties, anyway? Collins (1979) makes a very convincing case that the monopoly that colleges now enjoy over the credentials of teachers and others is historically a response to their inability to attract sufficient students without such a monopoly. The trouble with the highly publicized cases of incompetent teachers is that they take attention away from the far more problematic "normal" operation of teacher training institutions.

At the very least, schools of education and teacher training institutions are as venal as teachers' unions, despite the fact that most of the individuals involved are marked by a great depth of human concern. That is just the point. If they were not on the whole such nice people, such thoughtful and obviously well-intentioned people, they could not get away with it. We still tend to define social problems in Good Person/ Bad Person terms. If the professions are good at nothing else they are good at retaining for themselves the image of Good Persons, earning a kind of license that the disreputable seldom enjoy. All the public outcry about the quality of teachers has failed to translate itself into equally vigorous outcry for accountability from the "nice people" who train them.

Poorly trained teachers are unlikely to make reasonable demands on or hold reasonable expectations for their students because they have not themselves been exposed to reasonable expectations. Some teachers—I assume them to be a minority, but a significant one—begin their careers with a trained incapacity to expect much from their students. Those who do not learn minimal expectations before they come to an inner-city school are likely to learn it soon after. Inner-city schools, as we have seen, develop a culture of failure. Failure is the expected outcome of any activity. Thus, Estelle Fuchs (1969) found that the young student-teachers with whom she worked typically felt after their initial contact with inner-city children that the children were capable enough learners. As time went on, they increasingly picked up the message from older teachers that this was not the case at all. Rosenfeld reports the same pattern : "When I first came to Harlem School, I was apprised that the children were slow learners, had low I.Q.'s and were not interested in learning. Most of the children, I was told, were of poor families—many on welfare—and had parents who were busy, or unconcerned about school affairs." (Rosenfeld 1971:49). Hentoff (1979) quotes another New York City teacher: "When I first came here I was told, 'Don't knock yourself out—these kids can't learn.' " The doctrine of the inevitability of failure becomes, in a twist worthy of Orwell, a way to avoid feeling like a failure since failure that cannot be avoided cannot be regarded as personal failure.

Ability grouping must contribute something to the lowered expectations of teachers for those in lower groups.[6] At the high school level, the higher tracks get the better teachers, and those teachers prepare more carefully and use more imaginative approaches than they do with the lower tracks (Persell 1977:89), presumably a reflection of their expectations. The pattern is again that students have unequal access to resources within a school (a pattern taken into account neither by the early studies of the impact of school resources nor by many discussions of the value of school integration). At the least, ability grouping must institutionally reinforce expectations deemed appropriate to each level without institutionalizing procedures to guard against having low expectations translated into poor teaching.

Similarly, whatever the worth of some programs for the "culturally deprived," taken as a whole such programs may serve as an implicit endorsement of the idea that the children are too warped to be taught outside of such programs. Only with special facilities, special techniques, and special funds, it seems, can these special children be rendered educable. If that is the sort of message teachers get from all the programs tried over the last decade, these programs may be actively reinforcing the attitudes that helped to necessitate the programs in the first place. These programs come with built-in contradictions and the ones which are successful have to first overcome that. In any case, there is some evidence that pulling students out for special classes is ordinarily associated with lower rates of learning (Passow 1982).

The assumptions of classroom teachers, as one teacher told Robert Coles (1971), are constantly being shaped by the assumptions made downtown. In the more disorganized city systems, the central administrative apparatus, in its ready acceptance of failure, in its failure to see that teachers are adequately supervised or evaluated, and its consequent reluctance to punish failing teachers, tells teachers that failure is the norm. Downtown has to give up on teachers before they can give up on the students.

It is also likely that the division of labor within schools nurtures low expectations. The fact that the teaching process is fragmented diminishes any one teacher's sense of responsibility while it makes it more difficult for that teacher to maintain an awareness of what previous poor teaching has done to a child, all the more so since school norms frequently prevent teachers from observing one another in class. A teacher is better posi-

tioned to see the deficiencies in a child than the history of school relationships that may have produced them.

At the junior high level and beyond, organizational fragmentation
may have other consequences. History teachers may have trouble getting
students to do the work because students cannot read. Since few history
teachers know much about teaching reading, it becomes that much harder
for them to insist on the kind of performance they might otherwise
expect, unless they are willing to penalize students for not knowing
what they cannot teach. The specialization of teaching means that errors
made at earlier points in the process cannot be corrected at later points.
Indeed, subject-matter specialization, from the junior high level on, means
that most inner-city children are probably attending schools in which
the vast majority of teachers have hardly more than a layperson's knowledge of how to teach basic reading and computational skills. Yet without
those skills students are unlikely to profit much from the "specialized"
subject matter that higher-level teachers are prepared to teach. In an
ideal world, schools of education might respond to this by turning out
many more remedial basic skills specialists and, at least temporarily,
fewer majors in other fields. Given the politics of education in this world,
such a solution is unworkable for many reasons, not least of which is
that it would work to the detriment of those education professors who
train prospective teachers in areas other than basic skills. When the
needs of children and those of educational professionals are at cross-
purposes, we can expect urban schools to continue whatever arrangements best fit professional needs.

Perhaps what matters most is that, as currently structured, schools
reward teachers for holding low expectations of students and penalize
teachers for high expectations. By and large, teachers are allowed to
determine the amount of work students, and therefore they themselves,
will have to do. The lower the expectations, the lower the teacher's work
load. If you give true-false tests instead of essays (since the kids can't
write anyway), you don't have a stack of essays to carry home at night.
If you don't assign many books (since they would not/could not read
them anyway), you don't have to spend much time reviewing books.
Every classroom movie (since deprived children relate better to audio-
visual techniques) reduces the amount of time spent preparing lectures.
An added attraction of the movie is that after you've shown it, you can
ask if there are any questions, and when there are none, you can have
the satisfaction of complaining about how hard it is to motivate these
students.

The problem is not fundamentally that teachers are lazy. Take an
example from Westside. Well into December, I watched a teacher skill-
fully kill a class period doing nothing in particular. She began the period
by reviewing the names and locations of the country's largest cities,

which had been the subject of the previous lesson. The review went well and she gave no indication that she was dissatisfied with their level of knowledge. Nonetheless, she decided to devote another class period to the same material, passing out puzzles on the subject. The students had hardly started on them when there was an interruption. A former student, a poet, visited the class. With some prodding from the teacher, he read some of his latest work. This entertainment took up the rest of the class period. At the end of the class, she told students to hand in their puzzles, even if they had not finished, thus indicating that the assignment was not to be taken seriously. After class, the teacher told me that some teachers were still being transferred in and out of the building, so it was difficult to get into the important material. If she did that, the kids who had to switch classes would be penalized. (This makes sense only if one assumes that the incoming students would not have started the important material.) Therefore, she had been assigning "little projects" like the puzzle and some material from *Senior Scholastic Magazine*. She thought this was the kind of thing that would help them on IQ tests, but she was not sure. Essentially, in December she had not yet begun to teach, and she was delaying purely out of a sense of service to her students.

She really believed this, as nearly as I can tell. She saw herself as in a situation where teaching would be a disservice to her students and, of course, once she decided she was not going to teach, it hardly mattered whether she not-taught with a puzzle or a poem. It is hardly likely that she could see herself as exploitative. She was doing what was best for her students. If it happened that she did not have to read papers that evening, just as she did not have to prepare a lecture or outline a discussion the evening before, that was quite incidental to her sincere good intentions.

At least, I think teachers were ordinarily sincere in their explanations for not teaching. Still, as was the case here, some teachers were so clearly uneasy about discussing their teaching with an observer, so fulsome with unrequested explanations, as to imply more conscious ambivalence than I am allowing for. On the whole, in any case, it is not so much that teachers are lazier than anyone else as that the cult of futility gives some of them a perfectly plausible rationale for not teaching and the undemanding administrative structure allows them to act on that rationale and even rewards them for doing so.

Working hard in an environment where everyone works hard is one thing. Working hard while surrounded by colleagues some of whom barely work at all is quite another. The fact that some teachers in failing schools continue to put so much of themselves into their work despite a climate which both allows and encourages them to do otherwise is thus all the more interesting. It is not clear what their deviation from the norm does to their collegial relations. It may be that some of the best teachers in urban schools come to occupy a position akin to that of the rate-buster in industry; that is, they become unpopular mavericks. It would be helpful to know more about how such people keep their engines fired up and how they negotiate potentially uncomfortable relations with other teachers.

We do not measure teacher quality in any way that has anything to do with peformance; teachers, more than most other workers, are in a position where they can afford to reduce the effort they put into their jobs without jeopardizing the material rewards of the job. Teachers, of course, have traditionally opposed any suggestion that rewards be tied to performance, citing measurement problems which, while substantial, are not so very different from the problems inherent in grading students. It would be difficult to make an empirical case for the idea that most of the criteria of competence with which teachers have grown comfortable—National Teachers' Examination, higher degrees, extra course work and, more debatably, years of experience—relate more than tenuously to student growth. (Coleman did find that years of teacher experience and high scores on verbal ability tests—the latter presumably an index to the quality of intellectual training—do correlate with student learning more strongly for minority students than for others.) In contrast, elite private schools pay much less attention to "objective" measures of teacher competence, relying more on informed judgment.

Public school teachers, of course, are hardly likely to lose their jobs for reasons of incompetence. During the time I was at Westside, for example, Chicago, employing 27,000 teachers, fired just six for all reasons during the average school year. At that time the average cost of firing a teacher to the school system was about $25,000 which is undoubtedly part of the reason why firings are so rare (Banas 1975). Similarly, in the period 1963–69, only twelve of New York City's more than 55,000 teachers were released for reasons of incompetence (Boggs 1970:191). Nor have things changed too drastically since. Between 1978 and 1980, New York City, with a superintendent much more willing than most to insist on teacher performance, was able to dismiss only two of 50,000 teachers for incompetence (Maeroff 1982:167). Between 1971 and 1976, Finlayson (1979) can find only eleven cases of *attempted* dismissal for reasons of incompetence in all of Pennsylvania, which works out to one such case for every 50,000 teachers—a ratio much at variance, he notes, with the estimate of the American Association of School Administrators that one teacher in ten is incompetent. Any estimate of the proportion of incompetent teachers is an invitation to a quarrel. (A former director of the Council for Basic Education says that 40 percent of them are illiterate [Benjamin 1981:54]). Whatever the "real" number is, by whatever definition of competence, we can be certain that inadequate teacher performance is not among the major determinants of teacher job security.

More important, teachers in many urban systems, especially those in inner-city schools, are unlikely to be evaluated in any serious fashion. Terry Herndon, president of the National Education Association, claims, "Most districts make virtually no investment in the evaluation of teacher performance" (Maeroff 1982:169). Copperman (1978:195) says that the most common complaint from the elementary school teachers he interviewed was that principals fail to observe classes; this may explain why a study of western New York elementary teachers found that only 2 percent felt that their supervisor or principal functioned mainly as an educational leader (Heichberger and Young 1975). It does not seem likely that the average principal spends more than 10 percent of his or her time on *all* matters directly related to instruction, evaluation included (McIntyre and Morris 1982). David Rogers (1969:336–37) cites a five-year period in which just 252 of the then more than 54,000 teachers in the New York City system were given unsatisfactory ratings. Those receiving such ratings were often simply transferred to another school. He adds, significantly, that "the performances of principals are subject to even less measurement and control than those of teachers."

Some observers have claimed recently (for example, Saiter 1981) that there is a discernible national move toward closer monitoring of teacher behavior, despite the prospects of court fights and union opposition. In Seattle four years of experience with an elaborate evaluation plan has made it significantly easier to remove questionable teachers. More important, satisfactory teachers got even better. Evaluation of teachers is more art than science, but there is reason to think that supervisors can in fact measure teacher performance. Murnane's (1975) study of sixteen New Haven schools serving Black students found a consistently significant relationship between the ratings that principals gave teachers and the achievement of students. As difficult as it is to specify in the abstract the qualities that make a good teacher, principals who make an effort seem to be able to identify them.

How low expectations are generated and sustained is much less problematic than how it is possible for the school to let teachers carry them out. How is it possible for teachers—particularly, I am sure, those of the urban poor—to receive so little supervision from the enormous administrative superstructures that have developed in most cities? The underlying problem may not be so much sheer bureaucratic ineptitude, although that is not lacking, as administrative priorities and vested interests that frustrate educational goals, a pattern David Rogers calls "bureaucratic pathology."

The general effectiveness of the administration of public schools is open to question. Deal and Celotti (1980) studied 103 northern California

elementary schools in thirty-four school districts of widely varying socioeconomic character. With some exceptions, they found methods of
classroom instruction to be virtually unaffected by administrative factors
at the school or district level. The three levels of organization—district,
school, and classroom—operated pretty much independently of one another, as did individuals at any given level. Such a situation, they note,
is not necessarily bad in that it suggests classroom teachers can be flexible. Doubtless some of that flexibility sometimes lends itself to a choice
not to teach. It may also mean, as the authors note, that teachers, subject
to little pressure from above, may cave in too readily to pressures from
below, giving students unwarranted influence over instruction.

If administrations elsewhere are equally divorced from the substance
of the educational process, it appears that most school boards are incapable of doing anything about it. The evidence generally indicates that
"school boards virtually never set district policy in substantive areas
such as personnel evaluation and training, curriculum, or discipline"
(Copperman 1978:197). Rogers's study of the New York City school
bureaucracy similarly finds that board members devote very little time
to substantive educational questions. Board members may not even think
of their role as educational policymaking. Their role becomes, as Kerr
(1968) puts it, that of legitimating decisions made elsewhere. Kerr says
much about the processes by which boards become impotent. In the
two suburban districts he studied, board members deferred educational
questions to the professional staff, particularly to the superintendents,
in accordance with a belief that professionals deal most effectively with
such questions and require autonomy to do so.

Several factors led to this abdication of responsibility. Board members
were generally quite ignorant at the beginning of their tenure, not only
of educational practices and philosophies, but of board operations as
well. Their socialization was partly dependent upon older board members who had already accepted the norm of deference to the professional
staff and partly upon those professionals themselves, who thus found
themselves in the enviable position of being able to teach their nominal
supervisors how to supervise. Even experienced board members depended on professional staff for the information on which they based
their decisions. (Whether boards should hire their own staffs continues
to be a subject of debate.) Both of the superintendents in the Kerr study
deliberately steered board members away from the discussion of educational policy, an issue that occupied no more than 13 percent of board
time in either district.

It is not that board members are uninterested in education. Blanchard
(1979), polling a sample of members of the National School Boards Association, found that the issues they actually dealt with as board members were quite different from the issues they had, as candidates for the

board, expected to encounter. Prior to becoming board members, they had thought they would be dealing with curricular matters, expenditures, and the hiring of teachers—in that order. They found the bulk of their time going into collective bargaining, expenditures, and new building programs. If people interested enough in schools to run for board positions (about 95 percent of all boards are elected) are so misinformed about what boards actually do, the general public must be still more ignorant. Like Kerr, Blanchard found that the period of adjustment to the position is fairly lengthy. It took a year for the average board member to feel comfortable in the role. Superintendents were named as most influential during that period of adjustment in orienting board members to their jobs, with this being slightly less true in urban areas. More optimistically, Blanchard found signs of growing discontent with norms calling for deference to superintendents.

More assertive boards, though, need not be more responsive. The Kerr study shows that the boards were unlikely to function as representatives of the public because of deference to the professional staff and, moreover, because of their low opinion of the public. Given the public's special interests and their lack of familiarity with the legal and financial complexities of board activity, the public often appeared to the board to be composed of so many interfering, uninformed nuisances. The board thus concealed as much of their work as possible through such devices as engineered unanimity, executive sessions, informal and closed meetings for delicate discussions and open meetings for matters of boring routine. Members of elite strata could more easily force their concerns onto such boards, but their interests are only marginally involved.

One of the richer recent studies on the isolation of school decision makers is Marilyn Gittel's *Limits to Citizen Participation* (1980). Studying Los Angeles, Boston, and Atlanta, she finds significant variations among the three professional bureaucracies in degree of openness to the general public, with Los Angeles the most open, Atlanta the most closed. "Degree of openness" she defines to include the level of decentralization, the availability and representativeness of decision makers, and a flow of free information from the bureaucracy. As one would expect, the more receptive the bureaucracy is to citizen input, the more input it gets. Citizens in open Los Angeles make far more presentations to the board than do citizens of closed Atlanta. The school systems were more likely to be open with respect to narrow questions—Who shall be principal of this or that high school?—than more fundamental questions— By what criteria shall we choose principals? When it comes to *effective* involvement, however, some citizens are more equal than others. As judged by school decision makers, middle-to-upper income citizens groups were much more influential than groups of poorer citizens. After we allow for that exception, though, the most important finding may be that as much as they differed in their operating styles, all three systems ordinarily excluded citizens from effective involvement. The variations in openness were a sort of sham, "allowing for a greater or lesser degree of involvement without power" (Gittel 1980:212). The best we can say is that school systems, like many of our institutions, represent a *Herrenvolk* form of democracy, to use the South African term, responsive to some of the people some of the time, but unlikely to respond to the poor except in moments of crisis.

To the more obvious devices excluding lay persons from meaningful participation in governance, add the bloated and intimidating language of the professional educator, a language offering the poorest ratio of information to words used of any known idiom. Like misleading report cards, social promotion, and the use of mid-level administrators to keep parents at arm's length, such language helps keep parents ill informed. Having thus contributed to the processes making urban parents ineffective advocates for their children, school officials proceed to join the general lament about the lack of interest on the part of inner-city parents. Gittel (1980:170) finds that accurate information on what is going on in schools can be an important stimulus to the active involvement of low-income parents. A promising development, illustrated by the Parents' Union of Philadelphia (Hentoff 1980) is the use of trained parent advocates who are not so easily buffaloed.

Both Gittel and Rogers suggest that the tendency to exclude parents from school board deliberations may be sharpest where the parents represent racial or ethnic groups, particularly so if they are defined as militant. Thus, urban parents' groups find themselves in a triple bind. If they approach boards hat in hand, they may find their concerns absorbed by platitudes, buried under buck-passing and stonewalling. If they are more aggressive, their style itself becomes an excuse for the board to tune them out. If they do manage to get more than cursory consideration, they may learn only that the board is not really governing the schools in any case. From the viewpoint of parent-activists, fighting the bureaucracy is like punching clouds. The fragmentation of power and authority robs them of any clear target, except perhaps the classroom teacher, visibility being one of the chief virtues of rednecks.

If it is the case that boards frequently have little or no impact on educational direction and that effective power lies in the hands of the upper-level professional staff, might not that fact work to the best interests of the children? Sometimes it does, perhaps, but it is hardly the sort of thing one wants to depend on. Professional staffs of big-city systems often build "pathological bureaucracies," a phrase Rogers uses to cover bureaucratic structures whose traditions, structure, and operation subvert their formal missions. Among the elements of pathology as Rogers finds them in New York are overcentralization, unnecessary layers of hierarchy, isolation of units in the system from each other and consequent development of chauvinism within units, exercise of informal peer norms sanctioning conformity to traditions at cross-purposes with educational goals, a pattern of rebellion from lower-level supervisors alternating with overconformity, insulation from "clients," and, most familiarly, decision-making procedures that make it difficult to pinpoint responsibility.

The consequences of these conditions are pathological only with reference to the official goals of the administration. Not long ago, a (rather unusual) chancellor of the New York City system charged that too many teachers, administrators, and contractors were more interested in serving their own interests than those of children (Chambers 1979). For serving those interests, a structure making responsibility difficult to pinpoint—because decisions are made in committee, because there are so many organizational units involved, because information about decision making does not flow smoothly across units, because outside inquiry is minimized—is the purest blessing, allowing bureaucrats to claim professional perogatives without assuming a commensurate degree of responsibility. The informal norms that develop are also largely self-serving. Rogers describes norms that are largely protectionist, requiring, for example, loyalty to one's comrades or one's unit, allegiance to educationally dubious forms of credentialism that render career ladders predictable and, to a degree, manipulable, and allegiance to the tradition of promoting only insiders to important positions. Upper-level professional staff have a deeply vested interest in forms of pathology which make them autonomous, but which also tend to make them ineffective administrators.

Not every urban system has every problem mentioned here, but within a given system, the negative impact of whatever administrative failure there is will fall most heavily on the children of the poor. In schools with greater resources—a tradition of success or parents who are relatively respected by school officials or students whose in-school learning is constantly reinforced by out-of-school experiences—administrative inadequacies, even if present, may be largely neutralized. Perhaps middle-class kids have traditionally not been so much "school-ready" as relatively "school-proof." The urban poor, on the other hand, generally send their children to school with the resources to learn, if taught, but not with the resources to neutralize the consequences of administrative failure.

The self-serving professional subculture interacts with broader cultural assumptions about education and society. Presumably, the assumptions made by both administrators and teachers about the educability of students reflect widespread and very old assumptions about race and status and intelligence. There has never been a time in our history when meeting a "dumb" nonwhite person or "dumb" poor person has been grounds for surprise. Only the culturally sanctioned explanations for that phenomenon have changed. Orthodoxy has moved from the position that stupidity among the urban poor is ordinarily inevitable and immutable to the position that it is theoretically possible for the poor to attain an adequate level of intellectual functioning, but the practical tools for realizing that objective have yet to be invented. The social science documentation for the latter position is, of course, immense. The socially legitimate attenuated forms of racist and elitist ideologies, in combination with the vested interest of administrators in any idea that deflects blame away from them, may shape the assumptions that shape administrative behavior.

Culturally grounded assumptions about educability, structural irresponsibility, and the self-serving character of the educational bureaucracy do not by themselves account for administrative failure. Administrators have strictly limited formal power, and even less authority; with it they must confront problems of considerable complexity. Levy said of the administrators under whom he taught (1970:130):

[They] are caught in a crossfire of parental anger, supervisory dissatisfaction, teacher disrespect, and child rebellion. All their activity is directed toward ducking the crossfire. But in doing so they unintentionally administrate and sustain those policies which undermine the interest of parents and children. It is ironic but not illogical, given society's relationship to its lower-class youth, that the very activities which enable administrators to survive in the school insure the children's failure.

This captures the way administrators feel—harried, misunderstood, unjustly accused, and powerless to do much more than they are doing about the conditions of the schools. Here, too, however, we have to distinguish between alienation as powerlessness and alienation as the feeling of powerlessness. Administrators can be very demanding, even authoritarian, about educationally unimportant matters like some of the lesser clerical duties of teachers. On more pertinent matters, they clearly do much less than they have the power to do. Certainly, administrators can evaluate teachers if they choose to. They ordinarily cannot do that, however, without arousing substantial opposition; they cannot do it easily. It may not be so much that the courts, teachers' unions, parents' groups, national testing services, and various regulatory agencies have stripped administrators of the power to be effective as that the growing power of those groups has made the path of least resistance increasingly attractive to administrators, much as teachers capitulate in the face of students they think cannot be easily taught. Too many administrators are, in the ghetto vernacular, unwilling to "pay the cost to be the boss."

Much of what we have been calling bureaucratic pathology describes virtually any large formal organization to some degree. We find group-think, the displacement of official goals, avoidance of outside scrutiny and of personal responsibility almost everywhere. The difference is that in some organizations there is a bottom line, a point below which prog-ress toward achieving nominal goals cannot slip, lest heads roll, pro-cedures get revamped, policies scrapped. The bottom line in urban schools is excessively low; in fact, it is essentially nonexistent in that there is no level of failure among poor children that will cause administrators to be removed. At times of crisis or if schools begin failing middle-class stu-dents, administrators may be called to account. Ordinarily, no one is watching the watchers.

It is not true that no one in such a system cares for poor children. Schools, as educators have repeatedly and accurately pointed out, are being asked to do too many things, to give too much to too many, and they cannot do it all. Teachers ask for job security, a degree of autonomy in their daily routines, and a sense of professional justification, and they get it. The faculty of teachers' colleges ask that their nests not be dis-turbed, and they get that. Supervisory personnel ask for autonomy, particularly from outside interference, for power without responsibility, for manipulable and predictable career ladders and secure fiefdoms, and they get all of that, by and large. A system can only be asked to do so much. Serving the vested interests of the educational profession and the interests of inner-city children at the same time is a bit more than most city school systems are up to.

There is hardly anything new about portraying the upper adminis-trative levels of school systems as inefficient and self-interested. It is curious, though, how that knowledge can be used or not used. In my experience, the most withering critiques of urban administrations come from urban teachers. Yet if one asks the same teachers to explain the failure of urban children to learn, they overwhelmingly point to the inadequacies of the parents and the children. What they know of ad-ministrative inadequacies, which, one would think, might be presented as at least part of the answer, seems to get stored in some separate file. A 1975 survey of Chicago school teachers (Banas 1976) found that 75 percent of them rated the performance of the Chicago Board of Education as either fair or poor. The superintendent received about the same rat-ings. This suggests that teachers were overwhelmingly either critical of or lukewarm to the governing structure. Still their "consuming con-cerns," Banas found, were the various inadequacies of parents and chil-dren. Administrative inadequacies were acknowledged, but not seized upon.

The academic debate is similar; either it's bad teaching or it's dumb kids. Those who have studied both cultural deprivation and teacher expectation have produced works that are properly called "classic" in the sense that everyone in the field knows what they say. No study of administration has gripped our imaginations as *Pygmalion* has done, much less the work of James Coleman. Works as strong as Persell's and Hurn's, the former admirable for the breadth of its empirical coverage and its concern with synthesizing levels of theory, the latter for its plain hard-headedness, discuss teaching, with slight exception, as divorced from administration, very much the mind-set with which I went off to Westside High School. Benjamin (1981:120) points out that the push for accountability has led many states to adopt competency tests for students and teachers, but no state has taken similar steps to institute account-ability for those who supervise. We all know in a general sense that leadership in urban schools is of questionable quality, but that seems to get compartmentalized away from our underlying conception of the basic problems in urban schools. Oliver Cox, we may be sure, would see in that a continuation of the tradition of seeing the rednecks rather than the Bourbons, asking all other questions before we ask, who has the power and how is it being used?

For teachers, of course, thinking more carefully about the links be-tween what administrators are and what children learn would require that they think more carefully about their own role, since they are the link that intervenes. Certainly, for those who view the school from the outside, the problem is partly that the administrative dimension is rel-atively invisible, not so much a part of our shared personal experience as the teacher-student relationship and thus not so much a part of the background imagery out of which we frame questions and propose an-swers. Put differently, the fragmentation of the educational process ren-ders some elements of the process nearly invisible, thereby inviting a kind of structured irresponsibility from administrators.

But urban schools are more than bureaucracies, more even than public bureaucracies, which are probably generically more susceptible than others to certain forms of corruption. They are bureaucracies of profes-sionals, partaking of the mystique with which this society has ordinarily surrounded its professions. We have already had an example of that in the willingness of school board members to defer to the judgments of educational professionals. Those in all professions claim high ideals of service, exclusive mastery of some extensive and important body of knowledge, and the consequent right to go about their professional activities free of the interference of "unqualified" outsiders. Some profes-sions have been notably more successful than others in getting their claims taken seriously. No doubt, the public is a good deal more cynical about such claims than it used to be, but there is a hierarchy of plau-sibility. Spending enormous resources trying to understand why poor children do not do well in school makes no sense unless one assumes that they are by and large in something that could reasonably be called school; that is, one has to accept the claims of the educational profession to be making an earnest effort to teach in the ghetto and failing. Accepting those claims is apparently much easier than accepting the idea that the poor do not learn because they are not taught. The idea that the poor are intellectually inadequate seems to be vastly more plausible than the idea that professions respond more predictably to power and their own self-interest than to anything else; yet there is hardly anything unusual about the professions failing to serve a population that has negligible power. Even the relatively low-status education profession seems to have retained enough of the professional mystique to minimize questioning of its essential claims, which helps explain why those who are at the center of the profession have not often been scrutinized as being at the center of the problems of urban education despite what we have long known about their failings.

How much we know may often not be the critical determinant of how a problem gets approached. Not all that we know informs consciousness. How rapidly we accumulate new knowledge may be much less significant than how we juxtapose the bits and pieces of knowledge we already have. To borrow an example from chapter 5, what I take to be the most important development in the discussion of urban education since the initial popularity of the teacher expectation approach is the current interest in effective urban schools. There, too, it is not so much that startling new findings have come to light as that we are being forced to look in a new way at things we have always known.

What passes for the education of the urban poor is a system in which a great many children never encounter a serious and sustained effort to teach them, a system that nurtures a community of low expectations and then permits people who are theoretically paid to teach to translate those expectations into poor teaching and lax administration and even rewards them for doing so. Students are encouraged to withdraw or rebel or, at best, to learn far less than they might. It is also a system in which problems manifest themselves in ways that obscure their origins, partly through social and organizational fragmentation that prevent the individuals who make the system possible from having much sense of individual responsibility. It is a system highly successful at producing what many of those at the top most want it to produce, sustaining itself by distributing smaller and less tangible benefits to those lower in the hierarchy, but always offering at least a little something for everybody. There is some consolation here in that the interests of the professional bureaucracy which get in the way are not so much diametrically opposed to the interests of children as divergent from them. That leaves some room for flexibility and even makes it possible for leadership at the mid-levels of the systems to move in a positive direction even without the support of the hierarchy. Vested interests are perhaps less important in the creation of problems than in frustrating attempts at their resolution. In any case, we don't have to worry too much over the importance of administration as a "cause" of the problem. We ought to hold administrators to a more stringent standard. Voltaire said at the death of a powerful cardinal that the man went to his grave guilty of all the good he had not done. The administrative function is separated from the rest not by the negative contributions that are made but by the positive contributions that administrators could make and do not.

The social psychology of this problem is complex. Teachers' expectations are a key element certainly, but we don't want to stress them to the point of forgetting that they are, after all, only a part of an institutionalized system which must be addressed as a system, not as a collection of individuals who happen to share similar expectations. "Alienation" may cover more of the relevant feelings of actors at all levels in the system than any other single term, if we take it to mean a sense of personal powerlessness, the feeling of personal inefficacy. Here as with students, though, it is not always clear how much of "I can't" means "I can't" and how much is merely the safer form of "I won't."

Asking why low-income students do not learn sets up a false problem. Framing the question thus reinforces the official line. It assumes that there is an educational profession making a credible attempt at teaching them. Social service agencies, Ronald Edmonds has argued, tend to serve those they have to serve. The poor don't get an education because they haven't been able to demand it and those who could do so on their behalf have other interests. We are getting precisely what we are asking for and then we have the gall to act surprised at it.

Elite Interests and Miseducation

We will not fully understand urban education until we understand its connection with other sectors of society, the economic sector in particular. It is clear now that the traditional ways of seeing the linkages between schooling and subsequent economic status, derived from attribute-meritocracy thinking, are either dubious or fallacious. That is, contrary to traditional assumptions, the economic return on schooling cannot be well explained by what one learns in school (Berg 1971; Newman et al. 1978; Jencks 1972). The importance of educational credentials seems vastly disproportionate to their productive value (Berg) and are perhaps best understood as a means by which certain groups maintain a monopoly over certain sinecures by controlling access to the credentialing process and a means by which employers identify certain character traits of dubious productive value (Collins 1979). This implies that better education alone is hardly likely to be the means of economic salvation for the slums, a position Christopher Jencks was pilloried for taking ten years ago.

We have entered an age of an overeducated labor force, a phrase Freeman uses to denote a society in which economic returns to continued education are markedly lower than has traditionally been the case. Indeed, in the late 1970s only half of those getting college diplomas got college-graduate level jobs. Given recent history, it seems likely that if poor youth in massive numbers begin earning educational credentials, there will also be an equally massive upgrading of the kinds of entry-level credentials required by the job market, leaving their relative position unchanged or only marginally improved. Rather than being made economically more valuable by the credentials, poor youth will devalue the credentials they acquire. Among other things, this means that those minority-interest organizations that stress attaining group mobility through acquiring credentials will have adopted an inherently self-defeating economic strategy for their constituencies as a whole, though it should work very well for a few individuals, so long as their numbers remain small.

Better education alone, then, is hardly likely to be the path to economic renewal. Still, as Bowles and Gintis point out, greatly improved education of the poor would remove an important justification for the maldistribution of wealth in this society. More fundamentally, education is prerequisite to the full possession of one's faculties. As the education available to them improves, we may hope that the children of the poor will be better able to contribute to the shaping of their own means for redressing economic inequality.

Thus far, the problem of urban education has been portrayed as being peculiarly and particularly a failure of leadership—a revelation of the ineffectiveness of intellectual leadership—a failure that gives free reign to a variety of vested interests against which the poor cannot compete. That does not partake so much of the RAP thesis as do those arguments laying all the blame on bad teachers, but neither does it clearly address the matter of how the interests of more elite strata are involved. That involves some complicated issues, which I would like to speculate on briefly.[7]

Teachers might be taken as the first line of defense in class struggle (or the second, if one considers the culture promulgated by the mass media as the first). That is, for most poor children, teachers are the first representatives of officialdom, the first referees in the race for status and privilege in the outside world. It was stressed in chapter 1 that the attribute ideology to which teachers are powerfully attracted is just one expression of a deeper ideological stance which has historically been of special use to social elites. Choosing to define the world in terms of the inadequacies of children and parents, teachers opt for that definition of the situation which, of all those readily available, is least threatening to the powers-that-be.

Defending their own class interests, teachers inadvertently defend elite interests as well, becoming real and symbolic protectors of the status quo. This is ironic, since people who choose to become school teachers are, as judged by the standards of the status quo, rather poor material themselves. In general academic ability, education majors consistently rank near the bottom among college students (Swift 1976:35–36). If one takes the meaning system of meritocracy seriously, this society consistently assigns the most minimally competent members of the moderately privileged classes to teach, to serve as buffer and mediator between the established order and the teeming masses. If the meritocracy thesis had much basis in fact, we would expect that society would do whatever was necessary to see that only the brightest were allowed to teach. (It is possible, though, that if teachers were recruited from among abler students, they would be somewhat less prone to conservative world views.) The point is not that teachers are stupid—that follows, I said, only if one takes meritocracy seriously—but it might not be too much to accuse them of having a form of false consciousness, one in which the distancing device of professionalism plays a major role (Grace 1978). Inner-city teachers are defending a system under whose rules they are not particularly valuable people.

The systematic miseducation of the poor may or may not be essential to elite interests. Such miseducation is clearly acceptable to elites, though. "The at least tacit approval of dominant groups can be inferred by what they allow to exist without intervention and by where they send their own children to school" (Persell 1977:170–71). Meaningful intervention would mean that elites would act as they ordinarily do when their interests are at stake—that is, they would systematically press for a system in which administrative or pedagogical failure was punished and success rewarded, a system like that in which their own children are taught. The minimal interpretation to put on the acceptability of miseducation to elites is that the education of the poor is simply an issue of marginal concern to those best placed to demand change.

That marginality, the ideological concordance of interests between educators and elites and the existence of a stratified school system, allows for elite default. The schools are in very safe hands, the children of elites are in very safe (but different) hands and elites may comfortably withdraw from any direct involvement except sporadic and largely symbolic expressions of concern, creating a vacuum of power into which steps the educational profession, armed with an endless variety of excuses for selective teaching.

It is also possible that slum schooling may serve elite interests in another way—they may give to those who are destined to fail plausible and relatively acceptable explanations for their failure. Little is written on the subject, but it may be useful to speculate on how graduates of slum schooling feel about the relationship between their education and their economic status. How does a place like Westside look in retrospect?

Some years ago, about the time when the junior college movement had first begun to flower, Burton Clark wrote a piece entitled "The Cooling-Out Function of Higher Education" (1975). At the outset, he noted a significant problem:

Democracy asks individuals to act as if social mobility were universally possible; status is to be won by individual effort, and rewards are to accrue to those who try. But democratic societies also need selective training institutions and hierarchial work organizations permit increasingly fewer persons to succeed at ascending levels. Situations of opportunity are also situations of denial and failure. Thus democratic societies need not only to motivate achievement but also to *mollify those denied it to sustain motivation in the face of disappointment and to deflect resentment*. (Emphasis added, Clark 1975:393)

Clark goes on to point out that the junior college helps to manage the tensions inherent in that situation. It minimizes the emotional impact of failure by providing alternative routes of "achieving" for those whose grades would keep them out of more competitive schools and it makes the realization of failure a gradual, rather than a sudden discovery. Perhaps the same argument can be applied to Westside and to schools like it. Most graduates of Westside are going to be failures by the prevailing social standards, but Westside may help cool-out its victims. It makes their failures more palatable and makes such discontent as they do feel politically meaningless.

Slum students are as much exposed as anyone to the idea that intelligent people are entitled to get more from life and that, as these things are judged, they themselves are not terribly intelligent people. For many graduates of slum schooling, it must be impossible to completely avoid situations which stir up ambivalence about their intellectual capacity. When you sit down to take an employment test or the Armed Forces Qualifications Test, or to try to decipher the help-wanted ads, the situation confronts you with your own inadequacies. Ogbu and Stinchcombe argue plausibly that in-school problems are partly attributable to a lack of articulation with after-school life. Once you get out in the world, you may encounter situations so constructed as to make you at least wonder if your problems do not really arise from your lack of ability, an unpleasant notion to face squarely.

It is not clear that graduates of schools like Westside have to face it squarely, though. The teacher who said that the function of Westside was to keep the niggers happy but ignorant was exactly on the mark.

Graduates or dropouts know, after all, how much they played around in school, how little they worked. They were accomplices in their own miseducation and as graduates they may have to accept some of the responsibility for not trying when they had a chance. That may not be a very pleasant thought, either, but as compared to fully confronting the idea of their own stupidity, it may be fairly attractive. They can tell themselves that they were not stupid, they were just too fun-loving, too high-spirited and crazy when they were young. The reasons for failure are still internal, but now relatively acceptable.

The graduates of slum schools know that such schools offer a poor education. Why do they not blame the schools for their subsequent failure? That may not be so easy to do as one might think. After all, many teachers are nice people, if nothing else. Recall that status-degradation from teachers did not appear to be much of a problem at Westside. A study of eight San Francisco high schools by Dornbusch and associates found that Black and Chicano students were more likely to perceive their teachers as friendly and warm than either Asian or Anglo students. Low achievers perceived teachers as giving more praise than high achievers. It was very much as if teachers were trying to be nice to students in lieu of teaching them, which is not an uncommon pattern. If Westside graduates remember their teachers as nice people, on the whole, or at least not as particularly evil people, it is that much more difficult to think of these people as having participated in an exploitative process at their expense. In fact, it may be easier to see how other students hampered their growth.

Nonwhites have another shield against failure. The Westside graduate who fails an employment test can readily tell himself that he didn't really fail; he was cheated, he was failed because of his race rather than his performance. It is a vague sort of racism, though. Does it lie with the racist who constructed the test, the one who administered it, the one who graded it, or some other? We have, to paraphrase Sennett and Cobb, an image of racism without a face. Its impersonal character does not lessen its value as a buffer against a sense of personal inadequacy, but it does lessen the suitability of racism as a focal point for discontent. People do move against injustices that are abstract and vaguely defined, but they are more likely to act when there is a clear target. Teachers, of course, could serve to give racism a face, but enough of them are nonwhite and enough of the others are so nice that they really don't offer good villain material. Perhaps this partially explains why so much student misbehavior at Westside is aimed at maximizing student autonomy rather than at deliberately making life as hard as possible for the teacher, the latter pattern seemingly more common among younger students.[8]

The process of schooling may be so diffuse, its problematic side contributed to by so many, including students, that it may not be easy for graduates to understand exactly what the school has done to them and how. The same fragmentation of process that encourages professional irresponsibility discourages the most victimized from responding to their problems politically. Those who learn to internalize the idea that they are themselves responsible are no threat to social order. Those who are more bitter and other-blaming, may have no specific others to blame, making it less likely that their bitterness will crystallize into anything politically threatening.

There is not much room in this society for the people we send to inner-city schools, but it is also not socially acceptable to tell them that. Slum schools may help to "cool out the marks" by keeping bitterness unfocused. That does not resolve the contradiction between the promise of unlimited mobility and the reality of restricted opportunity, but it deflects attention away from it.

Learning from Real Kids

The behavioral and particularly the academic problems that we once thought of as exclusively characterizing schools for the poor have increasingly become characteristic of schools for everybody, at least in milder forms. It is instructive to watch what happens when schools begin to fail "real kids," that is, middle-class children.

If undemanding teaching, for example, has long been a part of the problem in ghetto schools, it is also a part of what accounts for the national decline in scholastic achievement. During the seventies, for instance, the average grade given to college students rose, even while the scores on college entrance examinations were falling. Faced with a population that does not correspond to the traditional image of what students should be, colleges capitulate rather easily, much as public schools do when faced with inner-city children. We do not know all the underlying reasons for that phenomenon, but at the individual level, some of the elements are obvious.

Consider, to take a situation I know well, a college instructor of sociological theory faced with a decision about whether to flunk a senior because of an atrocious lack of writing skills. No matter how compelling the case for a failing grade may be, it is not an attractive choice. Flunking the student is hardly likely to raise the instructor in the esteem of his colleagues. They, after all, were willing to give the student enough passing grades to get him or her this far. Then, too, the instructor would be failing the student for reasons falling outside the instructor's area of expertise. The practical importance of the area in which the instructor can claim expertise is probably not all that relevant to the student in any case. More sociology majors become clerks than become sociologists, and clerks really don't need to know that much about Durkheim, though increasingly they do need a college diploma. Flunking the student will not earn the teacher a larger paycheck in the future. Indeed, if his department is scrambling for enrollments, too much of that sort of thing might land him on the carpet. All the teacher would get from failing the student would be a distasteful session in the office with either a shattered or an angry student who is likely to feel that at the last possible moment and for no rational reason, someone has snatched away what was supposed to be a passport to a secure middle-class future.

It is easy for the individual teacher to find reasons not to act, and the system has no mechanism exerting pressure in the opposite direction. Such a system is workable while things are going along smoothly, but it need not take much to throw it off track, and when that happens there is no institutionalized procedure for self-correction. Everyone can say, yes, there is a problem, but it is not my job to respond to it. Even when the root problems would be fairly responsive to reform, it may be very difficult to direct the necessary resources to them until a crisis definition is imposed. This is very much like some of the problems in urban education, except that here the definition of crisis is likely to come sooner and be taken more seriously.

Indeed, learning how people react to the problems of real kids may be the most instructive part of this. We're going to have competency-based education. Exit exams for students, entry exams for teachers. Back to basics. All of this may be wrong-headed and simplistic, but it illustrates how social definitions inform social policy. There has been plenty of discussion about how the problems in the schools reflect problems outside the schools—the general erosion of respect for formal authority, the influence of the mass media, the increase in family instability, and so on. Predictably, this talk comes disproportionately from professional educators. What is important, though, is that the policy reaction has been to *ignore* that and concentrate on what can be done to make schools function more adequately. The assumption about real kids is that if schools do what they are supposed to do, real kids will learn. Notice, too, that the problems of real kids draw a reaction from elites who were not very active in the debate over urban education. State legislatures, for example, have been very aggressively involved, showing a hitherto unsuspected willingness to insist on accountability from educators, no matter how clumsy the vehicles they choose for doing that. Perhaps the real summary difference between real kids and others is that social power moves on behalf of real kids with a directness and a vigor that it seldom musters for children who matter less.

The explanations for the general achievement decline that we get from the educational right (Armbruster 1977; and, on the whole, Copperman 1978) see much of the problem as the fruit of the ideas and policies of the educational left which have been very visible during the period of the decline.[9] Thus, we are seeing attacks on open education, open admissions, on trying to make course work relevant to students, and on giving students some voice in shaping their education—none of which is in reality incompatible with good academic standards, although it is fair to say that these ideas have frequently been implemented in ways that do contribute to a deterioration of learning. In a way, the left set itself up for this by overselling its critique of traditional education, by framing issues in terms of simplistic polar opposites. All evil to the traditional way of doing things, all virtue to the alternatives. Even authors who have not presented their ideas so simplistically have often been read that way. There has also been a tendency among some theorists and practitioners to present ideas which might be quite good under some circumstances—I think of the open classroom this way—as curealls to be pushed regardless of actual social circumstance.

Historically, the stance of American education toward nonwhite students in particular has been that they can be failed because of their performance or passed in spite of it, but they cannot be taught. After a decade of flirting with passing them despite their performance, we may find ourselves pushed back toward failing them because of it, toward simply equating being demanding with being a teacher. The current climate of reaction lends itself well to a fetishizing of demands and structure, which is part of what is involved in the back-to-basics movement. As much as the children of the urban poor, even more than most others, need educational environments that ask more of them, simply abstracting demands from the total context of teaching is regressive. They need more demanding environments, but they also need environments that are supportive, that provide feedback and the opportunity to respond to it, environments flexible enough to allow them to discover the nature of their individual interests and passions, environments in which they can feel that they matter and in which they can relate the particularity of their lives to the process of intellectual growth.

Perhaps this is naive, but I worry a little less about the possible reaction from the left. It is true that once the left/liberal forces did contribute something to the tendency to make a fetish of "niceness" or the affective, interpersonal dimension of the teacher's role. This sprung in part, probably, from the tenacity of mystical conceptions of inequality even among progressive forces, conceptions which in their simplest forms said that the problem of the poor is that no one likes them, no one treats them well, which led to a confounding of sympathy with policy. It would be possible in the developing debate for people to become even more entrenched in that position, but I don't think it probable. (However, it would not hurt to keep an eye on NEA.) Nat Hentoff (1977:86) said once that the most humane thing a school can do for its students is see that they feel competent in the world when they leave school, a position that seems much better understood now than it did a few years ago. Jonathan Kozol, whose work is often attacked as an example of the excesses of the left, has in fact written quite clearly about the need to balance off structure and demands with the needs for individual autonomy and self-directed growth (1972). There are more recent discussions from the left of the need to balance discipline with students' rights to humane treatment (for example, Walsh and Cowles 1979).

Perhaps we will come out of the discussion of the educational problems of nonpoor children with a better sense of how to balance the various needs of children. Even if that does happen, it is fully possible that the needs of the urban poor could be shunted aside in either the discussion or the policy that flows from it. It would not be the first time that what we learned about the needs of real people failed to influence our approach to people who are not socially real. To be less pessimistic, though, maybe it is only in the context of a national discussion about the needs of all children that we can summon the will to effectively address the needs of poor children.

This chapter has tried to address the factors shaping urban education. A good deal has been left out,[10] but some things seem very clear. Certainly, it seems clear that either a strict attribute interpretation (cultural deprivation/deficits) or a strict progressive approach (teacher expectations, usually) leaves out much that matters. Poor children do not bring to school all the resources that other children bring, but that is less important than the way in which the school typically reacts to them. Schools capitulate to problems they could address if they chose to, creating and nurturing destructive patterns that they could and should be neutralizing. It seems clear also that the failure of teaching in the inner city—and that is what we have, not a failure of learning—is best understood as an administrative failure.

The issues here are important, but they are not what is most important. The underlying question here has been the traditional one—what causes failure? That question overlaps with, but is not the same as: What do we know about achieving success? That, right now, is the really critical question.

Notes

1. Entwistle's work involves having children make word associations. Syntactic responses are those that make associations on the basis of the way words are normally used in sentences: "chair-sit." Paradigmatic responses are based on the category the first word belongs to: "chair-sofa." Paradigmatic responses are considered an indication of higher language development and are more frequently made by Black children.

2. The same research finds that low-income children typically do not watch

Sesame Street as regularly as middle-class children, which might be taken to reflect a less organized home life or less parental emphasis on watching.

3. Similar to *Pygmalion* and Leacock's work, this study finds that for nonwhite students being labeled as gifted is associated with being liked *less* by the teacher. Teacher affectivity and student achievement normally show a positive association. The anomaly deserves further consideration. Gollub and Sloan (1978) suggest it may be that teachers simply do not like students who surprise them.

4. The power of peer groups may account for the relative insignificance of status-degradation at Westside. Less optimistically, perhaps degrading behavior from teachers becomes less important because students get so much of it from other sources that the teacher hardly matters. Ghetto students can be particularly rough on one another and some of it must penetrate, as much as the students try to shrug it off.

5. Heyns (1978) offers a different variant of the problem. She proceeds as though what sixth- and seventh-grade students do over the summer is not a school effect, a position which would be more acceptable if applied to younger students. Still, her highlighting of the differences in amounts of summer learning between low-status and high-status students is very important.

6. Reviews of the literature on tracking (for example, Jencks et al. 1972) traditionally find mixed results, but no overall impact on learning. The evidence grows (Rosenbaum 1976; Persell 1978) that this is another case of misleading findings from works that look uncautiously at aggregate data and are not geared to questions of process. Some of the work suggesting that grouping does influence learning is experimental in design (Gollub and Sloan 1978). There is fairly good reason to think that track assignment is sensitive to status-cues even with ability held constant (Persell 1978; Schafer, Olexa, and Polk 1975).

7. It could be argued that over the past two decades, styles of racial exploitation have become more patronizing, meaning that nonwhites have come to occupy a status more similar to that traditionally held by women.

8. There are two ways of explaining elite involvement with which I am uncomfortable. One takes the position that schools for low-status populations teach conformity, punctuality, acceptance of external authority in lieu of independent thinking, self-discipline, and creativity. That is, schools teach the traits appropriate to those headed for the lowest rungs of a capitalist economy. The first objection is that some degree of these attitudes would be useful in any hierarchical economy, capitalist or otherwise. See Persell (1978:164). The second is that whatever ghetto children are learning, it is not taking orders. See Hurn (1978:203). The last explanation is the reserve industrial army thesis. Historically very useful as a partial explanation for the exploitation of nonwhites (see William Wilson 1979) and women, it is a less useful idea in an era when large employers respond to "high" wage demands by simply moving out of an area or threatening to.

9. Taking Collins further, we might suspect—as the right never does—that many of the underlying problems in schools result from the fact that staff and students have increasingly adopted a "get-over" orientation that legitimates getting the most you can for the least you can, an idea much honored by the right in the economic sphere. Put differently, the social relations in school have become too capitalist, too much oriented to the commodity form.

10. Among the things left out, the most obvious may be school integration and some of the issues surrounding it. That, I have to think, was always among the least useful ways to approach the question, reflecting the traditional concerns of mystical analysis with interpersonal interracial relationships. A more important omission is that of cultural disjuncture (such as Clignet 1974; Valentine 1975). Important as are the issues raised on this point, it may be more important right now to make it clear that curricular irrelevance in itself does not preclude learning. Perhaps the most significant failure is the ahistorical character of the chapter, a problem not easy to correct given available materials. (See, however, Franklin 1979.)

5

Schools That Work and Research That Doesn't

By definition, the radical and conservative wings of the American intellectual community manage to agree on very little, but many members of both groups have traditionally agreed that reform of urban education is very difficult to attain. Conservatives say it is difficult because the problems are deeply embedded in various pathologies and deficiencies of the urban poor. Others maintain that the problems are deeply rooted in the requirements of an exploitative economic system. In the one case, we cannot hope for change until we make better people of the poor; in the other, they cannot be helped until we create a more humane economic system.

There is little truth to either position in isolation, except in the sense that self-fulfilling prophecies create their own truth. Getting inner-city children to read, write, and compute competently in the early grades—a minimal definition of success, but appropriate for now—is simply not the herculean task that it is often made out to be. There are real difficulties, but their resolution depends upon neither the radical reconstruction of the Western world nor a major cultural overhaul of its poor. We know that because of those inner-city schools that do in fact work, work in many cases despite having access to no more resources than schools that fail. The examples we have of success in urban education tell us a great deal about what is possible and a great deal about how, presumably with the best intentions in the world, we manage to study problems in ways that help frustrate their resolution.

Saying that I am proceeding from a minimal definition of success puts it mildly.[1] No experience should be called educational unless it helps students work and think more creatively, ask questions more effectively, synthesize information from disparate sources, and better understand the nature of their own talents and interests. In that sense, this chapter will discuss successful inner-city schooling, not necessarily successful education. However, schooling, the acquisition of a foundation of basic academic skills, is a necessary prerequisite for education. The back-to-basics movement is dangerously primitive insofar as it reduces education to basic skills, but those of its critics who insist on defending less simplistic educational models to the point of refusing to see the rational kernel in back-to-basics are pushing a stance that is elitist in form, order-serving in its consequences, and remarkably indifferent to the priorities of inner-city parents. It is another example of either-or dogmatism. The examples of success that we have are less than what is possible and desirable, but we must appreciate what they are and what their existence means.

When Frank Macchiorola became superintendent in New York City, he criticized his board of education for its failure to disseminate information about schools that did well. He could have made the same charge against most of the other institutions from which the public expects information about schools. Indeed, the inability of educators to see beyond failure is predicated upon a broader and deeper insensitivity within other institutions. Popular media have done, I suppose, a somewhat better job of disseminating information about what works in inner-city education than have the social sciences. Some writers—I think particularly of Nat Hentoff of the *Village Voice*, Fred Hechinger of the *New York Times*, and William Raspberry of the *Washington Post*—have consistently covered what I consider the important issues. Still, high school football scores and board meeting trivia are much better covered than any substantive educational issue. It would be worth much to know more about the processes defining educational news.

The character of news coverage of education is also problematic in another way: too frequently it does what teachers do, packaging important information in ways that render it much less useful. The Marva Collins phenomenon is an interesting case in point. Having quit her job as a public school teacher, the story goes, Collins proceeded to establish Westside Prep on a shoestring in the heart of one of Chicago's poorest ghettos. The school is presented as a place where slum children learn at an incredible pace. Her school has been the "beneficiary" of a media blitz which brought her to the pages of several popular magazines and ultimately to the television screen in a made-for-television docudrama (Babcock 1982; Kellett 1978; Martin 1978). Undoubtedly the most publicized case of relatively successful inner-city schooling, it raises the question, Why that case? With dozens of better-documented cases around the country, some of them much older than Collins's Westside Prep, why has this case been selected as *the* case?

We cannot really know. I am sure Babcock is right that some of attention was the result of an earnest desire to have some good news from the ghetto, but that doesn't explain why this school and not, say, Holy Angels across town or May School on the West Side, got such ferocious publicity. Perhaps it is partly that the press is particularly attracted to the dramatic and in its absence is not unwilling to create it, however inadvertently. The unembellished story certainly has elements of the dramatic—a one-room school (initially), ten-year-olds reading Chaucer, a lone individual taking on the system and refusing the system's handouts.

Whatever the reasons, showering attention on a single school fosters the false impression of singular achievement, an impression fostered even more directly by the way Marva Collins is sometimes described: "superteacher," "miracle worker." Intent aside, these terms are much less a positive comment on Collins than a negative comment on inner-city students. It makes sense to call her a miracle worker if you assume she's teaching morons, making bricks without intellectual straw. It makes sense to consider her for the head of the Office of Education if there is a long-hidden secret to teaching poor children that she has found, a notion from which she has tried to dissociate herself. The wide-eyed awe with which apparent success is greeted is a way of reinforcing traditional assumptions about the ineducability of the poor. I cannot help hearing in some accounts, "Well, can you believe it!! Black kids— and they're reading!!" Leaving aside the insult, treating good inner-city schooling as miraculous reinforces the public mind-set that helps insure that most inner-city schooling will not be good.

This is sympathetic journalism, done in the hope of contributing to reform. Individual sympathy notwithstanding, the terms in which journalists have learned to conceive of the problem, the background assumptions they bring to it, insure that their work will have an order-serving potential. This, of course, is not an unfamiliar pattern in racial relationships. The point here is that the press itself has done much to create those background assumptions through its history of insubstantial coverage of educational issues and uncritical acceptance of administrative excuses for failure.

In this particular case, the media blitz created another problem. It was so intense that it guaranteed close scrutiny, under which cracks began to appear in the portrait. It has been charged that reading scores are not really as consistently high as was thought, that little besides reading gets taught, and that despite Collins's vocal stance against federal funding, she was accepting a good bit of it. The same process that creates the icon generates an examination that few icons are going pass. When this one fell, thousands of those educational professionals with an emotional and material investment in believing in the impossibility of success must have said, with reflief, "Told ya so." Having become the symbol of successful ghetto schooling, Marva Collins's fall from public grace may be used by those so inclined as grounds for dismissing all the other cases.

The case of Westside Prep is useful because it reminds us of the importance of careful verification, and social science descriptions of effective schools usually have it over the popular media in this regard. One relatively early study frequently cited in discussions of effective schools was done by George Weber (1971) of the Council for Basic Education. Starting with ninety-five schools nominated as successful inner-city schools, Weber managed to identify four in which students typically read at or above grade level. There may have been more successful effective schools, since Weber was unable to get corroborating data on several, but his mortality rate shows again that much which gets labeled as successful will not stand scrutiny. Weber took pains to be certain that the schools really were inner-city schools—that is, nonselective and serving a low-income population—and that the reading scores were genuine. In fact, to be on the safe side, he gave his own reading tests.

Weber felt that the successful schools differed in several ways from what is ordinarily found in slum schools, including what he judged to be unusually strong leadership, careful monitoring of pupil progress—with tests given as frequently as once a month—high institutional expectations, carefully sequenced instructional materials, and some individualized instruction, not necessarily of a very formal sort. He also believed that a phonics-based approach to reading and extra reading personnel were important. I suspect that they would generally not matter as much as the other factors, but that remains debatable.

Essentially similar conclusions were reached by the State of New York Office of Education Performance Review (1974) which studied two comparable inner-city schools, one more effective than the other, using a definition of "effective" not quite as stringent as Weber's. The schools were matched for socioeconomic composition of their student bodies.[2] In fact, the more effective school had a less favorable teacher/student ratio and a slightly more impoverished student body. On paper, the reading programs were similar. But the more effective school had teachers who were less pessimistic about the abilities of their students, though that must have been at least partly a reflection of their relative success. That school also implemented its program more carefully: teachers were more closely supervised, a sequence of instruction was taken more seriously, and activities of various teachers were coordinated. The study concluded that the achievement differential appeared attributable to factors under the schools' control, most particularly to the quality of educational leadership.

One of the more distinctive small-scale success stories comes from Gerry Rosenfeld, an anthropologist who taught for several years in a

Harlem grade school. In his fourth year of teaching, his sixth-grade class made unusual gains in reading. Rosenfeld noted several factors associated with the improvement. It was his second year with the same group of students, so he knew them and their families quite well. He developed an approach to the curriculum that was social studies centered, emphasizing the connections between the material and the personal lives of the children. Of course, such a curriculum also played into Rosenfeld's strengths as an anthropologist. In contrast to the more traditional, tightly structured approach of many of the better inner-city schools, the approach he used came to take on something of the character of the open classroom, with children individually choosing many of the activities and questions they wanted to pursue. Rosenfeld also had access to some extra supportive services, but nothing that would not have been available to any Title I school. What was most distinctive was that Rosenfeld took advantage of the informal cliques and networks that children naturally create among themselves, using them as teaching units and support networks. In the course of the year, the average student made over two years' reading progress and everyone gained at least a year, results that so astounded school officials that they insisted that the entire class be retested. At least we can be certain that the scores were real. Revealingly, the school made no attempt to replicate Rosenfeld's success, another case where it turns out to be harder for a school to learn from success than to attain a measure of it.

Cases like Rosenfeld's confirm the proposition that it is possible to create islands of sanity at the classroom level even in the absence of administrative leadership. Rosenfeld's success might also be taken as an indication of how important it can be for teachers to do what they feel comfortable doing, as long as that is not taken as an excuse for the abdication of administrative responsibility. I doubt that many teachers would feel as fully comfortable with Rosenfeld's curricular innovations and his stress on informal social networks as he did; this does not suggest that replication is impossible, but that attempts at replication take into account the strengths and weaknesses of the individuals involved rather than adopting whole a program that worked for someone else, somewhere else. The predilection for reducing things to simple formulae may be nearly as strong among educators as among social scientists, and indulging it is one of the surest ways to waste what we are learning about success in inner-city schools.

Rosenfeld felt the emphasis on the in-class social organization was the crucial change. At the same time, he shows just how difficult it can be to pin down the critical factors even when looking at something as small as a single classroom. Given as much detail as he gives, it is hard to say that this or that was most important. The more sophisticated quantitative works may be more likely to make us forget the problem than to solve it. One of the great virtues of detailed ethnographies like Rosenfeld's is that they make what we don't understand perfectly clear.

Nevertheless, there are some important quantitative works on effective urban schools. Ronald Edmonds, who has been particularly important in directing attention to successful schools, has been involved in a continuing series of investigations (1979). He first identified five schools within Model Cities areas of Detroit that were instructionally effective: math and reading scores were at or above the citywide average. He and a research team were able to match one of the effective schools on socioeconomic variables with a less effective school, suggesting that in that case at least, differences in student achievement could not be written off as reflections of differences in the social standing of pupils. Matching, however, I take to be a questionable procedure under most circumstances. More interestingly, Edmonds reanalyzed the Coleman data to find fifty-five instructionally effective schools in the northeast quadrant, effective in that, taking each school as an aggregate, they essentially eliminated the relationship between successful performance and social background. Schools that were instructionally effective for poor and Black children were indistinguishable from less effective schools on measures of pupil social background.[3] Similarly, another study done in low-income neighborhoods of Detroit (Lezotte and Passalacqua 1978) finds that knowledge of school attended significantly predicts learning even with pupil social class controlled.

Methodologically, one of the more powerful studies now available is *Fifteen Thousand Hours* by Rutter and associates (1979), a three-year longitudinal study of twelve inner-city secondary schools in London.[4] Much of the significance of the work stems from the fact that it concentrates on the kinds of in-school behavior and processes that the older works supporting the denial paradigm ordinarily ignored. The central finding is that schools do have a significant impact on learning, attendance patterns, rates of out-of-school delinquency, and in-school misbehavior. The good schools produce much better results than the others even when the social class background and intellectual ability of students have been statistically controlled. Results were significantly related to how much the schools emphasized learning as measured by the amount of time spent on instruction and planning, the immediacy and directness of teacher responsiveness, teacher expectations, the amount of homework assigned, and whether lessons started on time. Schools that did better on one measure ordinarily did better on the others. The good schools did not erase the impact of student social background but students of all ability levels and from all social classes did better in the better schools. These patterns were generally stable over a four- or five-year period.

With respect to discipline, what appeared to be important was consensus as to just what the policy was, rather than any particular combination of rewards and punishments. It is also of particular interest that positive results were associated with a school having a large proportion of its student population holding some kind of position of responsibility. This is another point on which there is almost certainly some causal influence in both directions, but it brings up again the significance of reducing alienation among students. Perhaps the most important point is that the authors felt that school outcomes should be understood not so much as a function of specific practices as a function of a particular ethos, the combination of attitudes, values, and behavior that gives a school its distinctive character.

An American approximation of the work of Rutter and his associates, both in method and in conclusion, is the work cited earlier by Brookover et al. (1978). Looking at a random sample of Michigan fourth and fifth grades, they concluded that school climate was just about as good a predictor of achievement as social composition for most schools and a decidedly better one for Black schools, but the study was not longitudinal. In some ways, another American approximation of *Fifteen Thousand Hours* is a study by Summers and Wolfe (1975). An important subargument in the discussion about the relation between schools and social status has been the position that school resources do not make more than a negligible difference in what students learn. Summers and Wolfe argue persuasively that resources in fact have a very significant impact on learning, depending on how they are used and at whom they are directed (depending, that is, on whether one considers them in their actual context). The studies suggesting the opposite looked largely at average tendencies within large aggregates of data. They asked whether a school had a chemistry lab, but not which students were allowed to use it. Summers and Wolfe looked at data that tied particular pupils to experience with particular resources, finding that some resources had opposite effects on different kinds of pupils—effects that would be canceled if only group averages were examined. Their sample included about 1,800 pupils from the Philadelphia school system, a random sampling of grade school and junior high students and a sample of senior high pupils skewed slightly toward low-achieving schools.

The least surprising finding is that all types of pupils at all age levels achieve more if they attend more classes and if unexcused absences and lateness are minimized. All elementary school students do better if taught by teachers trained at one of the more highly regarded colleges, especially low-income students. At the junior high level, class size below thirty-two is especially important for low-income students. Blacks perform better in smaller elementary schools. All students benefit from smaller senior high schools. Low achievers in general are especially sensitive to school resources. High-IQ Black students in the early grades typically do not do as well as white students with the same IQ, but if

Black and non-Black students have the same achievement levels in third grade, they typically grow at the same rate in later years, again suggesting the primacy of the first few years of schooling. Summers and Wolfe do not look at actual in-school processes as closely as Rutter and associates but their measurements are more sophisticated than those used in earlier studies and their data tie particular students to particular resources.

An earlier study by St. John (1973) of thirty-six urban sixth-grade classes looked more closely at teacher practices. For Black students, child-oriented as opposed to task-oriented teachers contributed significantly more to reading growth, improved conduct, and improved attendance. With several possible confounding variables controlled, fairness in teachers contributed both to improved conduct among students and a sense of control over their environment. Interestingly, the pupils of teachers who did *not* believe that test scores were a good indication of ability made larger gains in reading than teachers who believed in tests.

Several studies—by Coleman, Brookover and associates, Summers and Wolfe, and St. John—have indicated that low-income or nonwhite students are more sensitive to school atmosphere or teacher behavior than middle-class children, which I take to mean that while low-status children come to school with adequate resources for learning, they do not bring all the resources that more privileged students bring with them and are thus more dependent upon what schools do or fail to do for students. The significance of the generally low academic ability of schoolteachers—which is perhaps best taken as a reflection of overall quality of educational training—has to be considered in light of this relatively greater dependency of slum children on teacher characteristics. How significant a factor it may be relative to others is still an open question, but the evidence does constitute an argument for seeing that urban teachers get stronger academic preparation than they do now.

Within a few years, we might be able to speak of urban school systems that work. Starting in 1978, after ten years of declining scores, the District of Columbia schools, 96 percent Black, had test scores rise two years in a row. In 1979, Detroit students raised average reading scores in every grade from the first through the seventh, and New Orleans students raised both reading and math scores in every grade. Similar signs of progress were shown in Newark and Philadelphia (Maeroff 1980; Hechinger 1980). East St. Louis, where 70 percent of all students are on welfare, reportedly has its sixth graders performing almost at grade-level (Benjamin 1981:196). Early reports on a Milwaukee project built around effective schools research, particularly that of Edmonds, are very promising (Linda Austin 1981; Thomas 1981). Milwaukee guidelines now call for students in the late elementary school grades to be assigned two to three hours of homework nightly, which would give them a workload comparable to that of many private schools. We have seen individual cities raise scores before and be unable to sustain them; test scores are crude measures of the quality of schooling and are subject to manipulation and random fluctuation.[5] Still, these may be real gains. In 1980, the National Assessment of Educational Progress reported that nationally during the 1970s Black students improved more in math, science, and reading then did white students, with the gains concentrated in younger age groups.

For me, all examples of effective schools are interesting, but nothing drives the point home like Westside. Although I have not visited there in some time, the school is cited these days as another case of regeneration in urban schooling. The days of terror in the hall are just a memory. The dropout rate has been halved. The number of students failing two or more courses has gone from 40 percent to under 20 percent. The number of students going on to college is up by 50 percent. So nearly as I have been able to find out, the changes have been made with pretty much the same staff and with students from the same kind of background as when I was there. It is not at all scientific, but I have to feel that if Westside can do it, if that zoo can move in the direction of becoming a school, there is no good excuse for any school anywhere continuing to perpetrate the kind of educational fraud that defined the Westside I knew.

The important point about all the examples of success is that they indicate that failure is not so entrenched as both radical and conservative theory has implied. There is still much we do not know, but we have too many examples of success for all of them to be written off as interesting exceptions. Many of them involve no out-of-the-ordinary resources. Some of them involve schools that were, prior to reform efforts, even worse than the average for urban schools. Some of them involve older students. If some schools involve self-selected parents, staff, or students, many others do not. We know enough to be sure that success at teaching basic skills is attainable, not in every case, but surely in the ordinary case.

Exactly how is it attainable, though? What is it that makes successful schools successful? An impressive variety of approaches seem to work, but overall what stands out is their simplicity. Few of them are doing things that would be called creative outside the context of inner-city education. It is hard to improve on Robert Coles's language: the schools that work are just those that make a determined and businesslike effort to teach.

Certainly, we find little exotic pedagogy. The apparent improvement in the Washington, D.C., system, for example, came under the superintendency of Vincent Reed (who resigned in late 1980 after a dispute with his board). Reed appears primarily to have done two things (Means

1979; Feinberg 1981). He made progress toward straightening out an administrative apparatus that was once so disorganized that the school system could not figure out how many employees it had. Second, he introduced a competency-based curriculum and it may be significant that he did it with a lot of citywide fanfare. The new curriculum is just a very detailed, step-by-step lesson guide in the basic skill areas, with set standards for what students should have learned at various points, but allowing for adjustments for the needs of individual students. The curriculum is particularly strong about insisting that students don't go to stage B until they are clearly comfortable with A. It is similar to Benjamin Bloom's mastery learning system which has also been used successfully with poor children. Still, the most creative part of both is the label used. In effect, Washington, D.C. is giving teachers a lesson plan and convincing them that they are expected to teach it.

The same message comes through from the more elaborate summaries of the research literature. According to Ronald Edmonds, drawing from his own work, from several other studies, and presumably from his experience as a New York City administrator, the most critical characteristics of effective schools are: strong, sometimes even tyrannical, leadership; high expectations; order without rigidity; the highest value placed on acquisition of basic skills; and some means by which pupil progress can be monitored frequently. It sounds much like Rutter's description of effective inner-city secondary schools, or like Weber's description of good grade schools. It also sounds like the model of teaching that emerged from my interviews with Westside students—that is, a no-frills model.

Clark, Lotto, and McCarthy (1980) confirm most of Edmonds's points and add some detail. Using 97 studies culled from a base of 12,000 and supplementing those with interviews with researchers on effective schools, they find, like Edmonds, that style of leadership is a crucially important factor in an effective school, even though the professional characteristics of leaders—that is, the criteria by which we decide who gets to be a principal—matter little. The effective leader frames goals and sets standards of performance; that is, does what principals get paid to do. The in-service training programs that make a difference tend to be those targeted to specific goals, the more specific, the better. Some successful programs have substantial levels of parent involvement and lower than average adult/child ratios, the latter suggestive of the Summers and Wolfe findings. While successful programs commonly have access to federally funded special projects, changes in facilities and financial resources by themselves make little difference.

What Clark et al. say about curriculum and instruction sounds just about like what the District of Columbia is doing. Successful schools have specific curricular goals as opposed to implicit or assumed ones, structured learning environments, and frequently some form of individualization—the latter meaning essentially that teachers are flexible enough to respond to particular needs. Clark et al. find, too, that successful schools often employ diagnostic/prescriptive teaching styles involving continuous evaluation and remediation, which recasts the point about flexibility and confirms what Edmonds says about the need for continuous monitoring of student progress. Beyond that, Clark et al. find no particular curricular approach or instructional strategy consistently related to success. They conclude, safely enough, that the distinguishing characteristics of maverick schools are neither so different nor so surprising as to be unattainable by large numbers of urban schools.

A summary by Gilbert Austin (1979) comes to similar conclusions. Austin looks at studies done by four states—New York, Delaware, Pennsylvania, and Maryland—of schools that overachieve, given their socioeconomic composition. Not all of them were inner-city schools. Among the factors characteristic of the group as a whole were strong principal leadership, including principal participation in the instructional process and high expectations held by principals for staff and student performance; teachers rated as more responsive, warmer, and holding higher expectations than is typical; more satisfactory parent-teacher relationships; more time devoted to instruction; a stronger sense of self and a feeling of controlling their environment among children. Austin holds that the major determinants of school effectiveness seem most pronounced in the early grades.

Summaries like these should be wary of speaking of "determinants." Just listing the correlates of success can confound the consequences of success with its preconditions, does not necessarily separate the essential from the merely coincidental and, most pertinently, says nothing about the historical process by which success is achieved. Some of the most important factors are not easily susceptible to precise measurement. Nevertheless, what we know is more important than what we do not know. We know that studies employing a variety of methodological approaches and looking at a large number of schools in widely differing circumstances point strongly to the conclusion that what inner-city schools need most is serious and sustained teaching—that among the elements of serious teaching are constant feedback and monitoring of progress, high expectations, responsiveness to individual needs of students, clear goals, and clear articulation between goals and curriculum. The question is not so much what will work; commenting on compensatory education, Edward Zigler (quoted in Tavris 1976) said that contrary to the then widely held opinion that nothing worked, it was his reading of the research that everything worked, if done with a sense of commitment. As with the various attempts at hall reform at Westside, what matters is not so much what is done but the attitude with which the institution does it.

In fact, reading through the literature on effective urban schools creates in me the sensation of being back at Westside watching program after program succeed in clearing the halls. One wants to say, is this all it takes? This unspeakably corrosive process can be dramatically improved so easily? Here as there, one almost wants the real answer to be more complex. From one perspective, this is all very important research, but from another it is just absurd. Strip these summaries down and they all say that teachers should know what they want to teach and should let students in on the secret; that teachers should keep an eye on how students are doing and should not simply keep repeating the approaches that have failed in the past; that teachers should have faith in the ability of students to learn; that principals should make sure that teachers do all of the above. These are simple ideas, honored as "research findings." Seldom have we so richly deserved our reputation for making the obvious obscure. That these "findings" are regarded as new and important—and make no mistake, they are important—is a testament to the absurdity of the overall discussion of urban education.

Two aspects of this research do deserve some additional comment— the role of principals and the role of parents. The indispensability of leadership from the principal's office is indicated by everything we have looked at (see also Shoemaker and Fraser 1981). Someone has said that there are plenty of bad schools with good principals, but almost no good schools with bad principals. The kinds of behaviors these studies point to—visible involvement in the instructional process, setting clear goals and standards—are no more than what principals ought to be doing in any case, but these summaries may be a little misleading here. The leadership of many successful principals is aptly summarized by those activities, but it also must take a particular quality of doggedness to introduce administration into a school that has grown accustomed to not having it. Additionally, some of the more detailed descriptive works (for example, Hentoff 1977) suggest that success for many principals is associated with unusual personal strengths. Some seem unusually skillful at negotiating or challenging the bureaucracy, at inspiring confidence or at moving people through sheer force of personality.

Just as no one instructional method is a precondition for success, various leadership styles seem workable. Charles Silberman's widely read Crisis in the Classroom illustrates how different successful principals can be (1970:99–111). (On this, see Hentoff 1967, 1977.) Part of that discussion concerns two schools, both located in Harlem and both with student populations scoring far above the levels of nearby schools. Moreover, test scores did not drop as students moved into the higher grades, although such declines are a common problem with ghetto students who achieve a measure of success.

The principals involved were as different as they could be, except that both insisted that teachers teach. Silberman describes one principal as observing classrooms constantly, giving teachers a great deal of supportive feedback and reviewing and correcting each teacher's plan for teaching reading every week. The other principal comes off as much less involved in the day-to-day specifics of the reading program. Indeed, he did not know what texts were being used, much less how they were being used. He administered reading tests every few weeks, though, projecting each time what level of competency each student should demonstrate at the next testing. If a student failed to perform as expected, the teacher was expected to explain what happened and what was going to be done about it. This principal kept a chart on his wall showing the progress of each student, another way to announce institutional priorities unambiguously.

Neither school served children from the poorest sections of Harlem, which has sometimes been taken as grounds for discounting their success. The more instructive truth, though, is that the same schools, serving the same kind of student body, were typical failing ghetto schools before they got principals who turned them around, principals who managed to do that despite the same bureaucratic and financial constraints that other New York City principals labor under and presumably despite having to work with teachers pretty much like the teachers in other Harlem schools. We have here two vastly different styles of leadership being employed and both seem to work.

If there is a common thread, perhaps it is that both styles offer some clarity of purpose and involve at least the hint of threat. Another case where the threat of sanctions for poor teaching and administration was a part of what led to reform is Brooklyn's Wingate High (Hechinger 1978; Savage 1979). Once rated a bad school even by the standards of Brooklyn, since Robert Schain became principal in 1971, Wingate has raised test scores substantially and has dramatically increased the proportion of its students going on to college. There is no one factor that accounts for the change of course. The curriculum was revamped to make it both more rigorous and more interesting (qualities that are too often discussed as though they were mutually exclusive); teachers were given an expanded role in decision making (a point to be developed further when we discuss James Comer's discussion of the need to share power), an intensive reading program was started; teachers in all subject areas emphasized basic skills. More to the point here, Schain has been described as ruthless about getting rid of teachers and supervisors who failed to perform. He says himself that at the beginning of his tenure he probably issued more unsatisfactory ratings than any principal in the city.

Like much of the discussion elsewhere in this book, these examples underscore the importance of a principal's being willing to make demands on teachers. Doing so is not incompatible with being supportive of teachers nor with sharing authority with them. Invoking a reasonable level of demands on teachers does not have to mean firing them or, more commonly, harassing them into "voluntarily" transferring to other schools. That path to reform is too appealing to some. Doubtless there are teachers who cannot be reformed, but recall that one of the points of the discussion of Westside in chapter 2 was the remarkable malleability of teacher behavior. Those who envision wholesale firings of teachers make the very same mistake that teachers have been making in their conceptualization of students, or that researchers have been making in their assumptions about inner-city schools—the mistake of confusing what *is* with what is possible.

Demands are a relatively visible aspect of leadership behavior. Because of that, there is the danger that as research on principals develops, demanding principal behavior will be seen apart from its context and misconstrued. Recall that the first principal at Westside was willing to be demanding in his way. Unfortunately, his inconsistency and his inability to create an overall sense of educational direction meant that his demands were seldom seen as legitimate and thus they seldom did much good. Demands have to be seen as a part of an integrated leadership style.

Some of these summaries point to the significance of parental involvement, while others do not. James Comer stresses it. Edmonds notes that the quality of parent-school contact may matter more than its quantity, and sees more effective mobilization of parents as the best hope for the future. Robert Benjamin "did not uncover a single instance where parents had been a critical factor in shaping a successful school" (1981:198). If it were merely a question of theory, we probably would not want to think of extensive parental involvement as a precondition of reform. For practical purposes, though, whether parental involvement is necessary does not matter. What matters is that parents are a resource, potentially an unusually effective resource, and we need to marshal all the resources we can. The most promising of recent developments may be the growth of a new wave of parents' groups concerned with exercising clout in the schools (Fernandez 1980; Marburger 1980). The days of siphoning off the energy of parents with PTA bake sales may be behind us. Some of these new groups have been very instrumental in disseminating information about effective schools and about effective educational practices. Some—and in this respect and others the Parents Union of Philadelphia (Hentoff 1980) is something of a model—have begun to exercise something akin to an oversight function with respect to administrators, at least to the point of letting administrators know that they can no longer govern in the dark.

Knowing what we know of what effective urban schools are like says very little about the process by which we can create more of them. There is a great need for more studies of the histories of good schools. Until we get them, I know of no road maps to follow, but James Comer has a good deal to say about the problems and possibilities to look for along the way. Much of what he has to say takes us back to a consideration of the distribution of power in schools and of what that distribution means for human relationships. Comer has long maintained (1975) that we need to pay more attention to the quality and tone of the human relationships affecting urban schools, and more recently he has demonstrated how crucial those relationships become in the process of making change. His *School Power* (1980) is essentially the story of a dramatic turnaround at King Elementary School in New Haven. In 1969, King's fourth graders ranked twentieth of the city's thirty-one elementary schools in reading and ranked thirty-first in math. In 1978–79, they ranked tenth in reading and math, behind only the city's most prosperous schools. Student attendance was second or third best in the city, and teacher attendance was the best. By the fourth year, parent attendance at important school functions had gone from 15 to 30 per event to between 250 and 300, this in a school with 360 students.

Comer's description of the process of transformation is the most precise one I know. Invaluable as they have been, some descriptions of effective urban schools run on so about the dedicated teachers and eager students as to seem almost saccharine. Not so with Comer. His work gives a history that includes petty jealousies and backbiting, power plays, obstructionist cliques and personality disputes, misfires and misunderstandings. Ah, the stuff of real life!

The program was built around the premise that the application of basic social science principles to every aspect of a school program would improve the climate of relationships within a school as well as the academic and social growth of its children. A mental health team, comprised of Yale professionals in psychiatry, social work, early childhood education, teacher training, and program evaluation was the entity primarily responsible for helping school staff apply social science principles to daily problems of schools. They brought no particular theoretical framework with them, but developed an approach reflecting various theories and disciplines. Among the important ideas growing out of their approach was the philosophy that all persons involved with a program, including parents, should be involved in its planning and decision making but, importantly, that no one should be allowed to paralyze the person held responsible for the program's outcome. Participation in decision making legitimated decisions and increased commitment to making them work. Broadening the base of involvement allowed some leadership to emerge, as it ordinarily will, from unlooked-for quarters. Having representatives of all segments involved helped to get accurate information out before misinformation could undermine a program. Workshops and in-service sessions were aimed at specific goals. Workshops were used to break down some of the social distance and distrust between parents, teachers, and members of the intervention team. Some workshops were aimed at specific instructional goals, others were aimed at teaching parents to evaluate teachers, others at how discussions of how principles of child development were reflected in the home and the school. Members of the mental health team were available to teachers for ongoing advice and consultation on specific problems. I am leaving out much, of course, but over a period of time teachers learned to take the needs and fears of children more fully into account, to respond in nonthreatening ways to small problems before they became big ones, to see the role they played in creating negative patterns in children. They found themselves responding to children much more analytically, supportively, and creatively. Developing a positive climate of human relationships in the school, incidentally, did not automatically lead to improved learning. That problem had to be dealt with separately. The instructional program they developed was fairly flexible, much more sensitive to the interests of individual teachers and students than some of the highly structured programs we will look at momentarily.

It sounds nice, but getting there was a very painful process. During the early years of the program, the climate of relationships made everything vastly more difficult than it had to be. The first year in particular was just one fiasco after another. Two schools started the program, but internal problems in one were so severe that the school dropped out after five years. It took several years to make any real academic progress at King School, which is comparable to what Weber (1971) says about how long it took the schools he visited to establish successful programs. King School teachers were intimidated by the Yale professionals and their jargon and feared being used by them. Parents were intimidated by the teachers and were leery of Yale's motives and impatient with the pace of change. At one time they threatened to picket one of the schools; at another point they actually did pull off a boycott. With his building in chaos, one principal was fearful of "repressing" kids and saw repression in every suggestion for reform. A well-meant suggestion that one teacher observe another could be read as personal criticism and reacted to so defensively as to negate whatever value the original suggestion may have had. In principle, everyone liked having a voice in decision making. In practice, not everyone wanted to put in the time required. "Racial issues, generation differences, teaching and discipline approach differences, the status of one's college, and finally just petty personal issues were always beneath the surface and occasionally flared into interpersonal and interclique conflicts" (Comer 1980-98).

In that kind of destructive and suspicious climate the best idea or the best program in the world may do little more than create another problem, unless it is introduced in a manner that takes that climate into account. For that reason, one of the chief virtues of *School Power* is the clarity of its insistence on a holistic viewpoint, one that is sensitive to the interrelatedness of problems and particularly to the climate and tone of the human networks within which they exist. Comer is thus emphatically not trying to sell any particular pedagogical program. His process model, as he calls it, amounts to a mode of introducing change that attempts to negate a destructive social climate through broad-based participation in planning and decision making, the sharing of power and expertise, and the need to remain flexible enough to respond to the peculiarities of any one school's situation. He stresses a style of work that is open, task oriented, and nonaccusatory, a style of work that won't aggravate problems it is trying to resolve. Since the various problems in urban schools are interrelated, they are often not effectively addressed singly or if the problem of coming up with the right instructional program is divorced from the problem of developing an effective work style. Therefore, Comer warns repeatedly against borrowing elements from the program of a successful school and expecting them to work as well someplace else. The magic may rest not in the individual elements of a program but in the way the elements fit together as a whole, or in the way the staff members feel about the program and one another. Certainly one of the reasons that successful reform efforts often cannot be replicated is that replication too frequently involves testing isolated fragments of a program in the belief that we are testing the whole.

The fragmented nature of the processes sustaining failure makes a fragmented vision of how change should be introduced particularly likely and particularly counterproductive. The idea that there is some single factor, which we can isolate and manipulate, that will make everything better is one of the most common expressions of a nonholistic viewpoint. The search for the One True Way has been nearly as pervasive an obstacle to reform as the general air of pessimism and despair. If we raise self-concepts *or* use open classrooms *or* make coursework more relevant *or* make teachers more demanding *or* raise expectations *or* use programmed instructions *or* give teachers merit pay *or* raise the cultural level of the home, the schools will straighten themselves out. Regrettably, social science research has contributed both to the general air of pessimism and to the idea that there is a single magic variable out there somewhere.

The methodology of social science research reinforces this kind of thinking, but perhaps it is simply in the nature of things for intellectuals to take discrete ideas too seriously, to overestimate the practical differences among ideas. The first principal at Westside High often thought like an intellectual in this respect. That is, he gave ideas a value irrespective of their context, irrespective of the real-world situation in which they have to be played out. Once he settled upon the idea of untracking English classes he was going to go ahead with it no matter how threatened teachers felt. He was going to go ahead without trying to create a simultaneous sense of direction, at least, on low reading levels, the mess in the halls, and poor attendance patterns—all problems that interact with the problem of tracking to a certain extent. He was so focused on the idea—probably a good one in the abstract—that he failed to consider the context in which he was working; that is, the climate of social relationships and the interrelatedness of problems. Another expression of the same style of thought is the tendency to define problems in technical terms, stripped of their human dimensions. If we employ personnel thus-and-so, we can clear the halls. In fact, the morale of Westside personnel was so poor, their manner of relating to supervisors so counterproductive, as to sooner or later undercut the impact of virtually any mode of employment.

Put another way, we may be tempted to put too much emphasis on the nature of certain programs and too little on the interaction among those implementing the programs. Work style very often may be much more important than the particular ideas or programs we get so excited about. Think of a political group that puts great energy into settling obscure questions of ideology when in fact its members relate to one another in such destructive ways that it would not matter at all if the group came up with *the* indisputably correct program because their internal social climate renders them incapable of executing it. In the case of urban schools, what programs are implemented may matter less than whether problems are worked on in a way that takes into account the alienation, despair, and irresponsibility that characterize urban schools, and the various stakes, real and imagined, that people have developed in the status quo.

One of the most instructive aspects of Comer's discussion, then, is its insistence on a holistic rather than a fragmented view of the problems. Equally important is his forthright discussion of the question of power—the dimension of reality Oliver Cox (1948) accused students of inequality of shying away from. We might think of it as an argument for the penetration of the principles of participatory democracy into schools, short, of course, of those extreme forms of democracy that guarantee that nothing can get done. Insistence on such sharing of power is being heard more frequently nowadays, under the labels "school site management" or "school-based management." These are calls for parents and teachers to have an effective voice in decisions from which they are traditionally excluded—hiring and firing, curriculum, funding allocations, and so forth. They are not calls for parents and teachers to assume power in trivial areas or to take merely advisory roles. Salt Lake City (Morgan 1980) and the states of South Carolina, Florida, and California are among the places where these ideas have been taken farthest. In effect, we have a revival of the ideas of community control and decentralization of schools. Whatever the name, the important thing is taking authority away from remote central administrations and redistributing it among teachers, administrators, parents, and in some cases, students.

In noneducational activities, we know a great deal about what happens when workers gain more authority over their work. Blumberg says: "There is scarcely a study in the entire literature which fails to demonstrate that satisfaction in work is enhanced . . . or productivity increases accrue from a genuine increase in workers' decision-making power. Findings of such consistency, I submit, are rare in social research" (quoted in Bowles and Gintis 1976:79–80). Conversely, we also know that the alienation of teachers and parents encouraged by the present structure can be inimical to even a minimal sense of responsibility and virtually precludes the full employment of any individual's full creative and productive capacity. It generates apathy where we most need a sense of personal involvement. According to the Schools Commission of New South Wales, Australia, "when it is considered that schools for so long have been 'fortresses,' actively discouraging parental involvement or trivializing it when it is allowed, the cause of the problem becomes apparent. Apathy is closely related to a lack of power" (quoted in Marburger 1980:11). That is true of the apathy of teachers and students as well. It is true in some degree not only of apathy but also of that larger climate of futility, mean-spiritedness, and mutual suspicion that saps the best energies of many institutions. People who participate in decision making have one less reason to be on the defensive. People who interact as equals over a period of time are less likely to be continually suspicious of one another. Substantive involvement in the shaping of an educational process by those who are going to be charged with implementing it gives them a vested interest in seeing that it works. Indeed, one of the chief advantages of a more participatory model may be that it can help neutralize the interests that various groups have in maintaining the status quo. It makes reform, for example, a much more attractive idea to teachers' unions that have contributed so much to the problems up until now. The picture at the administrative level is not so clear. On the one hand, some of the reforms we have discussed have been initiated from the top. On the other hand, administrators in general have the most to lose from new power relationships. At that level, the vested interests involved are of a different magnitude, and it is not clear how responsive people at that level will be. Past attempts by successful

principals to work with other supervisory personnel have met with un-
receptive and skeptical, if not cynical, responses (Hentoff 1977; Hechinger 1978).

Broadening the base of decision making so that parents and teachers
have more authority is obviously not a necessary part of reform, and it
will certainly generate new problems of its own, but in many respects
sharing power is the most appealing possibility. If the alienated cannot
easily accept responsibility for their behavior and the powerful seldom
have to, sharing power more equitably is one way to create a climate
with remoralizing potential, one in which people have a chance to dis-
charge their responsibilities rather than denying them, and a chance to
hold accountable those who refuse to do so.

In particular, expanding parental power is attractive for another reason, because of the likely abuse and misuse of the growing body of
research on effective schools. We have to work from the assumption
that all developments, even the most benign, will be turned against the
poor if at all possible. If that sounds cynical, consider what happened
to the discussion of accountability. Ten or twelve years ago, no idea
seemed saner. The popular way to act on it, though, has since taken
the form of competency exams for students, another celebration of the
idea that children perform in school according to the attributes they
bring with them. The new attention to effectiveness in urban schools
may similarly be distorted into a tool for reinforcing what already exists.
Deborah Meier (1982) points out that the new initiatives are easily distorted into grounds for the perpetuation of unequal education in new
forms. Many effective programs are based on tightly structured, closely
monitored teaching of specific skills. It is a short step from there to the
position that inner-city education, of necessity and in its totality, should
be highly structured. Such a position will be attractive to some because
it fits well with the traditional priorities of conservatives—structure,
discipline, control, a one-way transmission of knowledge. It also accords
well with traditional assumptions about the limited intellectual capacity
of inner-city children. Those most committed to an attribute interpretation are more likely to retreat a step than to yield their position altogether. Thus we may get a more efficient bureaucratization of teaching,
which would be a slight improvement over what we have now. Education for the poor would continue to be impersonal and inflexible,
sacrificing any attempt at developing more complex cognitive skills.
Already some schools seem to be confounding the teaching of word
attack skills with the teaching of reading, producing students who read
words without comprehending sentences.

Whether inner-city children, as they come to school, have any particular need for structure is an arguable point; I doubt that they do. On
the other hand, teachers accustomed to failing need something that will

structure their behavior in such a way as to counter their low expectations of students and bad habits. Because they leave so little to teacher interpretation or skill, highly structured programs should be much more replicable than more loosely organized programs. Still, it is quite clear that several successful programs have not involved the close-order drill of the structured programs. Where we have teachers with Rosenfeld's commitment to his subject matter and his students, or teachers with the analytical bent developed at King School, it is not necessary that teachers follow a script. The highly structured approach may be a very useful element in some situations, but it is dangerous to treat it as the One True Way.

The opposite danger is just as real, the danger that highly structured programs, being ideologically unacceptable to some liberal educators, will not be used even when it would be especially sensible to do so (with a staff of inexperienced teachers, perhaps, or in the case of an administration unskilled in interpersonal relationships, or in the absence of adequate support from effective curriculum specialists).

Consider the range of reactions to Benjamin Bloom's mastery learning, for example. Bloom agues that with adequate teaching 80 to 90 percent of all students should be able to master the curriculum at a level of competence now reached by only the top students. (Actual experience seems to show that something on the order of 75 to 95 percent of all students could learn what the best 25 percent learn now [Trogdon 1980:390].) Adequate teaching starts with identifying concrete teaching objectives and organizing small units of material into a logical sequence. Student progress is assessed after each unit and students are given a chance to relearn whatever material they failed to learn the first time, with the material presented in a different fashion the second time around. (Edmonds [1981] makes this point more generally, pointing out that successful schools refused to simply keep on doing things that had failed in the past.) The assumption is that student aptitude defines the pace at which students learn, and the teaching approach through which they learn best, but not whether students learn. Mastery learning has quite a record of successful applications (Benjamin 1981; Levine 1982; Vogel 1980), but it is still fiercely resisted by some educators who charge that it violates principles of humane learning, interferes with creative teaching, and stresses only the acquisition of narrow skills.

Anyone who sees mastery learning as unduly regimented is likely to see Distar, a commercially developed program for teaching basic skills, as satanic. The scripted lessons break skills down into smaller units than does mastery learning, assume no knowledge on the part of the student and no talent beyond minimal literacy on the teacher's part. Distar minutely prescribes teacher behavior down to the point of telling teachers when, with what words and in what tone of voice, students should be praised. Teachers are closely supervised to minimize the possibility of ad-libbing. Students are expected to answer teachers in unison. Not surprisingly, Distar is almost universally described as being a draining experience for teachers.

Distar is glorified rote learning, it is derived from a very questionable body of theory, it pays too much homage to the false idea that students can learn material only in some ordained sequence, but it also has a very respectable history of successful application, especially in the early grades. Its record is all the more impressive because it has ordinarily been instituted over substantial opposition. The best argument for the value of Distar comes from the evaluation of the federally sponsored Follow-Through program, the extension of Head Start. The evaluation pitted nine different instructional philosophies against one another, including models emphasizing the development of self-esteem, models stressing bilingual education, and some stressing self-directed learning. Over a nine-year period, Distar was a hands-down winner on both academic and non-academic (development of self-confidence and sense of responsibility) measures. The second best model was also a highly structured program.

Distar's relatively strong showing did not lead to a large number of adoptions. Benjamin argues (1981:94) that the results of the evaluation were played down by Office of Education bureaucrats who had an ideological investment in defending the more "progressive" models, which they did by hiding behind methodological nitpicking. He might have added vested material interests, since whose friends get funding would be directly affected by how the evaluation was regarded. As of 1980, he reports, all Follow-Through models were funded equally, irrespective of measured performance.

A program must both work and be ideologically acceptable to those with the power to implement it. I have no doubt that the fear of the educational liberals, the fear of needlessly regimented, unimaginative schooling, is based on real possibilities. Still, the least appropriate reaction is to totally eschew highly structured models under all circumstances. (On the other hand, proponents of the highly structured models have not helped their case any by claiming their various methods—they are far from agreeing on one—to be the alpha and omega of education.)

Still, more is operating here than justifiable fear. Radical educators may become so involved with their ideological agendas that they cannot hear the demands of slum dwellers, demands that I understand to amount to: "Get my child reading and writing by any means possible, and then let's talk about creativity and self-actualization and anything else you like." The priorities and interests of even the most sincere radicals cannot of course overlap entirely with the priorities of the poor.[6] In some cases, that opens the door to a form of ideological pimping in which radicals exploit the symbolic value of the poor as a stick with which to thrash the bourgeoisie or as the means to prove to themselves that they are in fact radical. To restate a point from chapter 1, the law of contradiction operates on formally change-oriented ideologies. Sympathy for the most victimized and outrage at their condition push one toward one formally progressive ideological system or another. Commitment to the people involved becomes confounded with commitment to the ideology. Ideology begins as a means to liberation and then becomes an end itself, becomes ossified into a dogmatic little code reflexively defended under all circumstances—both when it is in the interests of the poor and when it runs counter to their interests. If the most backward elements of the educational right are perfectly willing to shape an educational system worthy of *Brave New World*, the most dogmatic elements of the educational left are perfectly willing to countenance the continued cretinization of the urban poor in the name of their greater liberation in the not too distant by-and-by.

None of this has anything to do with evil intentions, but that of course is never the problem. The problem is that there is no reason to think that the welfare of the urban poor is going to have as high a priority for anyone else, including their allies, as it does for the urban poor. Other groups have contributed much to attempts at reform and will continue to do so, but that is not enough to rely on. Their search for solutions will occasionally be taken off track by priorities which they do not share with those most affected by the problem. Parents must be involved if only to protect themselves from their friends when that becomes necessary. Involvement here means power: the ability to reward people and to hurt people. Power is fairly dependable. The clear-sightedness of researchers, the dedication of teachers, the leadership of administrators, the desire of reformers for a restructuring of access to privilege—these things must be cherished when we can get them, but they are hardly dependable. What is currently happening in New York City, if I understand it, is that very sensible reform initiatives are being pushed by a core of people at the top. There are at least two problems with that. There is the familiar problem of people at lower levels of the system either sabotaging or slowing down reforms which they had no role in shaping. More to the point here, what will happen when the political winds shift again and the current crew gets dumped out? If people at the bottom of the system—teachers and especially parents—play no role in creating reform, they are dependent upon the staying power of Good People at the top and that won't do at all.

It would be a dreadful error to think that because others cannot be depended on, parents can or should go it alone. The danger is again that of romanticizing parents. Educators and researchers do have valuable experience and knowledge that is inaccessible to most parents, even if educators have less such knowledge than they think they have. Parents can add balance and direction to the discussion; they can encourage those who have other kinds of expertise to use it in ways more useful than the ways experts would choose, if left to their own devices; but expecting parents to simply take over urban school systems is a bit much.

I have argued that one of the most attractive routes to the reform of urban education involves broadening the base of decision-making power. In a sense, this turns the world on its head. It is like arguing that treating students with warmth and kindness is important because if we do they will learn more. People are entitled to decent treatment and it is degrading to have to justify decency on the basis of its implications for test scores. That again is buying into the official line. People are similarly entitled to an effective voice in the decisions that affect their lives. That is an end in itself as important as academic reform narrowly conceived.

Actually, it is more important. Bowles and Gintis maintain that education has the best chance of contributing to a more humane society if educational reform is coupled with broader political concerns; schools are not independent of their social context. Experiences in one sphere of life, they note, tend to be generalized to others (Bowles and Gintis 1976:70). To the extent that is true, more broadly based participation in school governance may be significant not only because of what it may do for schools but also for what the experience of exercising power will do to encourage people to question their exclusion from decision making in other areas of their lives. While she doesn't present the case as closed, Rothschild-Whitt (1979:522) reads the available evidence as suggesting that being a part of a participatory decision-making structure develops feelings of self-confidence and political efficacy, or what James Farmer might call an expanded sense of the boundaries of the self. It develops, that is, the feelings that an educational experience should develop. What is important is what that participation will do for those parents and teachers who experience it and what they in turn will be able to do for their children and students as a result.

Some of what we learn from examining urban schools that work is ironic. That no particular instructional strategy is a precondition for success, I find more than mildly ironic, having devoted no small amount of time to the search for the One True Way. Continuing to try to develop the most optimal methods for various combinations of circumstances is still important, but not so important as realizing what determined, unadorned teaching can do. That we should come to that realization so late is tragic. With the benefit of hindsight, we see that even if there were no evidence whatsoever for the proposition that what urban children most need is access to teaching, it would have made sense to try that idea first, to eliminate the possibility that the problem with urban schooling is inferior teaching, or lack of teaching, before doing anything else. Had it not been the children of the poor who were being victimized, we would have done so automatically. That we come to this approach after almost two decades of trying virtually everything else must say something about the feeble efficacy of scholarship as a tool of reform and about the power of race and poverty to obscure the real sources of problems. It suggests that the assumptions that those who are poor and dark are in some extraordinary and negative way different, that they are somehow incapable of responding to the kinds of solutions to problems that the rest of us take for granted, are so profoundly engrained that the most earnest desire for change is no protection against them.

I find it especially ironic that I should end up arguing for a style of reform that includes giving greater power to urban schoolteachers. I began this work with a great deal of hostility toward teachers and that hostility was built into how I defined the problem. There were days I left Westside early because I simply could not stomach talking to any more teachers. I still have some of those feelings. It seems clear to me now, however, that such hostility toward teachers on the part of those who write about schools, while often richly deserved, is itself a part of the problem. It contributes to the siege mentality among teachers which automatically closes them off from perspectives they would profit from. More important, I now make a firmer distinction between what teachers are and what they can be. That is, I no longer expect that what teachers do under a set of intensely alienating and demoralizing conditions is all that teachers can do or be. As with students, a change in those conditions can produce remarkably different patterns of behavior. My earlier failure to see that was—irony of ironies—rooted in the same style of thought that characterized Coleman and other attribute thinkers. Like them, I tried to interpret behavior apart from its situational context, which inevitably means confounding people with their response to a situation.

If it is true in the ordinary case that when schools believe in inner-city children and teach accordingly, the children will in fact master basic skills, it is also true that not every case is the ordinary case. With individual students from severely troubled homes, perhaps, or with older students who have developed particularly self-destructive habits, or with individual schools serving areas of highly concentrated poverty, change may require more resources or more sophisticated approaches. As important as leadership is, it brings no guarantees. There will be principals doing all the right things and yet not producing better results. We may very well find that the political system imposes constraints on the extent to which successful schools can be replicated. We are a very long way from understanding the processes by which effective urban schools are created. Still, given where we have been, that is less crucial than simply acknowledging the fact that such schools exist. Robert Merton once commented that one success tells us more than a thousand failures: one success tells us what is possible. Knowing what is possible puts us in a position to stop asking, "Why failure?" and to start asking how we replicate success. That is not an easy question, but it is a much better question than the ones we have had.

Looking Where the Light is Bright

Looking back at the history of the discussion of urban schooling from the plateau we have recently reached, we realize how long it has taken us to reach it. We have really outdone ourselves this time. We have spent two decades, with research costs in the hundreds of millions of dollars, to produce a research literature whose major practical import is as follows: if you want poor children to learn, you have to make sure that someone teaches them. That oversimplifies the situation somewhat. Not all of the work has been intended to be policy-oriented and some of it has made enduring contributions apart from what it has taught us about the reform of urban schools. Still, considering the magnitude of the effort, it seems to have taken us a long while to get where we are now. If it weren't tragic, it would be funny.

In part, it has taken so long because it has taken us so long to consider the implications of effective schools. That is not the only avenue we might have taken that would have been more efficient than the avenue we have taken, but it was one of them. There was virtually no literature on effective urban schools until perhaps 1979 or 1980. There have always been "schools where children learn," to use the title of Joseph Featherstone's book (1971), and there have always been people writing about them, but it is only recently that the available material has become a literature in the sense of being a body of research and publications that are conscious of one another, interact with one another, and are widely read and discussed. In that sense, we have reached the first new plateau since teacher-expectation theory became recognized as the standard counterargument to cultural deprivation theory.

The Coleman report is the colossus that towers over this debate. Andrea Wilson (1980) looks back at Coleman in light of what we know now about the significance of school resources and effective urban schools. We can see now, she says, that Coleman did not emphasize or sufficiently address himself to what goes on inside the school. The new work does not so much contradict Coleman as throw new light on aspects of the problem that he and others did not consider. Wilson is far too gentle; she does not say enough by half. It has to be said that Coleman and the school of thought he helped to inspire advanced the mischievous idea that school failure among the disadvantaged could be understood without considering the process of teaching. The things he did not "sufficiently address" were logically necessary to the interpretation he advanced; that is, that influences of home background were the most important determinants of learning for policymakers to consider. We ought not play down the fact that the Coleman report set a framework for discussion and policy that has survived for fifteen years despite who knows how much criticism; we should not forget that in those years a great many flesh-and-blood children have been miseducated who might have been helped if the nation's experts had not spent so much time barking up the wrong tree and at one another. On many questions, we can console ourselves with the thought that nobody out there is listening to us anyway, unless listening happens to be convenient. However, on the question of improving education for the urban poor, I think the social sciences did have an audience at one time, had a chance to be of service, had more than adequate resources, and simply failed. This has been an intellectual clown show with poor people paying the bill. Glossing over that in the tradition of academic civility insults those we have already done so much to injure and helps to condemn us and them to more of the same in the future. Let us review once again the methodology of denial.

The organizing question was the wrong question. We have traditionally asked: "Why failure?" That is not, in all probability, the way inner-city parents would have framed the issue. Surely we framed it as we did because failure is typical and we tend to confuse the typical with the significant. This contributes to the low status of case studies, an approach that lends itself well to the study of effective schools. Case studies do get done, but they get little attention. The framing of the organizing question also reflects the traditional concern with identifying original causal factors and assuming that by doing so one is making a contribution to changing something. The problem, of course, is that the original causal forces, even where they can be identified, may no longer be the factors sustaining the pattern nor the most efficient way to change it. Remember that Edmonds says that the Coleman data identified fifty-five effective schools in the Northeast. Had Coleman been less concerned with "ultimate" causal factors and more concerned with change, he might have separated those schools out for intensive study and in 1966 that might have put us on a more fruitful path toward educational reform.

Benjamin Bloom (1980) maintains that one of the most promising recent developments is the increased attention being paid to what he calls alterable variables, the factors in a situation that we can reasonably hope to change. This means paying less attention to the significance of family background, whatever it might be, and more attention to things more amenable to public policy control, like time actually spent on instruction. His other examples include interest in cognitive entry characteristics as opposed to intelligence (the former referring to the particular skills and information needed to master a particular body of material as against "generic" aptitude); in formative rather than summative testing (that is, tests used primarily as feedback to guide teaching rather than as a means to evaluate students); in the teaching behavior of teachers as opposed to their static professional characteristics; in parental behavior as opposed to parental social status. Choosing these emphases represents a conceptualization of teaching and learning as a process. They mean that the question becomes not "What factors created failure?" but "Of those factors we can control, which have the best chance of changing it?" Better still, in Elizabeth Freidheim's language, they represent a shift from asking what is and why to asking what is possible.

The common reaction to experimental effects in educational evaluation research also illustrates the exaggerated concern with original causation. It often happens that some program or instructional strategy is successful when first tried but cannot be replicated because the initial success was due to the climate of expectancy associated with the experiment. Teacher expectation theorists warn against it implicitly and explicitly, but the common reaction to that phenomenon is to treat it as having marred an experiment. The experimental effect is seen as preventing an assessment of what is really important, the particular program under evaluation. If the primary interest is "What works?" the experimental effect is a substantive finding in itself. It suggests that enthusiasm and a vested interest in success and in the methods used are often more important than the methods themselves.

Methodological fashion also lends itself to the presumption that we will find some single factor that explains the whole problem. Monocausality is held in principle to be a fallacy, but in practice we assign much value to isolating individual variables. Supposedly after one has isolated several variables pertinent to a particular problem, one can then synthesize results into some approximation of real-world conditions with interaction among multiple factors. In practice, we seldom get to that stage. The popularity of experimental work in particular may lead to an exaggerated concern with single-factor analysis.

James Comer, who comments on that problem, also points out that working with teachers has come to be thought of as less prestigious than doing and publishing research. Such a status distinction encourages us to frame and pursue questions that are so divorced from the ways in which practitioners confront problems that much policy-related work, from the teacher's viewpoint, is irrelevant from the moment of its conceptualization. Academics have ordinarily separated the problem of achievement from that of misbehavior. One does not often find both discussed in a single work, ethnographies excepted, prior to the mid-seventies. Had we been in day-to-day contact with people in the schools, I doubt we could have made that kind of separation. The inability to consider things from a variety of perspectives, the refusal to consider them holistically, is partly a function of professional vanity, vanity that limits us to doing research *on* people rather than *with* them or *for* them.

The prestige of originality is also a problem. One of the highest accolades we can bestow on intellectual work is that it is original. If what we most want to do is change inner-city schools, then it is not clear, especially now, that more new knowledge is called for. We might get farther faster by disseminating more widely such knowledge as we already have. We could try getting more inner-city parents to understand what we know of the impact of teachers' expectations on learning or what we know of the relationship between students' self-concept and achievement; or we could try getting school board members to understand what we know about the processes by which school boards are rendered impotent; or we could encourage teachers to think more about selective perception and how it is reinforced by the climate in a defensive in-group. The broader dissemination of information now commonplace among professional observers would make a more lasting contribution than one more "strikingly original" critique of American education. Broadly, the ideal intellectual product is now defined as being original, quantified, concerned with cause in the grand sense, and obscurely written. That very definition of knowledge is more than slightly racist and elitist in its consequences, leading us to pursue obscure little questions in ways that suit the professional prestige system rather than insuring that the work we produce has a chance to be of value to the people studied.

Even if professional pretensions were not a problem, it is hardly likely that methods alone could protect us from our culture. The idea that intellectual failure among nonwhite or non-middle class populations has its sources within those populations derives a certain background plausibility from its consistency with popular culture. Coleman set out expecting to find that unequal school resources were a key part of the problem of inadequate education for the urban poor. When that did not appear to be the case, it was quite natural, given the store of cultural ideas available to him, that it would occur to him and others that possibly the problems stemmed from attributes of the disadvantaged themselves (and had that been presented only as a possibility, little harm might have been done). As that idea became the academic orthodoxy, it delayed consideration of the damage done by social institutions; it is one of the contributions of progressive theorists that they forced consideration of just that issue. The orthodox academic versions of attribute theory were relatively sympathetic, but it was a demeaning kind of sympathy, close to the tradition of seeing the poor as nothing more than the products of their oppression, allowing little room for the possibility that some of the adaptions people make to low socioeconomic status enable them to

protect themselves fairly successfully from the worst potential consequences of their position.

That we are affected by cultural biases is inconsistent with the pretensions to scientific status common in the more traditional branches of
the social sciences, the same pretensions that partly account for the
exaggerated emphasis on certain methods of research. We have developed our own vested interests in ways of seeing and doing. The problem
has much more to do with the kinds of emphasis we put on methods
than with the methods themselves. It is not that we have too many
quantitative studies, nor even as James Comer more moderately puts it,
that we have an unhealthy imbalance in favor of controlled quantitative
work. We need more such work than we have, but we need quantitative
work that is aware of its own limitations and is therefore sensitive to
issues raised by other kinds of work. The trouble is that when research
has the air of science, we have been tempted to claim too much for it.
Modernity aggravates the problem. It means that chains of influence
become more complex, more fragmented, with contributions made from
a variety of sources, each difficult to measure or to understand separately. As the processes sustaining inequality retreat to "soft" processes,
"hard" methods, if not used and interpreted with modesty, may become
increasingly misleading.

Conventional wisdom has taken several misleading or downright erroneous positions until fairly recently. There was the position that school
resources do not matter, the position that compensatory education has
been a failure (which Jensen then took as a point of departure when
arguing for genetic racial inferiority), the position that reform of urban
education requires the cultural uplift of the poor, and the position that
ability grouping does not affect learning (the latter idea is still not as
clearly wrong as the others). Much of the evidence for these positions
came from studies with similar characteristics. There is now pretty widespread agreement that the supportive work for those conclusions concentrated on mean tendencies in aggregate data, often masking important
within-aggregate differences; it tended to minimize questions of social
process, often inferring it from distantly related substitutes; it tended to
infer causation from correlational data.

Coleman exhibited all these tendencies. The point is not that he and
others made errors—who doesn't?—but that the effects of the errors on
the policy debate would have been minimal if his interpretations had
been presented with a degree of modesty commensurate with the limitations of the design. In his case, this would have meant emphasizing
that he knew next to nothing about what went on inside schools as
strongly as he emphasized the correlation between home background
and achievement. The error was claiming too much for the methods;
however, what he did wrong is much less significant than that his work

could be so persuasive for so long within the academic community. This fact has much less to do with the quality of his methods than with their prestige. Similarly, the charge to Coleman gave him only two years to complete the research, which alone virtually eliminated certain research strategies. The real-world political constraints, however, have been largely forgotten in the assessment of Coleman's work, which may be another way of saying, "Let's pretend this is true science." Playing at being scientific on a question as vital as this one becomes, after a point, professional irresponsibility.

That many, perhaps even most, social scientists are no longer particularly committed to the claim to "real" scientific status, and the associated tendency to claim too much for their work, matters less than it once did. The consequences of an earlier generation's scientific pretensions have been thoroughly institutionalized in the reward structures and the socializing processes of the social science professions.[7] If researchers in education want their work published and listened to, there is an advantage in doing regression analysis, all apart from whether it is the most effective way to address the problem. Our work has to serve personal needs, professional pretensions, and intellectual fashion, which makes it all the more difficult for the same work to speak clearly to the issue of change.

Even before we got the literature on effective schools and the second-generation quantitative studies, progressive theorists emphasizing within-school processes had created a sizeable literature which by itself was a persuasive rebuttal to the pure attribute approach. In some cases, though, the kinds of ideological commitments which helped make that contribution possible precluded other kinds of contributions. Even though generated by a genuine concern for the most victimized, ideological commitments easily get reduced to formulae and become ends unto themselves. Keeping faith with the formula and proving the other side wrong becomes the most intense day-to-day motivation, which will not always be the most efficient way to contribute to change even where the other side is in fact essentially wrong. Ideological dogmatism leads to either–or formulations in which questions and facts and leads not easily handled by the sacred formula get overlooked or receive minimal attention. Teachers might have been more comfortable with teacher-expectation theory had it given a little more attention to the fact that many students are real problems, but that is a theme, I think, that runs counter to the political sympathies of some of the people who have produced the teacher-expectation literature. I do not disagree with the position that urban school failure may have to be traced ultimately to the injustices caused by the nature of the economy, but it is irresponsible to leap from that idea to the position that reform therefore requires simply restructuring the economy. At its worst, the left could be accused of reducing the poor to abstractions whose sole utility is to prove this or that point of dogma. One could say, at least, that the left has lately paid too little attention to the potential potency of those at the bottom, seeing them too much as a dependent class that has to be aided by their intellectual betters. Certainly, there is fear that, in this country's political traditions, talk about what the poor can do for themselves plays into conservative hands; this accounts for the emphasis on a kind of noblesse oblige toward the poor. That fear can be so debilitating as to prevent us from thinking about ways we might help improve the efficacy of the most reliable instrument of change the most victimized have—themselves.

The earlier references to professional irresponsibility cannot, of course, be taken literally. Unlike school administrators who insist that they ought not be held responsible for failure given the constraints of their situation, social scientists are well enough situated to be able to claim effectively that there is no conception of responsibility which applies to them even in theory. Accountability for educators can be discussed; the research community is so closed it is hard to even conceive of what accountability might mean in that context. When I refer to responsibility, I mean only that if there were a notion of responsibility that in fact applied to us, in all probability doing what we have done to the national discussion of schooling for the urban poor, for the reasons that we have done it, would constitute irresponsibility. Some of the most victimized would go further. They see researchers as exploitative, period. They see all the work we researchers do as an elaborate form of pimping off the poor. All our talk about good intentions and about how hard it is to do social research sounds just about as hollow to them as the excuses of school administrators sound to us. It is as hard for us to think seriously and calmly about whatever justice there is in that viewpoint—and certainly there is some—as for school personnel to think of themselves as being the problem.

That is, there are certain viewpoints we cannot accept, certain voices to which we are ordinarily deaf. Of these, the most important are the voices of inner-city parents. One of the ways we might have progressed more rapidly than we have done would be to take the views of parents more seriously. That would have given us a counterweight to our concern with ultimate causation. The concern of parents is: "What works? What is the best this school can do for my child, whatever his or her limitations?" Exploring that question thoroughly fifteen or twenty years ago would have been much more productive than taking the tack we opted for. Parents have given us other leads that we have not taken. The readily available example of effective basic education in the inner city has been the Catholic school system. Inner-city parents have indicated their belief that schools can make a difference for their children by sending their children to Catholic schools in large numbers, often at great financial sacrifice to the family. The strict response to that from researchers is that Catholic schools may in fact be superior, but there is no way to be certain because the students and parents involved are self-selected and we haven't the data to know if their superior record results from the fact that they have superior material or from the possibility that they do things differently. This is unassailable reasoning, but why don't we have the data? We have not exactly pursued the question with vigor, at least not until lately. (It is James Coleman [1982] who has raised the question very recently and doing so has required standing his previous analysis on its head.) A politically charged decision about what is worth studying is hidden behind methodological objectivity. We thereby lose valuable leads by not listening to parents, partly because it is hard for us to see how inner-city parents could know something we don't.

Another thing one often hears from inner-city parents is: "Do for my child whatever you do for rich kids." This charge represents an interesting adaptation to limited familiarity with educational practice. Had we taken elite upper-middle-class schools as the model for what we wanted in the inner city, we would have ignored the research that held that money does not matter, we would have put students in small schools where they could feel that they matter personally, we would have evaluated teachers with frankly subjective judgments from informed persons, asking those who did not perform to go elsewhere, and we would have given students a level of work that required them to stretch their talents.

Elite schools are hardly my idea of the best we can do, but in retrospect, treating poor children as we treat rich children looks like a pretty good idea. That, given its source, we could not take the idea seriously has to do in some part with a kind of ingrained arrogance against which neither ideology nor honest sympathy is adequate proof. It is an arrogance that permits us to see urban parents as either the villains in the piece or as its victims, but which generally prevents us from seeing them collegially, as people we might both teach and learn from.

On balance, the positive contributions made by social scientists are more striking than the negative ones. It is hardly likely that the social sciences could be less a conspiracy against the laity than the other professions. Certainly, there is no likelihood that they could be consistently responsive to populations that have no power over them. Still, to the degree that social scientists have been the architects of other people's misfortune, it is less understandable than it is with school personnel. Social scientists claim so much more and do not confront day-to-day pressures of the same magnitude.

There is blame to go around. Apportioning responsibility more precisely than that might be more satisfying than useful. John Simon, who has written an inspiring history of a successful alternative high school, notes that, having spent much of his adult life in a rage at the education system, he now finds his capacity for anger dwindling. "I no longer find villains wherever I look in our society. Instead I see a welter of confused people caught up in a system they cannot control and only vaguely comprehend, a system that encourages them to do as much for themselves and as little for others as they can get away with" (1982:215). The problem he describes is more political than educational. If we are to resolve it, we cannot continue to allow the education profession to question the humanity of urban students, but we also cannot defend those students by reducing teachers to cardboard villains. In the end, what makes shared governance an especially attractive route to reform is that it gives us an investment in one another. If urban schooling as a political problem is to be resolved—if it can be resolved—we will need that mutuality.

Notes

1. The works to be cited in this chapter employ a variety of definitions of success, but they generally mean work at or near grade level. That definition is most appropriate at the grade school level. The work of older students would have to be judged against more complex standards, about which we know less.

2. The New York State study does not identify the schools used by name. It is possible that one of their schools is among those examined by Weber, though not likely, judging from the descriptions. There is one case of overlap between Weber and Silberman.

3. Responding to Edmonds, Scott and Walberg (1979) point out that in Edmonds's reanalysis of the Coleman data there remains a correlation between family background and learning for individual pupils. This is to be expected. Even an overachieving school is unlikely to fully neutralize the advantage of privilege.

4. For a more critical view of Rutter, see the review by Cuttace (1982) which raises questions about the strength of Rutter's case for inference and indicates what sort of questions might profitably be addressed in future studies.

5. Teaching to the test is not the same as simply teaching the test. It is a matter of stressing those kinds of materials that are most testable—grammar and punctuation, for example—while deemphasizing less testable skills—the ability to write a coherent essay.

6. Grace (1978:59) points out that child-centered or progressive-romantic educational ideologies are conservative in another way if the stress on individual development and interpersonal relationships leads to a separation of pedagogy from wider structural questions. He also notes that establishing a new realm of pedagogical expertise serves the self-interest of educational professionals.

7. The significance of increasing skepticism within the social science community about claims to "true" scientific status is also lessened by problems of audience access. Those researchers who still espouse the traditional position are likely to have greater access to official policy-makers.

References

Acuna, Rodolfo. "Mixing Apples with Oranges." *Integrated Education*, March-April 1975.

Amidon, Edmund, and Ned Flanders. *The Role of the Teacher in the Classroom.* Minneapolis: Amidon Associates, 1964.

Anderson, R.C. "Learning in Discussion: A Resume of the Authoritarian-Democratic Studies." *Harvard Educational Review*, Summer 1959.

Armbruster, Frank. "The More We Spend, the Less Children Learn." *New York Times Magazine*, August 28, 1977.

Arnold, Millard, ed. *Steve Biko*. New York: Vintage, 1979.

Asbell, Barnard. "Not Like Other Children." In *Policy Issues in Urban Education*, edited by Marjorie Smiley and Harry Miller. New York: Free Press, 1968.

Austin, Gilbert. "Exemplary Schools and the Search for Effectiveness." *Educational Leadership*, October 1979.

Austin, Linda. "One-third of New Teachers Would Fail High School Test." *Dallas Times Herald*. September 7, 1981.

Ausubel, D. P., and Pearl Ausubel. "Ego Development Among Segregated Negro Children." In *Education in Depressed Areas*, edited by A. H. Passow. New York: Teachers College Press, 1963.

Averch, Harvey, Stephen Carroll, Theodore Donaldson, Herbert Kiesling, and John Pincus. *How Effective Is Schooling?* Englewood Cliffs, N.J.: Educational Technology Publications, 1974.

Babcock, Charles. "Critics Tarnish Image of Chicago's Super Teacher." *Philadelphia Inquirer*, March 24, 1982.

Banas, Casey. "Teachers' Answers to Money Questions." *Chicago Tribune*, February 19, 1975.

———. "Parents and School Boards Are Indicted by Teachers." *American School Board Journal*, February 1976.

Banfield, Edward. *The Unheavenly City*. Boston: Little, Brown, 1968.

Baratz, Joan. "Teaching Reading in a Negro School." In *Teaching Black Children to Read*, edited by Joan Baratz and Roger Shuy. Washington, D.C.: Center for Applied Linguistics, 1969.

Baratz, Joan, and Stephen Baratz. "Black Culture on Black Terms: A Rejection of the Social Pathology Model." In *Rappin' and Stylin' Out*, edited by Thomas Kochman. Urbana: University of Illinois Press, 1972.

Baughman, Earl. *Black Americans: A Psychological Analysis*. New York: Academic Press, 1971.

Beez, W. Z. "The Influence of Biased Psychological Reports on Teacher Behavior." In *Learning in Social Settings*, edited by M. B. Miles and W. W. Charters. Boston: Allyn and Bacon, 1970.

Benjamin, Robert. *Making Schools Work*. New York: Continuum, 1981.

Berg, Ivar. *Education and Jobs*. Boston: Beacon, 1971.

Berger, Bennett. "Black Culture or Lower-Class Culture?" In *Soul*, edited by Lee Rainwater. New Brunswick, N.J.: Transaction, 1970.

Bernstein, Basil. "Language and Social Class." *British Journal of Psychology*, September 1960.

Billingsley, Andrew. *Black Families in White America*. Englewood Cliffs, N.J.: Prentice-Hall, 1968.

Blalock, Hubert. *Toward a Theory of Minority Group Relations*. New York: Capricorn, 1967.

Blanchard, Paul. *New School Board Members: A Portrait*. Washington, D.C.: National School Boards Association, 1979.

Blauner, Robert. "Internal Colonialism and Ghetto Revolt." *Social Problems*, Spring 1969.

Bloom, Benjamin. "New Directions in Educational Research: Alterable Variables." *Phi Delta Kappan*, February 19, 1980.

Boggs, Grace Lee. "Toward a New System of Education." In *What Black Educators Are Saying*, edited by Nathan Wright. San Francisco: Leswing, 1970.

Boocock, Sarane. *An Introduction to the Sociology of Learning*. New York: Houghton-Mifflin, 1972.

Bowles, Samuel, and Herbert Gintis. *Schooling in Capitalist America*. New York: Basic Books, 1976.

Brookover, Wilbur, and Edsel Erickson. *Sociology of Education*. Homewood, Ill.: Dorsey, 1975.

Brookover, Wilbur, John Schweitzer, Jeffrey Schneider, Charles Beady, Patricia Flood, and Joseph Wisenbaker. "Elementary School Social Climate and School Achievement." *American Educational Research Journal*, Spring 1978.

Brophy, Jere. "Successful Teaching Strategies for the Inner-City Child." *Phi Delta Kappan*, April 1982.

Burkhead, Jesse. *Input and Output in Large City High Schools*. Syracuse, N.Y.: Syracuse University Press, 1967.

Campbell, Angus. *White Attitudes Toward Black People*. Ann Arbor, Mich.: Institute of Social Research, 1971.

Chakin, Alan, Edward Sigler, and Valerian Perlega. "Nonverbal Mediators of Teacher Expectancy Effects." *Journal of Personality and Social Psychology*, July 1974.

Chambers, Marcia. "Mayor Praises, Shanker Assails Schools Analysis." *New York Times*, January 19, 1979.

Chesler, Mark. "Contemporary Sociological Theories of Racism." In *Towards the Elimination of Racism*, edited by Phyliss Katz. New York: Pergamon, 1976.

Clark, Burton. "The Cooling-Out Function in Higher Education." In *The Sociology of Education*, edited by Holger Stub. Homewood, Ill.: Dorsey, 1975.

Clark, David, Linda Lotto, and Martha McCarthy. "Factors Associated With Success in Urban Elementary Schools." *Phi Delta Kappan*, March 1980.

Clark, Kenneth. *Dark Ghetto: Dilemmas of Social Power*. New York: Harper and Row, 1965.

Clignet, Remi. *Liberty and Equality in the Educational Process*. New York: Wiley, 1974.

Cloward, Richard, and James Jones. "Social Class: Educational Attitudes and Participation." In *Education in Depressed Areas*, edited by A. H. Passow. New York: Teachers College Press, 1963.

Cloward, Richard, and Lloyd Ohlin. *Delinquency and Opportunity*. New York: Free Press, 1960.

Cohen, Michael. "Effective Schools: What the Research Says." *Today's Education*, April-May 1981.

Coleman, James, E. Q. Campbell, C. J. Hobson, J. McPartland, A. Mood, F. D. Weinfeld, and R. L. York. *Equality of Educational Opportunity*. Washington, D.C.: U.S. Office of Education, 1966.

Coleman, James, T. Hoffer, and S. Kilgore. *High School and Beyond*. New York: Basic Books, 1982.

Coles, Robert. *The South Goes North*. Boston: Little, Brown, 1971.

Colfax, J. David, and Jack Roach. *Radical Sociology*. New York: Basic Books, 1971.

Collins, Randall. *The Credential Society*. New York: Academic Press, 1979.

Comer, James. "Black Education: An Holistic View." *Urban Review*, Fall 1975.

———. *School Power*. New York: Free Press, 1980.

Cooke, Sandra and Jeanette Moss. "How Troubled Is Teacher Education?" *Teacher*, November–December 1980.

Copperman, Paul. *The Literacy Hoax*. New York: Morrow, 1978.

Coser, Lewis. "Two Methods in Search of a Substance."*American Sociological Review*, December 1975.

Costin, Frank, W. Greenough, and Robert Menges. "Student Ratings of College Teaching: Reliability, Validity and Usefulness." *Review of Educational Research*, December 1974.

Cottle, Thomas. "Politics of Pronouncement: Notes on Publishing in the Social Sciences." *Harvard Educational Review*, Summer 1969.

Cox, Oliver. *Caste, Class and Race*. Garden City, N.Y.: Doubleday, 1948.

Cruse, Harold. *Rebellion or Revolution*. New York: Morrow, 1968.

———. *The Crisis of the Negro Intellectual*. New York: William Morrow, 1967.

Cuttace, Peter. "Reflections of the Rutter Ethos." *Urban Education*, January 1982.

Davidson, Helen, and Gerhard Lang. "Childrens' Perception of Their Teachers' Feelings Toward Them as Related to Self-Perception, School Achievement and Behavior." *Journal of Experimental Education*, December 1960.

Davis, Allison. "The Motivation of the Underprivileged Worker." In *Industry and Society*, edited by W. F. Whyte. New York: McGraw-Hill, 1966.

Deal, Terence, and Lynn Celotti. "How Much Influence Do (and Can) Educational Administrators Have on Classrooms?" *Phi Delta Kappan*, March 1980.

Decker, Susan. *An Empty Spoon*. New York: Harper and Row, 1969.

Delone, Richard. *Small Futures: Children, Inequality and the Limits of Liberal Reform.* New York: Harcourt Brace Jovanovich, 1979.

Deutsch, Martin. "The Disadvantaged Child and the Learning Process." In *Education in Depressed Areas*, edited by A. H. Passow. New York: Teachers College Press, 1963.

Deutscher, Erwin. "Words and Deeds: Social Science and Social Policy." *Social Problems*, Fall 1966.

Dornbusch, Sanford, Grace Massey, and Mona Scott. "Racism Without Racists: Institutional Racism in Urban Schools." *Black Scholar*, November 1975.

Doyle, Wayne. "Teachers' Perceptions: Do They Make a Difference?" *Annals of the American Educational Research Association*, 1971.

DuBois, W.E.B. "Postscript." *Crisis*, April 1934.

———. *Souls of Black Folk*. Greenwich, Conn.: Fawcett, 1961.

Edmonds, Ronald. "Effective Schools for the Urban Poor." *Educational Leadership*, October 1979.

———. "The Characteristics of Effective Schools: Research and Implementation." Unpublished, October 1981.

Elkins, Stanley. *Slavery*. Chicago: University of Chicago Press, 1968.

Ellison, Ralph. *Shadow and Act*. New York: Signet, 1963.

Entwistle, Doris. "Developmental Linguistics: A Comparative Study in Four Subcultural Settings." *Sociometry*, March 1966.

———. "Developmental Socio-Linguistics: Inner City Children." *American Journal of Sociology*, January 1968.

Fanon, Frantz. *The Wretched of the Earth*. New York: Grove Press, 1968.

Farmer, James. *Freedom When?* New York: Random House, 1966.

Featherstone, Joseph. *Schools where Children Learn*. New York: Liveright, 1971.

Feinberg, Lawrence. "James Guines." *Washington Post*, January 4, 1981.

Fernandez, Happy. "Parents' Rights and Power as New Dynamics in the American School System." *NASSP Bulletin*, January 1980.

Feron, James. "Distar May Be Tough . . . ." *New York Times*, November 16, 1980.

Finlayson, Harry. "Incompetence and Teacher Dismissal." *Phi Delta Kappan*, September 1979.

Franklin, Vincent. *The Education of Black Philadelphia*. Philadelphia: University of Pennsylvania Press, 1979.

Freeman, Richard. *The Overeducated American*. New York: Academic Press, 1976.

Freidheim, Elizabeth. "Critical Theory as Consciousness." Unpublished, 1979.

Fuchs, Estelle. *Teachers Talk*. New York: Anchor, 1969.

Genovese, Eugene. *Roll, Jordan, Roll*. New York: Pantheon, 1974.

Gittel, Marilyn. *Limits to Citizen Participation*. Berkeley, Calif.: Sage, 1980.

Goldman, Harvey, and Richard Larson. "When Inner-city Teachers Are Given Free Time." *Journal of Negro Education*, Winter 1971.

Gollub, Wendy, and Earline Sloan. "Teacher Expectations and Race and Socioeconomic Status." *Urban Education*, April 1978.

———. "Teacher Expectations and Student Perceptions: A Decade of Research." *Educational Leadership*, February 1981.

Good, Thomas. "Which Pupils Do Teachers Call On?" In *The Sociology of Education*, edited by Holger Stub. Homewood, Ill.: Dorsey, 1975.

Gouldner, Alvin. "The Sociologist as Partisan: Sociology and the Welfare State." *American Sociologist*, May 1968.

———. *The Coming Crisis of Western Sociology*. New York: Avon, 1970.

Gouldner, Helen. *Teachers' Pets, Troublemakers and Nobodies*. Westport, Conn.: Greenwood, 1978.

Grace, Gerald. *Teachers, Ideology and Control: A Study in Urban Education*. London: Routledge and Kegan Paul, 1978.

Greer, Colin. Untitled review of C. Jencks, *Inequality*. *Society*, March–April 1974.

Gutman, Herbert. *The Black Family in Freedom and Slavery, 1750–1925*. New York: Pantheon, 1976.

Haller, E. J., and S. A. Davis. "Does SES Bias the Assignment of Elementary School Students to Reading Groups?" *American Educational Research Journal*, Winter 1980.

Hamer, Fannie Lou. "It's in Your Hands." In *Black Women in White America*, edited by Gerda Lerner. New York: Vintage, 1973.

Hansberry, Lorraine. *To Be Young, Gifted and Black*. New York: Signet, 1970.

Harding, Vincent. "History: White, Negro and Black." *Southern Exposure*. September 1974.

———. "The Black Wedge in America." *Black Scholar*, December 1975.

Heath, Robert, and Mark Nielson. "The Empirical Basis of Performance Based Teacher Education." *Review of Educational Research*, Winter 1974.

Hechinger, Fred. "Model Schools Teach a Lesson." *New York Times*, December 5, 1978.

———. "Improvement in Reading Linked to Broad Support for the Basics." *New York Times*, September 16, 1980.

Heichberger, Robert, and James Young. "Teacher Perceptions of Supervision and Evaluation." *Phi Delta Kappan*, November 1975.

Hentoff, Nat. *Our Children Are Dying*. New York: Viking, 1967.

———. *Does Anybody Give A Damn?* New York: Knopf, 1977.

———. "Schoolchild's Blues." *Village Voice*, March 26, 1979.

———. "Look for the Parents' Union Label." *Village Voice*, August 26, 1980.

Herndon, James. *The Way It 'Spozed to Be*. New York: Bantam, 1965.

Heyns, Barbara. *Summer Learning and the Effects of Schooling*. New York: Academic Press, 1978.

Hill, Robert. *Strengths of the Black Family*. New York: Emerson Hall, 1972.

Hobart, Charles. "Underachievement Among Minority Group Students: An Analysis and Proposal." *Phylon*, Summer 1963.

Hodgson, Geoffrey. "Do Schools Make a Difference?" In *The Sociology of Education*, edited by Holger Stub. Homewood, Ill.: Dorsey, 1975.

Horton, John. "Order and Conflict Theories of Social Problems as Competing Ideologies." *American Journal of Sociology*, May 1966.

Hurn, Christopher. *The Limits and Possibilities of Schooling*. New York: Allyn and Bacon, 1978.

Jackall, Robert. "Structural Invitations to Deceit: Some Reflections on Bureaucracy and Morality." Unpublished, 1980.

Jencks, Christopher, Marshall Smith, Henry Acland, Mary Jo Bane, David Cohen, Herbert Gintis, Barbara Heyns, and Stephen Michelson. *Inequality: A Reas-*

sessment of the Impact of Family and Schooling in America. New York: Harper and Row, 1972.

Johnson, Charles. *The Social Psychology of Education.* New York: Holt, Rinehart and Winston, 1970.

Jones, Alan. *Students: Do Not Push Your Teachers Down the Stairs on Friday.* Baltimore: Penguin Books, 1972.

Jones, Reginald, ed. *Black Psychology.* New York: Harper and Row, 1980.

Jones, Rhett. "Proving Blacks Inferior: The Sociology of Knowledge." In *The Death of White Sociology,* edited by Joyce Ladner. New York: Vintage, 1973.

Justin, Neal. "Culture Conflict and Mexican-American Achievement." In *Sociology of Education,* edited by W. Cave and M. Chesler. New York: Macmillan, 1974.

Kellet, Susan. "Marva Collins Resurrects the One-Room School." *People,* December 11, 1978.

Kerr, Norman. "The School Board as an Agency of Legitimation." In *Sociology of Education,* edited by R. Pavelko. Itasco, Ill.: Peacock, 1968.

King, C. E., Robert Mayer, and Ann Borders-Patterson. "Differential Responses to Black and White Males by Female Teachers in a Southern City." *Sociology and Social Research,* July 1973.

Kozol, Jonathan. *Death at an Early Age.* Boston: Houghton-Mifflin, 1967.

———. "Free Schools: A Time for Candor." *Saturday Review,* March 4, 1972.

Ladner, Joyce. *The Death of White Sociology.* New York: Vintage, 1973.

Lambdin, William. "Johnny Can't Write Because English Teachers Can't Either." *Washington Post,* August 31, 1980.

Leacock, Eleanor. *Teaching and Learning in City Schools.* New York: Basic, 1969.

Levine, Daniel. "Successful Approaches for Improving Academic Achievement in Inner-City Elementary Schools." *Phi Delta Kappan,* April 1982.

Levine, Lawrence. *Black Culture and Black Consciousness.* New York: Oxford University Press, 1977.

Levy, Gerald. *Class Warfare in Ghetto Schools.* New York: Pegasus, 1970.

Lezotte, Lawrence, and Joseph Passalacqua. "Individual School Buildings: Accounting for Differences in Measured Pupil Performance." *Urban Education,* October 1978.

Liebow, Elliot. *Tally's Corner: A Study of Negro Streetcorner Men.* Boston: Little, Brown, 1967.

Lifton, Robert. *Home from the War.* New York: Simon and Schuster, 1974.

Lightfoot, Sarah. *Worlds Apart.* New York: Basic Books, 1978.

Lucey, Paul. "Crisis in the Halls." *Journal of Secondary Education,* October 1967.

Lyons, Gene. "Why Teachers Can't Teach." *Phi Delta Kappan,* October 1980.

McCarthy, John, and William Yancey. "Uncle Tom and Mr. Charlie: Metaphysical Pathos in the Study of Racism and Personal Disorganization." In *Race Relations,* edited by Edgar Epps. Cambridge, Mass.: Winthrop, 1973.

McIntyre, John, and William Morris. "Time Management and Instructional Supervision." *Clearinghouse,* May 1982.

Mackler, Bernard. "The Little Black Schoolhouse." New York: ERIC Center for Urban Education, 1969. Microfilm.

Maeroff, Gene. *Don't Blame the Children.* New York: McGraw-Hill, 1982.

————. "Inner-city Schools Show Signs of Progress." *New York Times*, January 6, 1982.

Marable, Manning. "The Quiet Death of Black Colleges." *Witness*, August 1983.

Marburger, Carl. "Parents/Citizens: The Fourth Force in Education." *NASSP Bulletin*, January 1980.

Martin, Paul. "Marva Collins—A Teacher Who Cares." *Good Housekeeping*, September 11, 1978.

Means, Howard. "Vincent Reed Keeps on Picking up Peanuts." *Washingtonian*, January 1979.

Meier, Deborah. "Planning to Keep Them in Their Place." *In These Times*, June 1, 1982.

Merchenbaum, Donald, Kenneth Bowers, and Robert Ross. "A Behavioral Analysis of Teacher Expectancy Effects." *Journal of Personality and Social Psychology*, December 1979.

Merton, Robert. "Discrimination and the American Creed." In *Discrimination and National Welfare*, edited by R. McIver. New York: Harper and Row, 1949.

————. *Social Theory and Social Structure*. New York: Free Press, 1957.

Mills, C. Wright. *The Sociological Imagination*. New York: Oxford, 1959.

Morgan, Stanley. "Shared Governance: A Concept for Public Schools." *NASSP Bulletin*, January 1980.

Moynihan, Daniel. *The Negro Family: The Case for National Action*. Washington, D.C.: Government Printing Office, 1965.

Murnane, Richard. *The Impact of School Resources on the Learning of Inner-City Children*. Cambridge, Mass.: Ballinger, 1975.

Murray, Albert. *The Omni-Americans*. New York: Dutton, 1970.

Myrdal, Gunnar. *An American Dilemma*. 1944. Reprint. New York: Harper and Row, 1962.

Naipul, V. S. *A Home for Mr. Biswas*. New York: Penguin, 1976.

Newman, Dorothy K., Nancy Amidei, Barbara Carter, Dawn Day, William Kurant, and Jack Russell. *Politics and Prosperity*. New York: Pantheon, 1978.

Ogbu, John. *The Next Generation*. New York: Academic Press, 1974.

————. *Minority Education and Caste*. New York: Academic Press, 1978.

Ornstein, Allan. *Race and Politics in School and Community Organizations*. Palisades, Calif.: Goodyear, 1974.

Passow, A. Harry. "Urban Education for the 1980's: Trends and Issues." *Phi Delta Kappan*, April 1982.

————, ed. *Education in Depressed Areas*. New York: Teachers College Press, 1963.

Payne, Charles. "The Civil Rights Movement as History." *Integrated Education*, May–December 1981.

————. "The Declining—and Increasing—Significance of Race." In *The Caste and Class Controversy*, edited by C. V. Willie. New York: General Hall, 1980.

Persell, Caroline. *Education and Inequality*. New York: Free Press, 1977.

Pitts, James. "The Study of Race Consciousness: Comments on New Directions." *American Journal of Sociology*, November 1974.

Piven, Frances, and Richard Cloward. *Poor People's Movements*. New York: Pantheon, 1977.

Powell, Douglas, and Paul Driscoll. "Middle-Class Professionals Face Unemployment." *Society*, February 1973.

Rainwater, Lee. "Crucible of Identity: The Negro Lower Class Family." In *White Racism and Black Americans*, edited by D. Bromley and C. Longino. Cambridge, Mass.: Schenkman, 1972.

Reed, Adolph. "Black Particularity Reconsidered." *Telos*, Winter 1979.

Richer, Stephen. "Middle-Class Bias of Schools: Fact or Fancy." *Sociology of Education*, Fall 1974.

Riessman, Frank. *The Culturally Deprived Child*. New York: Harper and Row, 1962.

Rist, Ray. *The Urban School: A Factory of Failure*. Cambridge, Mass.: MIT Press, 1977.

Rodney, Walter. *How Europe Underdeveloped Africa*. London: Bogle-L'Ouverture Press, 1972.

Rodriquez, Richard. *Hunger of Memory*. Boston: Godine, 1982.

Rogers, David. *110 Livingston Street*. New York: Vintage, 1969.

Romano, Octavio. "The Anthropology and Sociology of the Mexican-American: The Distortion of History." *El Grito*, Winter 1968.

Rosenbaum, James. *Making Inequality: The Hidden Curriculum of High School Tracking*. New York: Wiley, 1976.

Rosenfeld, Gerry. *Shut Those Thick Lips: A Study of Slum School Failure*. New York: Holt, Rinehart and Winston, 1971.

Rosenthal, Robert, and Lenore Jacobsen. *Pygmalion in the Classroom*. New York: Holt, Rinehart and Winston, 1968.

Rothschild-Whitt, Joyce. "Collectivist Organization: An Alternative to Rational-Bureaucratic Models." *American Sociological Review*, August 1979.

Rubovits, P. C., and Martin Maehr. "*Pygmalion* Analyzed: Toward an Explanation of the Rosenthal-Jacobsen Findings." *Journal of Personality and Social Psychology*, August 1971.

————. "Teacher Expectations: A Special Problem for Black Children with White Teachers?" In *Culture, Child and School*, edited by M. Maehr and W. Stallings. Monterey, Calif.: Brooks-Cole, 1975.

Rutter, Michael, Barbara Maughan, Peter Mortimore, and Janet Ouston. *Fifteen Thousand Hours: Secondary Schools and Their Effects on Children*. Cambridge, Mass.: Harvard University Press, 1979.

Ryan, William. *Blaming the Victim*. New York: Vintage, 1971.

St. John, Nancy. "Elementary School Classroom as a Frog Pond: Self-Concept, Sense of Control and Social Context." *Social Forces*, June 1971.

Saiter, Susan. "Uprooting the Failing Teacher." *New York Times*, January 4, 1981.

Savage, David. "Wingate: Brooklyn's Born Again High School." *Educational Leadership*, May 1979.

Schafer, Walter, Carol Olexa, and Kenneth Polk. "Programmed for Social Class: Tracking in High School." In *Sociology of Education*, edited by Holger Stub. Homewood, Ill.: Dorsey, 1975.

Schwartz, Audrey. "A Comparative Study of Values and Achievements of Mexican-American and Anglo Youth." *Sociology of Education*, Fall 1971.

Scott, Ralph, and Herbert Walberg. "Schools Alone are Insufficient: A Response to Edmonds." *Educational Leadership*, October 1979.

Seeman, Melvin. "The Urban Alienations: Some Dubious Theses From Marx to Marcuse." *Journal of Personality and Social Psychology*, August 1971.

Seligman, C. R., G. Tucker, and W. Lambert. "The Effects of Speech Style and Other Attributes on Teachers' Attitudes Toward Pupils." *Language in Society*, January 1972.

Sennett, Richard, and Jonathan Cobb. *The Hidden Injuries of Class*. New York: Vintage, 1972.

Sexton, Patricia. *The American School*. Englewood Cliffs, N.J.: Prentice-Hall, 1967.

Shoemaker, Joan, and Hugh Fraser. "What Principals Can Do." *Phi Delta Kappan*, November 1981.

Silberman, Charles. *Crisis in the Classroom*. New York: Random House, 1970.

Simon, John. *To Become Somebody: Growing Up Against the Grain of Society*. New York: Houghton-Mifflin, 1982.

Stanfield, John. "Urban Public School Desegregation: The Reproduction of Normative White Domination." *Journal of Negro Education*, Spring 1982.

State of New York Office of Education Performance Review. "School Factors Influencing Reading Achievement: A Case Study of Two Inner-city Schools." Washington, D.C.: ERIC microfilm, March 1974.

Stebbins, Robert. "The Meaning of Disorderly Behavior: Teacher Definitions of a Classroom Situation." *Sociology of Education*, Spring 1971.

Stinchcombe, Arthur. *Rebellion in a High School*. Chicago: Quadrangle, 1964.

Summers, Anita, and Barbara Wolfe. "Which School Resources Help Learning." *Federal Reserve Bank of Philadelphia Review*, February 1975.

Swift, David W. *American Education: A Sociological View*. Boston: Houghton-Mifflin, 1976.

Tabb, William. *The Political Economy of the Black Ghetto*. New York: Norton, 1970.

Tavris, Carol. "Compensatory Education: The Glass Is Half Full." *Psychology Today*, September 1976.

Taylor, Howard. "Playing the Dozens with Path Analysis: Methodological Pitfalls in Jencks *et al.*, *Inequality*." *Sociology of Education*, Fall 1973.

————. "IQ Heritability: A Checklist of Fallacies." *Journal of Afro-American Issues*, Winter 1976.

Teachman, Gerard. "In-School Truancy in Urban Schools: The Problem and a Solution." *Phi Delta Kappan*, November 1979.

Thomas, Clarke. "Schools Can Teach All Students, Educator Says." *Pittsburgh Post-Gazette*, September 19, 1981.

Torrey, Jane. "Illiteracy in the Ghetto." *Harvard Educational Review*, May 1970.

Trogdon, E. Wayne. "An Exercise in Mastery Learning." *Phi Delta Kappan*, February 1980.

U.S. Commission on Civil Rights. *Teachers and Students: Differences in Teacher Interaction with Mexican-American and Anglo Students*. Washington, D.C.: Government Printing Office, 1973.

Valentine, Charles. "Deficit, Difference and Bicultural Models of Afro-American Behavior." *Harvard Educational Review*, reprint no. 5, 1975.

Vogel, Robert. "Mastery Learning, Boon to Upstate City, Stirs Wide Interest." *New York Times*, November 16, 1980.

Walsh, Kevin, and Milly Cowles. "Social Consciousness and Discipline in the Urban Elementary Schools." *Urban Review*, Spring 1979.

Weber, George. *Inner-city Children Can Be Taught to Read*. Washington, D.C.: Council for Basic Education, 1971.

Wilson, Alan. "Social Stratification and Academic Achievement." In *Education in Depressed Areas*, edited by A. H. Passow. New York: Teachers College Press, 1963.

Wilson, Andrea. "How Powerful Is Schooling?" *New York University Education Quarterly*, Spring 1980.

Wilson, William. *The Declining Significance of Race*. Chicago: University of Chicago Press, 1979.

Yetman, Norman, and Hoy Steele. *Majority and Minority*. Boston: Allyn and Bacon, 1971.

Index

Ability grouping, 108–10, 131, 153 n.6

Absenteeism, 91–92, 161; at Westside High, 56, 57, 73 n.3

Academic achievement. *See* Educational achievement

Accountability, 142, 150, 174, 186. *See also* Responsibility

Acuna, Rodolfo, 114

Administration of schools, 135–44; problems of, 68–70, 131; reform at Westside High, 67–71; style at Westside High, 53–54, 71

Administration-teacher relationships, at Westside High, 53–55, 63–64, 66, 67

Administrators, alienation of, 140

Alienation, 40, 73, n.4, 127, 140, 144, 173; of students, 118; of teachers, 63, 117

Alterable variables, 181–82

An American Dilemma (Myrdal), 11

Anomie theory, 11

Apathy, 173

Asbell, Barnard, 120

Assemblies, in Westside High, 55

Attendance of classes, 91–92, 161. *See also* Absenteeism

Attribute theories, 9–10, 11, 13, 14, 104–6, 183–84; interpretation of studies, 57–58; and progressive theory, 21

Austin, Gilbert, 165

Babcock, Charles, 156–57

Back-to-basics movement, 151, 156

Bad Person concept, 13

Baldwin, James, 9, 24

Banas, Casey, 141

Baratz, Joan, 106

Beez, W. Z., 113, 114

Benjamin, Robert, 142, 168, 176

Biko, Steve, 40

Births, out-of-wedlock, 25–26

Black colleges, 33; criticism of, 30–31

The Black Family in Slavery or Freedom (Gutman), 32

Black history, Harding's view of, 28

Black life, and progressive theory, 22

Blacks, intra-racial relations, 22–23

Blaming the Victim (Ryan), 25–26

Blanchard, Paul, 136–37

Bloom, Benjamin, 164, 175, 181

Blumberg, 173

Bowles, Samuel, 145, 178

Bronfennbrenner, Urie, 105

Brooklyn, Wingate High, 167

Brookover, Wilbur, 116, 118, 121, 161

Bureaucracy: citizen involvement in, 137–38; professional, urban schools as, 142–43

Bureaucratic pathology, 135, 138–39, 141

Capitalism, 32

Catholic schools, 186–87

Causal analysis, 19–20

Celotti, Lynn, 135
Central tendency, 34, 104
Change: possibility of, 72; and success, 63
Chesler, Mark, 8–12
Chicago, Ill.: job security of teachers in, 134; West side of, 43–44
Civil Rights Commission study, 16–17
Civil rights movement, 12, 13, 23, 41 n.2
Clarity of instruction, 79, 80–82, 88, 89
Clark, Burton, 147, 164–65
Clark, Kenneth, 111
Class attendance, 91–92, 161. *See also* Absenteeism
Class differences, and rebellious behavior, 125–26
Classroom, social process in, 19
Classroom behavior, students' explanations of, 82–95
Classroom discipline, 82–90, 160–61; by inexperienced teachers, 121–22
Class struggle, teachers in, 145–46
Cloward, Richard, 11
Cobb, Jonathan, 121
Cognitive entry characteristics, 181–82
Coleman, James, 18–20, 33, 104–5, 117–18, 134, 142, 180–85, 187
Coles, Robert, 45, 131, 163
Collective responsibility, 40
Colleges: Black, 30–31, 33; problems of, 149–50
Collins, Marva, 156–58
Collins, Randall, 130
Comer, James, 63, 126, 168, 169–71, 182, 184
Commitment, 121, 165
Communication: among intellectuals, 41–42 n.4; student-teacher, 52–53
Compensatory education, 105, 165
Competency-based curriculum, 164
Competency tests, for teachers, 128–29

Concern, by teachers, 79–80, 81, 82, 88–89; and student behavior, 96
Conservative attitudes, 36–37
Control, locus of, 117–18
Copperman, Paul, 135
Cottle, Thomas, 16
Cox, Oliver, 11, 12, 13, 142, 172
Credentialism, 130
Credentials of education, 144, 145
Crisis in the Classroom (Silberman), 166
Crisis of the Negro Intellectual (Cruse), 36
Culturally deprived, programs for, 131
Culture, influence on social sciences, 15–16, 19
Curricular goals, 164

Davis, S. A., 110–11
Deal, Terence, 135
Decision-making: and education reform, 178; in school administration, 137–38; shared, 173–74
Declining Significance of Race (Wilson), 30
Delinquency theory, 11
Demands on students, 76, 79–80, 100; and classroom behavior, 83, 85, 88, 89, 91, 92, 94–95; and expectations, 114–15
Demands on teachers, 66–68, 70–71, 89, 104, 167–68
Denial theories of inequality, 9–14, 34, 37, 39, 103, 127; methodology of, 14–20; and progressive theory, 21, 27, 36
Differential distribution of opportunity, 11
Discipline. *See* Classroom discipline
Disorder, in Westside High, 50–51, 55–57, 58
Disruptive behavior, 120–21
Distar, 116, 175–76
Dornbusch, Sanford, 113, 116, 148
Driscoll, Paul, 16

DuBois, W. E. B., 31, 101; *Souls of Black Folk*, 7

Economic deprivation, 118
Economic opportunity, and educational achievement, 125
Economic value of education, 144–45
Edmonds, Ronald, 6, 144, 160, 164, 165, 168, 175, 181
Educability, assumptions about, 139–40
Education: economic value of, 144–45; news coverage of, 156–58; schools of, 129–30; successful, 155–56; of teachers, 128–30, 162
Educational achievement: decline of, 149–51; and economic opportunity, 125; and fate-control, 118; and social status, 103; and teacher expectation, 115
Efficiency ratings of teachers, 64
Elite interests, in education of urban poor, 145–47
Elite schools, 187
Ellison, Ralph, 22
Embeddedness of racism, 8
Empowerment, individual, 41 n.2
Entwistle, Doris, 105
Equality, statistical, 33–34
Evaluation of teachers, 68–69, 135, 140
Expectations: and achievement, 112–17; and behavior, 126; of schools, 128. *See also* Teacher expectations
Experimental effect, 182
Exploitative relationships, 38
Exploitative systems, 23
Extracurricular activities, at Westside High, 55

Failure, 5, 61–62, 72, 104, 112, 148; of administrators, 140; in inner-city schools, 130–31, 152; at Westside High, 59. *See also* Teacher expectations
Family background, and educational achievement, 18, 121

Family life, Black, 25–26
Fanon, Frantz, 36
Farmer, James, 29–30
Fate control, 117–18
Featherstone, Joseph, 180
Feiffer, Jules, 37
Fifteen Thousand Hours (Rutter et al.), 160–61
Finlayson, Harry, 134
Follow-Through program, 176
Formative testing, 182
Fragmentation: of educational retardation, 110; organizational, 131–32; of social process, 37–38
Freeman, Richard, 145
Freidheim, Elizabeth, 35, 182
Fuchs, Estelle, 130
Futility of effort, 64–66; teacher's sense of, 117; student's sense of, 118, 121

Generation differences, and behavior problems, 123
Gintis, Herbert, 145, 178
Gittel, Marilyn, 137–38
Good, Thomas, 113, 114
Gouldner, Alvin, 13, 20
Gouldner, Helen, 107–10, 111, 120
Gutman, Herbert, 20, 32

Haller, E. J., 110–11
Hallway reform at Westside High, 59–68
Hamer, Fannie Lou, 34
Hansberry, Lorraine, 35
Harding, Vincent, 22, 28
Hechinger, Fred, 156
Helpful Outsider, dilemma of, 35–36
Hentoff, Nat, 131, 151, 156
Herndon, Terry, 135
Historical-cultural theories of inequality, 10
"History: White, Negro and Black" (Harding), 28
Home backgrounds, and educational achievement, 105–6
Home from the War (Lifton), 37

Home-school interaction, 111
Homework, 115
Hurn, Christopher, 113, 116, 142

Ideological approaches to education,
   176–77
Illegitimacy, 25–26
Incompetent teachers, 134–35
Individual empowerment, 41 n.2
Individualization, 164–65
Inequality, 7, 32; and educational
   achievement, 103; rationalization
   of, 37–41; studies of, 18–20, 36–37
Inequality (Jencks), 19
Inequality systems, 23, 24
Information transmission, in West-
   side High, 51
Inner-city life, 118
Inner-city parents, 123–24
Inner-city schools, 7, 61, 143; educa-
   tional achievement at, 103–4; fail-
   ure in, 111, 130–31; relationship
   with parents, 123–24; successful,
   156; teacher-student relationships,
   107–10
Inner-city teachers, 62, 63, 72–73, 146
Inspiration, 76
Institutional failure, rewards of, 62
Intelligence: Black, 22–23; genetic
   theories of, 27–28
Interpersonal relationships, 12; in
   classroom, 16–17
Interviews for Westside High study,
   47–49
Intraracial relationships, 22–23
Isolation, racial, 12

Jacobsen, Lenore, 112–13, 128
Jaspers, Karl, 40
Jencks, Christopher, 19, 145
Jensen, 184
Job security for teachers, 134
Johnson, Charles, 114
Junior colleges, 147
Justin, Neal, 17

Kerr, Norman, 136, 137
Kindergarten, track placement in,
   108–9

King, C. E., 114
King Elementary School, New Ha-
   ven, Conn., 169–71
Kozol, Jonathan, 152

Labor force, overeducated, 145
Lambdin, William, 128
Lambert, W., 106
Language: of denial theories, 14; of
   professional educators, 138; of pro-
   gressive theory, 23, 35; of sociol-
   ogy, 15
Language skills, of Black slum chil-
   dren, 105, 106–7, 152 n.1
Leacock, Eleanor, 114
Leadership, 5, 142, 169, 179; of prin-
   cipals, 166–68; and success of
   schools, 158, 164, 165
Learning environments, structured,
   164
Left, ideological, 184–86; educational
   theories of, 150–52, 176–77
Levine, Lawrence, 24
Levy, Gerald, 119, 121–22, 140
Liebow, Elliot, 11
Lifton, Robert, 37
Limits to Citizen Participation (Gittel),
   137–38
Longitudinal studies, 16
Lotto, Linda, 164–65
Low-achieving students, 114
Lower-class life-style, 27
Low social status, and language, 107

McCarthy, Martha, 164–65
Macchiorola, Frank, 156
Mackler, Bernard, 105
Maehr, Martin, 114
Mastery learning system, 164, 175
Media coverage of education, 156–58
Meier, Deborah, 174
Merton, Robert, 11, 128, 179–80
Methodology of denial theories, 14–
   20
Mexican-American students, 16–17
Middle class, Black, 29
Middle-class students, 125–26, 139,
   149–52

Mills, C. Wright, 18
Minorities, opportunities for, 125
Misbehavior: benefits of, 122; students' explanations of, 82–95
Monitoring of teachers, 135
Monocausality, 182
Morale problems, 44
Moralistic theories of inequality, 11
Moral majority, 13
Moral questions of inequality, 27
Moral stature of poor, 25–26; and statistical equality, 33–34
Moynihan, Daniel P., 10
Murnane, Richard, 135
Murray, Albert, 18
Myrdal, Gunnar, 11, 13
Mystical theories of inequality, 9, 11–14, 17–18; and teacher expectations, 117

Negro history, Harding's view of, 28
New Haven, Conn., King Elementary School, 169–71
News coverage of education, 156–58
New York City: education in, 177; evaluation of teachers, 135; job security of teachers, 134

Ogbu, John, 124–25, 147
Ohlin, Lloyd, 11
Opportunity theories of inequality, 11
Organizational fragmentation, 131–32
Organization of school, 49–50; and disruptive behavior, 126
The Outpost, 46
Outsider, dilemma of, 35–36

Parental involvement, 168
Parents, urban, 36; and discipline problems, 122–24; and educational reform, 177–78; and educational research, 186–87; and school administrations, 137–38
Parents' Union of Philadelphia, 138, 168
Pathological bureaucracy, 135, 138–39, 141

Peer groups, 121, 153 n.4
Persell, Caroline, 113, 142
Physical attributes of teachers, 85
Pitts, James, 12
Poverty, and educational inadequacy, 125
Powell, Douglas, 16
Power, questions of, 103–4, 172–74
Power differentials, 23, 34
Preschool factors, 7
Principals, leadership of, 135, 165, 166–68
Problems, approaches to, 171–72
Professional bureaucracy of education, 142–43
Programs, special, 131
Progressive theory of inequality, 10, 18, 41, 183; conservative potential of, 20–37; research, 185
Public schools, administration of, 135–44
Pygmalion in the Classroom (Rosenthal and Jacobsen), 112–13, 128, 142

Qualifications of teachers, 128–30
Quality of teaching, 47, 75; and classroom behavior, 83, 92, 95; and expectations, 113

Racial inequality, genetic theories of, 27–28
Racial isolation, 12
Racial relationships, theories of, 11–12
Racism, 8; of failure, 148
Radical educators, 176–77
RAP (Redneck-as-Patsy) theory of inequality, 9, 11, 13, 14, 18; and progressive theory, 21; and teacher expectations, 117; teachers in, 127
Raspberry, William, 156
Rationalization: of educational retardation, 110; of inequality, 37–41
Rebellion in a High School (Stinchcombe), 125–26
Record-keeping, at Westside High, 52, 53, 57
Reed, Adolph, 123

Reed, Vincent, 163–64
Reform: administrative, at Westside High, 67–71; approaches to, 103–4; decision-making, 173–74, 178; obstacles to, 171; participation in, 63, 168; of urban education, 155
Research, 186; methodology and reform, 171; problems of, 182–84
Resources of school, 161
Responsibility: avoidance in Westside High, 58–59; collective, 40; and denial theories, 14; and fragmentation of social process, 40; and progressive analysis, 21–22; school boards' abdication of, 136; in school systems, 139; and shared decision-making, 174; of social scientists, 186–87; of students, 36, 117–28, 148; for teacher education, 129–30; of teachers, 58–59, 131; views of, 25–26
Richer, Stephen, 114
Rist, Ray, 107, 110
Rodney, Walter, 20
Rogers, David, 135, 136, 138–39
Rosenfeld, Gerry, 108, 130–31, 158–60
Rosenthal, Robert, 112–13, 128
Rothschild-Whitt, Joyce, 178
Rubovits, P. C., 114
Rutter, Michael, 160–61
Ryan, William, 15, 25–26, 27

St. John, Nancy, 118, 162
Schain, Robert, 167
School boards, 136–39, 141
School climate, and achievement, 121
School-home interaction, 111
School Power (Comer), 169–71
Schools: failures of, 58; organization of, 49–50; poor, 43–44; successful, 5–6, 155–56, 181, 186–87
Schools of education, 129–30
School systems, 131, 135–44
Schwartz, Audrey, 17
Self-concept, 10
Self-destructive behavior, 126–27
Self-image of inner-city child, 119–20
Seligman, C. R., 106

Sennett, Richard, 121
Sesame Street, 111, 152–53 n.2
Shut Those Thick Lips (Rosenfeld), 108
Silberman, Charles, 166
Simon, John, 187–88
Single-factor analysis, 182–83
Size of class, 161
Slavery, 22, 32
Slum children, disadvantages of, 105–7
Slum schools, 43–44
Social change, 28–30, 32; progressive theory and, 21
Social inequality, approaches to, 7–9; denial theories, 9–10
Social interactions, 46
Social process, 16–17; in classroom, 19; and denial theory, 17; fragmentation of, 37–38
Social sciences: approaches to inequality, 7; cultural influences on, 15–16, 19; and educational reform, 181; responsibility of, 186, 187; scientific status of, 185; and urban teachers, 4
Socioeconomic status: and educational achievement, 103; and educational inequality, 18; and rebellious behavior, 125–26; and teacher expectations, 115–16; and track placement in schools, 108–9
Sociology: language of, 15; progressive theory, 20
Souls of Black Folk (DuBois), 7
Specialization of teaching, 132
Special programs, 131
Speech patterns, social significance of, 106–7
Stanfield, John, 12, 103
Statistical equality, 33–34
Status, language and, 106–7
Status-degrading behavior by teachers, 46–47, 75, 80–82, 153 n.4; and classroom behavior, 85, 88, 92, 96–99; in inner-city grade schools, 119; at street academy, 101 n.4
Status-supportiveness, 75, 91

Stinchcombe, Arthur, 120, 125–26, 147
Street academy, 45–46, 101 n.4
Structural unemployment, 38–39
Structured educational programs, 174–76
Structured learning environments, 164
Student body, social mix of, 18
Student interactions, 120
Students: misbehavior of, 82–95, 126–27; responsibility of, 36, 117–27, 148; in slum schools, 44–47; views of teachers, 48
Student's Reported Sense of Futility, 118
Student-teacher relationships, 16–17, 46, 52–53, 75, 76–82, 99–100; denial of, 81, 82; in elementary schools, 107–10; and expectations, 114; and quality of teaching, 96; student accounts of, 82–89; of transfer students, 94–95
Subject-matter interest, 91
Subject-matter specialization, 132
Success, 61–63, 72; in education, 188 n.1; at Westside High, 68
Successful schools, 5–6, 158–65, 181; Catholic, 186–87
Summers, Anita, 161–62
Superintendents of schools, 136, 137, 141

Teacher expectations, 7, 12–13, 20, 112–17, 118, 127, 130, 144, 185
Teacher-pupil relationships. *See* Student-teacher relationships
Teachers, 62, 63, 73, 146; and administration at Westside High, 53–55; avoidance of responsibility by, 58–59; commitment of, 121; deficiencies of, 58, 64–65; demands on, 66–67, 68, 70–71, 89, 104, 167–68; evaluation of, 134, 135, 140; exploitative behavior of, 61–62, 100; failures of, 61–62, 132–33; hostility toward, 179; inadequate, 127, 134–35; inexperienced, 121–22; job secu-

rity of, 134; late for class, 57; poorly trained, 130; and social scientists, 4; status-degrading behavior by, 46–47; student's views of, 48, 76–82, 148; successful, 45, 162; training of, 128–30, 162; young, 24
Teacher's Pets, Troublemakers and Nobodies (Gouldner), 107–10
Teachers' unions, 129, 135
Teaching: inferior, 110, 178–79; quality of, 47; successful, 165–66
Teachman, Gerard, 92, 95
Test scores, 162–63
Time-order of variables, 15–16
Torrey, Jane, 106
Track placement, 108–10, 131, 153 n.6
Training, teacher, 128–30, 162
Transfer students, 94–95
Tucker, G., 106

Unemployment, 16, 38–39
Unions: parents', 138; teachers', 129, 135
Urban education: problems of, 61; reform of, 176–78
Urban parents' groups, 138

Values, and achievement, 17
Vandalism, 99, 120
Variables: alterable, 181–82; time-order of, 16, 17
Verbal skills of slum children, 105, 106–7, 152 n.1
Vested interests: of education schools, 132; of educators, 141; of professional staffs, 139; in school systems, 135, 144; of social scientists, 184; in teacher education, 129–30
Victim-blaming theories, 9
Victims, views of, 24–26
Victim-system control theory of racism, 8
Villains, views of, 24

Washington, D.C., school system, 162, 163–64
Weber, George, 158, 170

Weber, Max, 38
Westside High, 43–101; improvement in, 163
Westside Prep, Chicago, 156–58
Wilson, Alan, 114–15
Wilson, Andrea, 180

Wilson, William, 30
Wingate High, Brooklyn, 167
Wolfe, Barbara, 161–62
Work style, 172

Zigler, Edward, 165

About the Author

CHARLES M. PAYNE is director of the Urban Education Project, a community education center in Orange, New Jersey. He has taught sociology and Afro-American studies at Williams College, Southern University, and Haverford College. His contributions have appeared in *The Race and Class Controversy* (ed. C. V. Willie) and *Integrateducation*.

F